FIRM OBJECTIVES, CONTROLS AND ORGANIZATION

Economics of Science, Technology and Innovation

VOLUME 8

The titles published in this series are listed at the end of this volume.

FIRM OBJECTIVES, CONTROLS AND ORGANIZATION

The Use of Information and the
Transfer of Knowledge within the Firm

by

GUNNAR ELIASSON
Royal Technical Institute (KTH), Stockholm

KLUWER ACADEMIC PUBLISHERS
DORDRECHT / BOSTON / LONDON

A C.I.P. Catalogue record for this book is available from the Library of Congress.

ISBN 0-7923-3870-7

Published by Kluwer Academic Publishers,
P.O. Box 17, 3300 AA Dordrecht, The Netherlands.

Kluwer Academic Publishers incorporates
the publishing programmes of
D. Reidel, Martinus Nijhoff, Dr W. Junk and MTP Press.

Sold and distributed in the U.S.A. and Canada
by Kluwer Academic Publishers,
101 Philip Drive, Norwell, MA 02061, U.S.A.

In all other countries, sold and distributed
by Kluwer Academic Publishers Group,
P.O. Box 322, 3300 AH Dordrecht, The Netherlands.

Printed on acid-free paper

Printed in the Netherlands

CONTENTS

Appended as diskette

A Chronicle of Events that Mark the Experimental Evolution of a New Information Product

Systems Components and the New Information Product Defined

The Content of the Business Information System
-- A Classification of Technologies

A Representation of the Business
B Analysis, Data Processing
C Communications
D User Contacts
E Applications

LIST OF FIGURES

LIST OF TABLES

FOREWORD

The business firm, large or small, is the source of welfare for millions of people in the industrialized world. It exists on the basis of *organized human competence*, a very scarce production factor in most of the world. Understanding the internal organization of the business firm and its rôle in economic growth is, therefore, a prime task of economics. Nevertheless, it took a long time for economic theory to recognize the existence of the firm as a decision unit in its attempts to explain what is going on in the economy.

This book has been organized as five mutually supporting research tasks. It is *first* of all an empirical study of the nature of the firm and its management and information system as they can be observed from the information available and used by the top managers. *Second*, this study clarifies the limited capacity of top management to understand what goes on both outside and inside the firm. To handle such observations in a systematic and scientifically acceptable way my presentation has to be organized around a relevant *theory of firm behavior*. This theory, in turn, has to be based on some systematic conceptualization of the environment in which the firm is thought to operate, i.e. a body of economic theory encompassing the entire economy. The *third* task then becomes to formulate, or rather outline the idea of the *experimentally organized market economy*, an economy populated by firms that look like real firms.

One strong theme of this book is that economics -- despite recent attempts to introduce the firm in its *existing* body of theory -- has a *very* long way to go before it understands the firm and the dynamic interaction of firms in markets. One reason is lack of understanding of the nature of the firm among academics. Another and more fundamental reason is that a theory of the firm that looks like the real firm may not be compatible with the body of received theory. Reading recent literature one soon finds that there are at least as many theories of the firm as there are ideas of what a market is. Hence, most of the many theories of firm management can always be derived from some theoretical notion of the firm and its environment.

Theory shapes our minds. Theory is like a pair of glasses that determines what we see and what we cannot see. The received body of economic theory is an intellectual heritage that will support us, or intellectually be in our way. Theories and ideas have guided the evolution of *business information systems*. The business information system is the language through which the firm communicates internally and "understands itself". *Fourth*, the story of the development of business information systems and the supporting information technology, therefore, is not only a study of the development of management technique but also a fascinating story about the experimental development of a "new" and very complex information product by a couple of dozen firms in the information and communications markets. This has taken place along roads littered with billion $ business failures. Thus, and *finally*, this book also provides an excellent *empirical demonstration of the relevance of the theory of the experimentally organized economy*. This documentation, therefore, occupies a sizable part of the book, including the Chronicle.

A critical dividing line in the organization of the firm can be identified between, on the one hand, the high-level *organizational choice problems relating to the long term* and, on the other, the short-term *coordination efficiency* of the organization which requires structural (organizational) stability. Can the two problems be addressed through the same "universal" information system, or be managed by the same "corporate language"? The answer to this question pushes far beyond the limits of received economic theory. It is, however, a practical question to ask. When, during the 1980s several large firms in the information market attempted to design *universal information systems* for firms, they unknowingly addressed some deep problems of language, addressed also by the philosophers. Billions of dollars were spent on these ventures. So the design of a universal business information system is, indeed, a very real problem to address. To do this, however, I have to formulate a relevant theory of how the firm relates to its market context. The theory of the firm, the theory of firm management and the theory and practice of internal firm measurement are almost always shaped on the design of a unit of measurement with a *given* organization. A business firm that survives is never "a given organization" and its contours are always diffuse and constantly changing. This text, hence, is partly concerned with the optimal design of business information systems in an experimentally organized market economy that constantly and in unpredictable ways challenges the capacity of the firm to survive. A universal information system is shown to exist neither in principle or theory, nor in practice. And if it can be designed, perhaps it should be designed completely independently of operations management's information requirements, the way responsibilities are structured today in large firms (Eliasson 1976, 1984b, 1990b, Thorngren 1970).

This book was originally planned as a straightforward empirical study on the *objectives, the controls and the organization of firms* -- in short their information system. It has, however, expanded far beyond my ambitions. To capture my task adequately, I have had to use a much broader brush than I intended, and to dig deeper into the fundamentals of understanding economics than was obvious to me from the start. Business micro reality has little to do with the economic theory that is being taught at universities. Micro theory was never intended to be used in a context like this. It has, nevertheless, very much influenced thinking about the actual design of business information systems. As a consequence of all these interacting problems, this book takes on an ambition that some would consider too comprehensive. But there is a comprehensive story to tell, and someone needs to do it.

The book is organized in three parts. In the intellectual *Part I* it is concluded that management science, built on classical economic reasoning has misguided thinking about management and business information systems design along the lines of centralized planning or even of automated production. To demonstrate that the alternative economic reference model -- the experimentally organized economy -- is developed. *Part II* begins by deriving the ideal business information systems design, based on the firm in the model of the experimentally organized economy and goes on to show that information systems in firms today look very much like that, focusing on identification and correction of business mistakes, rather than on the design of optimal strategies and plans.

The Chronicle in *Part III* illustrates how information industry has gradually changed its product development in recent years toward developing exactly that kind of product, based on easy *access* features, but that this development has taken place in new firms rather than in the old information firms.

More specifically *Chapter I* introduces the problem and the basic, empirical assumptions. *Chapter II* introduces the economy -- the theory of the *experimentally organized economy* -- that will emerge on the basis of these assumptions.

Chapter III presents ("derives") the nature of the firm, as it must be presented in the experimentally organized economy. *Chapter IV* introduces the firm information and control system in practice, based on a large number of interviews with firms in the U.S., in Europe and in Japan. *Chapter V* discusses, on the basis of the theoretical Chapter III and observed practice, whether the ideal, universal information system is at all feasible. If feasible, what should such an information system look like? This ideal system, of course, by the very questions asked, should come as close as possible to what we would consider a theory of the firm, formulated with the view of understanding the nature and internal dynamics of a firm.

Chapter VI goes on to tell -- again based on many interviews with firms -- what firms in the information sector have been attempting to do, in developing the ready-to-install general or Universal Business Information System (UBIS). *Chapter VII*, finally, documents this experimental evolution of a new product by way of summarizing a *Chronicle* of events. This Chronicle encompasses, as it turns out, the evolution of the modern information industry. The full Chronicle is appended to the book on a diskette.

This study has taken many years to complete. I am very grateful for the patience of its initiator and part financier, the *TELDOK* research foundation and in particular Bertil Thorngren, the chairman of the Teldok Board with whom I have had many enlightening discussions on the content of this book. The long gestation period has at least offered one advantage. I have had the opportunity to follow the development of a technology during one of its most dramatic phases and to study its introduction in industry, in several cases in individual firms that I have visited many times. The book has been written "in installments" when my time as the president of the *Industrial Institute for Economic and Social Research*

(IUI) has permitted it. This position, on the other hand, has involved a steady interaction with management people at all levels in firms, Swedish and foreign, that has allowed me to test my ideas. The ideas, the experience, the support and the enthusiasm of the then chairman of the IUI Board, Curt Nicolin, have been uniquely valuable for the progress of this study. Writing this book has thus above all been a great learning experience. The study continues along the themes of my 1976 book on *Business Economic Planning*, revisited in 1984 [in *Hur styrs storföretag* (How are Large Businesses Run?)] and summarized in my 1990 article *The Firm as a Competent Team*, only to be opened up again with this book.

Many people have read parts of this manuscript in various stages of completion. Parts of it have been discussed at seminars at the IUI, at Telia, at Université Paris II (ERMES) and at several other places. Bo Carlsson at Case Western Reserve University took the time to read the entire manuscript and I am very grateful for his suggested modifications. Pavel Pelikan, at IUI, with experience both from a formerly planned economy and from western so-called market economies has evoked deep discussions on the nature of those problems that confront both business decision makers and economic policy advisers that I think should be raised more often. Pontus Braunerhjelm, Erik Mellander, Karl Markus Modén and Sten Nyberg, also at IUI, Ingemar Hedenklint, earlier with IBM Sweden, and Harald Fries, earlier at IUI, have commented on various parts of the manuscript at various stages, as have Gérard Ballot at Université Paris II, P.G. Holmlöv at Telia, Bengt Stymne at the Stockholm School of Economics and Erol Taymaz at Middle East Technical University, Ankara. Discussions with Lars Arosenius and Håkan Kihlberg, earlier with IBM Sweden, Stellan Horwitz, Stig Larsson, Håkan Ledin, and Gert Schyborger, earlier with Ericsson Information Systems, Stig Hagström, earlier director at Xerox Palo Alto Research Center, Örjan Håkanson at Scribona, Martin Leimdörfer at Industrimatematik, Per Olofsson at IBM Sweden, Lars Ramqvist, CEO at Ericsson, and Sven Wallgren, earlier CEO at Esselte, have been very helpful for my understanding of the use of information technology in business. Without the help of my daughter Charlotte Eliasson, who has read and condensed a very large number of articles for the Chronicle it would not have been possible to complete this survey that concludes the book.

Most of this book consists of what I have learned through direct contacts with people in firms and in academia. The evidence I have collected -- I can only observe -- has not been consistent but rather blended with ideas and particular experiences, not least from failing firms; and my learning is still going on. This has been the challenge of the research task I have taken on that I simply had to conclude somehow, after a decade. I have arrived at my own interpretations, and synthesis of the whole, and an important part of it is my view on economic theory and the rôle it gives to the firm. I believe I have a message to tell. If one can talk about right and wrong in this context, all the errors are, of course, of my own making.

Stockholm, June 1995
Gunnar Eliasson

PART I

THEORY

I

THE ECONOMICS OF INNOVATION, COORDINATION, SELECTION, AND KNOWLEDGE TRANSFER

The theory of the firm, as well as actual business practice, builds on ideas about the market environment in which the firm operates. The intellectual perception of the firm and its market environment seems to have been experiencing more drastic change than the corresponding reality. It is, therefore, necessary to begin the presentation of the firm and its information and control system by properly setting the stage upon which it is supposed to act.

I.1   THE EXPERIMENTALLY ORGANIZED ECONOMY

It is natural to begin by defining the space (of business opportunities) in which the firm is supposed to operate. This space has been interpreted very differently over time by philosophers and economists. Karl Marx, for instance, saw no limit to the production potential of the "modern capital-intensive industrial organization of work". He borrowed this notion of unlimited production opportunities from Adam Smith. Adam Smith also saw no end to human ingenuity in devising increasingly more elaborate specialization patterns of production organization to achieve local economies of scale.

The check on unlimited production growth, according to Adam Smith, Karl Marx and George Stigler (1951) was the limited capacity of humans to consume goods. Hence markets became the limiting factor for production growth.

The marginalist economists[1], notably Walras, needed a transparent state space for agents to be able to optimize. The state space implicitly assumed to exist by theorists accordingly shrank, until it posed no mathematical problems. This assumption, which was rarely formulated explicitly, and hardly at all discussed in economic textbooks, disturbed many empirically oriented economists. Joseph Schumpeter (1911) reformulated the possibility of a very large state space in his treatment of the innovator and the unpredictable entrepreneur. This "Austrian notion" he gave up in his dismal (1942) analysis of the capacity of large firms to routinize innovative behavior, thus achieving internal knowledge-based scale economies of the kind proposed more recently by the so-called modern macro growth theorists. Eventually, or perhaps quite soon one firm (producer in Schumpeter's analysis) would dominate each market on the basis of its sustainable superior competence. Economies of scale still pose a fundamental theoretical problem in classical (static) economic theory, and for the same reason.

In that respect both Smith, Marx, Stigler, Schumpeter and the marginalists misunderstood the nature of production. To all three the firm was a goods producing factory. They forgot *quality*, for which there is no physical market saturation limit. And they had difficulties dealing intellectually with dynamics, or with *time*. Quality and time are still the intellectual harassments of economics. Product quality is the main technological instrument of competition of the modern business firm.

Introducing heterogeneous quality as a dimension of output removes the notion of a limited business opportunities space that characterizes the classical, full information model of economics. Instead a virtually unlimited set of *business opportunities* opens up, making it impossible to observe and understand more than a fraction of the whole. This is the way business people view their market environment. But theorists cannot deal with such *open-ended state spaces*. Some kind of closeness is needed to come up with the solution needed to say something precise, to make a decision or to advice on policy. Apparently the properties of state space are important for which body of theory you choose to work with. This is where the story of this book begins.

With quality of output being the key competitive factor, *knowledge* or *competence becomes* the key input in quality production, *the natural limiting factor to macroeconomic growth*, and the key to survival for individual agents in the market. Competence capital determines the economic value of the firm. Hence, the efficiency of the firm as a *learning organization* determines the rate at which its principal asset -- knowledge -- is accumulated. But learning is subjected to rapidly diminishing returns. Hence, the competence to subjectively understand state space defines the management competence of the firm. This competence depends critically on the selection and allocation of competent people (Eliasson, 1988c, 1990b, 1992c, 1995a). Hence, supporting the management task of hiring and allocating competence must be the most important function of the information system of the firm.

While capital equipment deteriorates in value from use, the stock of knowledge is for ever. Its economic value, however, diminishes from its diffusion to, and use by competitors. Hence, this study of the *economics of information in human decision making in organizations* starts from the notion of -- for all practical purposes -- unlimited business opportunities. It makes the *local*, not easily communicable *knowledge* to exploit these opportunities the limiting factor for local success, profits and growth. It introduces participation in market competition with other advanced producers as the active learning mechanism, by which each competitor adds marginal improvements to its knowledge base, thus contributing to the diffusion of industrial know-how through "technological competition", and enlarging the business opportunity set even further, perhaps -- for long periods -- even faster than it is being exploited.

The *opportunity set* of this practically oriented book on business behavior should be viewed as *international*, while the competence to access and to exploit it is typically *local* and related to the firm (internal). This means that each actor in the advanced game of international competition operates in a tiny little corner of an immense business opportunity set, on the basis of his, or her, or its, local competence, now and then coming up with new solutions or business combinations that can be profitably exploited until somebody has come up with an even better solution. This entire action is contributing to a further enlargement of the opportunity set and new possibilities to innovate and compete. In such an economy *predictability of micro outcomes will be very low*. (New business combinations will enter the market unpredictably as a deus ex machina, as argued already by Joseph Schumpeter 1911). Experimentation, trial and error will be the typical form of innovative learning. Because of that, some firms will temporarily earn above-normal returns. Others, because of technological competition, will earn below-normal returns. *A permanent capital market disequilibrium in the Wicksellian (1898) sense* -- when redefined, as we do here, at the micro level -- *becomes the normal order.* [Static, full-information equilibrium as economists often view the market situation, can never be reached (Eliasson 1985a, Chapter VII, 1991a).] The notion of equilibrium has to be replaced by a more or less balanced market process composed of millions of agents that coordinate themselves and the economy through dynamic competition in markets. Dynamic markets can be no more than the total action of all these agents. Spontaneous innovative activity maintains competition in dynamic markets and forces increased economic performance on all agents. This process is what generates economic growth in the (Eliasson 1987a, 1991a) *experimentally organized market economy*. The incentives that fuel such spontaneous, innovative activity, that maintains this permanent micro disequilibrium, the open market and free entry of agents in pursuit of profit, should thus be the paramount concern of political authorities. In this economy, *business mistakes* will be a *normal cost for economic development* (Eliasson 1992b).

While the notion of an *experimental organization of the economy* (see Eliasson 1987a, 1990a, 1991a) will be further elaborated later on, this is sufficient to introduce the nature of the economic information problem of the firm as the *economics of innovation and coordination*. This study is concerned with the technology of coordinating and reshaping business organizations ("hierarchies") in the experimentally organized economy.

I.2   THE BUSINESS INFORMATION PROBLEM -- CAN THE MIND OF THE FIRM BE AUTOMATED?

Simplicity is the trademark of theory. Theory is the organizer of facts and assumptions to understand observed phenomena. The hallmark of good theory is to use as few and as powerful explanatory variables as possible. However, good theory is also a way of organizing millions of disparate bits of evidence into a coherent and transparent whole, from which reliable and unbiased predictions can be drawn. Simplifying too much will distort your perception of reality.

There is normally a difference, sometimes a conflict between understanding and being able to communicate your understanding. There is always a large difference between "understanding in principle" and "operations know-how". In engineering the ambition is to achieve operational functionality. You observe theoretical principles when you design an airplane, but you don't design and run it on theory. Reliable and precise engineering information is needed. The same is needed to run a factory. Bad data or bad measurement systems are the common reasons for unsuccessful process automation whether it be a factory process sequence or the autopilot of a Boeing 747.

Bad or biased theory, however, is also the common reason for misrepresentations of reality in science. In natural sciences many principles can be regarded as natural laws that remain reasonably stable over time and can be experimentally determined. Engineering systems can be fixed structurally. For the entire business, however, the situation changes. Business leaders look for "stabilities" to be able to predict and control their firms. This is also theoretically possible in the classical economic model, founded on the assumption of a very small and transparent state space. How does the business information, control and decision situation change "intellectually" when we enter the experimentally organized economy in which the content of progress is structural or "organizational" change?

Engineering complexity in social science is close to overwhelming, but decision makers nevertheless have to act, and they ask "experts" for simple policy advice and rules of behavior. Hence, waves of fashion are commonplace in management and economic policy literature. Simplistic "few variable" solutions -- like the widely read book "In Search of Excellence", or in much Keynesian policy analysis -- are in demand, as are futuristic scenarios in which modern information technology is featured as being capable of designing devices that will soon take over the management mind functions of large business organizations, i.e. more or less what computers have long been doing to airplane designs. So this is clearly an important area of inquiry. Billions of dollars are constantly rolling in search of advice.

One key notion of this book, in fact, is the question how far up in a complex business organization that "grammar" can be brought in the sense of automating high-level decision making and making the corresponding knowledge communicable. The observant reader may recall business administration literature from the 1960s in which the management system ruled. The system -- not the people -- embodied the competence needed to run and to reorganize the firm. People could come and go. They were disposable.

The management automation question has in fact been asked very seriously, and several giant electronics firms have allocated huge R&D budgets to explore the potential of automated high-level decision making (see Chapter V). As we will see, the answer depends on the nature of technological and commercial predictability at the level of firm decision making. The case for universal information and decision systems depends critically on which theory of the economic environment of the firm you choose to think in terms of. Does the experimentally organized economy offer a universal grammar -- to borrow a notion from linguistics -- or a language which can handle all possible entrepreneurial problems, and communicate all needed industrial knowledge, as information, free of context? What are the limits for explicit grammar in business (Campbell 1982)?

As we will see, teams of competent people (Eliasson 1991b) not administrative systems or capital hardware dominate success or failure of business organizations. The world is, nevertheless, heading towards increased use of scientific methods to solve old decision problems. An expert system substituted for human judgment already in 1985 when it came to the final mixing of Campbell soups (*Business Week*, Oct. 7, 1985, p. 64 f; also see Chronicle). Not long ago you had to see a prototype flying before you started up production of a commercial airplane. Today aircraft producers can sell the same plane on the basis of computer analysis, and airlines commit themselves to firm orders on the basis of computer analysis of something that only exists in the body of computerized experience of aircraft producers.

So when will society be run by Johanneson's (1968) ultimate computer, and automated grammar brought into top executive offices -- the ideal situation of old-time central planners? In the experimentally organized economy there is no answer to this global planning problem. However, *every high-level executive knows that his next major decision problem might be very different from the last one, that the information he now has will be only partially useful in the future and will often give bad advice for his new decision experiment of today.*

I.3   THE FIRM AS A FINANCIAL DECISION UNIT

Joseph Schumpeter (1942, p. 123) once observed that double-entry bookkeeping was one of the major inventions of western civilization. It made rational profit and cost calculations possible in larger and larger organizations. It enlarged the potential span of organizational control. The firm, defined as a financial unit, is both defined in terms of its objectives (which are financial, profitability; Eliasson 1976a) and its "information system", its statistical accounts. This information system not only delimits the optimal size of the firm as a monolithic decision unit. It functions as a calculating device -- a financial control function -- that makes it possible for firm management to integrate profitability considerations and the real dimensions of economic activity in centrally taken decisions (Eliasson 1990b).

Any firm, even a small one, coordinates a large number of economic activities within its financial shell. Different goods and services are produced, inputs purchased, outputs marketed and distributed, often internationally, new products developed, etc. Coordinating all these activities is a typical information activity. The same coordination can also be achieved by the price system of markets. The efficiency of this coordination compared to coordination through the market determines the optimal size of the firm as a decision unit (Coase 1937). Expanding on those notions, *divisionalization* of large U.S. firms in the 1920s was heralded by Williamson (1981, p. 1555) as the "most significant organizational innovation of the 20th century". These classical ideas are all recognized in this study. We do, however ask the question whether, and how they have to be reformulated when we introduce the live firm based on heterogeneous competence capital, in the practically unlimited space of investment opportunities? What does competence and information mean in the experimentally organized economy?

I.4   THE FIRM AS A COMPETENCE ORGANIZATION

Coordination is only part of the business management problem. *The main long-term priority of owners and top management is to avoid getting the organization staffed with incompetence.* This priority also sets the standards of the top competent team itself (Eliasson 1990b). All activities to be coordinated, furthermore, have to be upgraded ("innovation"). The new competence thereby created has to be diffused through the organization ("learning"). The capacity of the individual, the team and the organization to learn, in turn, depends on the *receiver competence* (Eliasson 1990b, p. 277) residing in the organization. Such receiver competence is also influenced by upgrading, and the understanding of *organization-based receiver competence* will be an important part of this study. Since receiver competence is generally lacking, new competence cannot be communicated artificially, for instance in a classroom context. It is embodied ("tacit") in individuals or teams of people. The art of disseminating the new competence through the firm therefore is a matter of *organizational technique*, of allocating ("filtering") people through careers and job assignments. The competitiveness of a business firm almost entirely depends on its ability to create, accumulate, disseminate, and allocate human or team embodied competence.

Machines and labor hours have no economic value without a dominant competence to guide and control their allocation and use. This competence can be defined, and also generally learned and acquired, in a world that is transparent to its actors, or subjectively perceived to be. But suppose this is not the case, what then is competence?

I.5   HOW DO DIFFERENT PEOPLE LOOK AT BUSINESS?

The existence of the successful large business organization in a competitive and increasingly international market environment has always been a source of discomfort for policy markers, responsible as they are supposed to be for the welfare of the nation. Indeed, the business firm is not only a fact of economic life. It is the source of economic welfare for millions of people in the industrialized world. But it cannot be taken for granted, as witnessed by the lack of industrial competence in a large part of the industrially undeveloped world, including several formerly centrally planned economies in Eastern Europe that were once advanced industrial countries.

The business firm has a pronounced capacity for unpredictable innovative behavior. Being so, politicians are often asked by their constituencies to install orderly and predictable behavior in the business world, by squelching such disorderly behavior and keeping competition at bay. Economists often share that view. How could they otherwise "understand", to be able to write books? And how do you get the unpredictable adventurers at the top of large and small firms in the experimentally organized economy reined in so that responsible politicians can exercise judgment and impose order? Sometimes business people believe that overview is feasible and organize their firms as scientifically based planning machines. This was predominantly the case in the 1960s (Eliasson 1976a). Did or does this mean more efficient economic performance?

The firm, in fact, is a source of intellectual trouble in modern economic theory. It represents a disturbing market imperfection ("a temporary monopoly") in the competitive general equilibrium setting of modern economic theory that should have been competed away "to the short-term benefit of all". At the same time the source of that imperfection, i.e. superior competitiveness, is a superior, innovative competence, that we want to see in action. It drives the economic growth process (Eliasson 1991a). If we put on a different set of glasses, however, the same market imperfections become the source of technological competition that creates economic growth and benefits all. So economists and politicians alike have a problem to make the two views consistent.

The real business market imperfections called firms, it perhaps should be remarked, carry on their life irrespective of economic theory, but not entirely undisturbed by policy makers influenced by economic advisors who base their advice on economic theory. And firms are definitely not unaffected by each others' behavior. According to standard theory in which market imperfections lower economic welfare, policy makers are concerned about the growth of monopolies and design "antitrust policies" to remedy the situation. According to an extreme version of that theory, the central policy authority can be demonstrated to be the superior allocator of resources, on the basis of a superior overview. This is the argument for central planning. This notion of economics comes out strongly in so-called static general equilibrium theory, a mandatory requirement for all economic majors of western universities. The same intellectual position is not unfamiliar to Corporate Headquarters people in large firms, trained as they are at the same universities. This was especially the case before the disorderly economic situation of the 1970s, when scientific management teaching flourished.

According to another version of the same body of theory, the more superior as an innovator and a competitor the firm is, the more it will dominate the market. Eventually one firm will take over in each market and establish a monopoly, and the most efficient economic order will rule. This "dismal" -- as he thought -- prediction of the aging Joseph Schumpeter (1942) was in fact almost identical to the argument for central planning. The problem was that Schumpeter thought this outcome, contrary to his 1911 position, as empirically unavoidable.

Obviously economic analysts do have an intellectual dilemma, choosing the right theory for understanding what is going on. Theory is essential for organizing both our thoughts and facts. But theory also represents a prior choice of view that biases one's outlook, decisions and advice. The choice of right ("optimal") theory for the particular problem is the most important art at all levels, whether we are scientists, politicians, business decision makers or individuals managing the family portfolio of assets.

Therefore, the themes of this book are

1. An argument for the necessity of developing the art, or the competence, of choosing the right perception, or model, of the firm and its environment.
2. The management technique of designing and using the model correctly and changing it when necessary, since it will *always* be more or less misleading (biased).

This technique can be observed, analyzed and documented. It will take up a significant part of the book. The most important business competence, however, is the choice of management technique. This art is extremely difficult to document, especially if you don't have such experience of your own and do not write for those who have a similar experience. I will not follow the common armchair tradition and neglect this part.

I.6   HOW TO MANAGE BIGNESS EFFICIENTLY?

This study is based on interviews with users (notably big firms) of variously designed business information systems and designers of the same systems for the markets in Europe and in the U.S. For obvious reasons, Swedish firms dominate the interviews on the users' side, even though many U.S. and European and some Japanese firms are also included in the sample. The large, international Swedish corporations illustrate the problems of this particular study. They are innovative within traditional well-defined technologies and they are efficient. During the postwar period a group of rapidly growing, international and very old Swedish firms have emerged as premier performers in different international market segments. They base their commercial success on a dominant position in world markets but they also, together, dominate the Swedish economy (see Table II.3). These firms make up the foundation of current Swedish economic welfare. In that respect, this group of engineering firms have taken over the dominance of the previously dominant Swedish basic industries. These "new" firms, however, are based on an old technology, namely the large-scale factory organization around the new machine tools that initiated the industrial revolution more than 150 years ago, and that Karl Marx observed and frequently referred to as exhibiting an unlimited production potential.

The competitive position of the large business firms is based on acquired technological, organizational and commercial competence. The nature of that competence capital cannot be measured, except by studying how it has been developed, how it is maintained and upgraded. The large western firms, predominantly operate on old technologies in markets for mature products. Hence, this becomes a study of the organizational and commercial competence of big business. It is, therefore, of particular interest in this study to understand whether success in the past makes the organizational transition into new technologies more, or less, difficult.

The rapid emergence of successful, large firms operating on old technologies in markets for mature products explains the reasonably smooth transition of the Swedish economy from the potential disaster of the 1970s. In that respect, Swedish manufacturing development ran counter to the development in other industrial nations (Carlsson 1992a, 1994). While the average size, and the dominance of the largest firms have increased in Sweden, the opposite development has taken place in Germany, the U.S., Japan etc. The Swedish firms, by the way, are becoming less and less rooted in Sweden-based economic resources, and less and less tied to Sweden by top level competence and ownership. In that sense, Swedish economic welfare has become increasingly dependent upon the extremely competence-intensive information activity needed to build, operate and constantly reorganize giant business organizations, i.e. on the competence that is the concern of this study. This competence, consisting of talented, experienced and educated human beings, furthermore, needs a suitable economic, cultural and political climate to develop, feel at home and stay. What will the new European situation, after EU and the possible revitalization of the formerly centrally planned Eastern economies mean for the relative attractiveness of national economic environments?

Since technological development apparently is in favor of smaller scale, the question is: what is the rationale for the contrary development in Sweden and what does this mean for the future? Has Swedish manufacturing industry become locked into the wrong technology?

I.7   THE ACCOUNTS OF THE KNOWLEDGE-BASED INFORMATION ECONOMY

In his famous 1776 book, Adam Smith made the division of labor the source of the wealth of nations. Specialization of work involved an organizational and technological know-how through which economies of scale were achieved at each "workstation". New technology, or organizational competence, pulled productivity growth along at the rate it was created ("innovation"), commercially implemented ("entrepreneurship") and diffused through the economies ("learning").

The more specialized the work process, however, the more geographically dispersed physical production became and the more distributed the knowledge base of the economy. Hence, the larger the transactions costs needed for *transport* and for *communication* to *coordinate* economic activities.

The creation and transmission of knowledge, and the coordination of economic activities can occur *in markets through competition*, or *in hierarchies through administrative techniques*.

Sometimes knowledge cannot be transmitted as coded messages, as information, but is embodied in human beings or groups of human beings; it is *"tacit"* (Polanyi 1967). Tacit knowledge, including all kinds of competence up to the ultimate competence, that to select competence (Pelikan 1989), involves a particular form of competition, which we call *selection* or *filtering*. Selection of competence must mean the selection of competent people. Thus, the information system of a firm must be oriented towards supporting that selection. The most general filter activity is the choice of *organizational structure*, including work specialization itself, exit and entry of new activities, etc. This classification scheme is presented in Table I:1. It can be demonstrated that the bulk of production costs in an economy, and in manufacturing, is devoted to these forms of information processing (Eliasson 1990a).

Table I.1   The statistical accounts of the knowledge-based information economy

1. Choice and selection	*Filtering* - entry - exit - mobility - careers
2. Identifying business opportunities (exploring state space)	*The creation of new knowledge* - innovation - entrepreneurship - technical development
3. Coordination	*Disciplining* - competition (in markets) - management (in hierarchies)
4. Learning	*Knowledge transfer* - education - imitation - diffusion

Source: Modified version of Eliasson, G., *Technological Competition and Trade in the Experimentally Organized Economy*, Research Report No. 32, IUI, Stockholm 1987, p. 12.

With tacit knowledge embodied in human beings or groups of human beings, the allocation of competence through the mobility of human beings becomes the critical function of the economy. The knowledge-based information economy rests on an information technology embodied in its organizational structure: organizational change means a change in information technology that in turn generates macroeconomic productivity growth. One can envision -- as was done already by Ricardo (1821) -- a totally specialized economy with no direct manual production labor, all labor input being devoted to creating and transmitting new knowledge, coordinating the production process through competition and administrative technique, and allocating competence through filtering. In this "extreme" economy all technical change will have its origin in organizational change or change in the information technology of the economy. This notion of technological change is not as far-fetched as it may appear. A survey of technological change as commonly done by economic historians means a listing of the "major innovations" like the steam engine or electricity, thought to have pulled the growth processes of industrial nations along. Such a listing, on closer scrutiny, will reveal that most of these innovations have a generic quality and are involved in the central and communication techniques of the economic system (Eliasson 1988b, 1990a, pp. 18 ff). In the beginning most of these information and coordination communication techniques were physical ("transport"). In modern postwar times techniques influencing the information processing capacity of the economy are becoming increasingly important, including the internal administrative systems of firms and the capacity of markets, notably financial markets, to coordinate allocation processes in the entire economy.

Coordination occurs in markets through competition and in hierarchies through administration or management technique. The relative efficiency of the invisible and the visible (management) hands determines the sizes and kinds of agents in the market (Coase 1937). The market is the combined competitive action of all firms. This means that a minimum requirement of relevant economic theory is to be explicit about the endogenous combinations and recombinations of "institutions" (agents, rules) in markets, a demand economic theory has hardly even began to look at.

It should also be noted, that understanding agent competence and behavior is much more than understanding how transactions costs are minimized within hierarchies through mimicking the signaling of prices in markets. Control of a hierarchy means imposing competence on the administrative system through policy, forcing a direction on the organization. Hence, the organization of the hierarchy, or the firm is itself the result of an experimental, self-organizing process that evolves endogenously in the market.

I.8   THE NECESSITY OF TACIT COMPETENCE

The competence of the organization called a firm to act as a monopoly, earning a return above the interest rate is largely "tacit" and unique, and difficult or impossible to communicate. It has to be, because otherwise all other firms would immediately learn that competence and eliminate its economic value.

It has been argued in many classical texts that tacitness is an irrelevant property; if you spend enough resources ("costs") you will eventually learn. This is wrong both in practice and in principle. Some knowledge is incommunicable in principle due to lacking receiver competence on the part of users (Eliasson 1990b, pp. 276 f), and if it is acquired through experience or on-the-job learning, it will always become somewhat different from what had been learnt before. The very large size of state space or the set of investment opportunities is therefore partly, perhaps largely, a consequence of the extreme variation in knowledge that resides in a large population of agents (*heterogeneity*) and the consequent limitations of agents' ability to understand each other's behavior (*receiver competence*). Limited access to more than a fraction of that diversified (Eliasson 1984b, p. 254, 1987, pp. 25 ff) knowledge base makes each individual *boundedly rational* (using Simon's 1955 term) in the sense that he is capable of understanding only a fraction of the whole. Hence, *a significant part of the total knowledge base of an economy is tacit and has to be communicated by other means than by coded messages*. This is why markets become so important.

The proof of existence of tacit knowledge builds on the assumption that individuals are heterogeneous. I, then, demonstrate that tacit knowledge must occur in teams of two or more members. Assume that

(a) heterogeneous individual knowledge endowments or

(b) heterogeneous preferences

(c) or both

characterize economic agents. Identical individual knowledge endowments, but different preferences can be transformed into different *decisions* (the exercising of economic competence). Identical preferences, but heterogeneous knowledge endowments (restrictions) will also produce different decisions. Individuals will have a limited capacity to understand and to predict each other's behavior. They will be boundedly rational in Simon's sense, but differently so. This establishes heterogeneity of "competence" in the sense of understanding other actors' behavior on the basis of a common information signal. Hence, different responses to the same signals should be expected among individuals, and so on.

With different knowledge endowments and different preferences (determining individual responses) each individual will be unable to communicate all he knows, and unable to learn everything other agents know or will do. Hence, *tacit knowledge* arises in groups of individuals of more than two. Since the capacity to understand varies among individuals there will always be certain things that I cannot communicate to others and vice versa. Tacit team knowledge arises (Eliasson 1990b, p. 276 f). This is a strong proof since tacit knowledge can be demonstrated always to arise in a group of two as long as the two individuals are not identical in *all* respects. There will always be something about your wife that you don't understand. The mirror image of tacit knowledge, hence, is bounded rationality. This has been demonstrated without recourse to the assumption of complexity or of a very large number of individuals, or of an extremely large state space, including all possible future investment opportunities based on decisions today. Introducing the possibilities of differently structured *receiver competences* (Eliasson 1986b, pp. 57, 95; 1990a,b)[2] and a reasonably large and/or heterogeneous state space makes perfect foresight and situations of full information theoretically impossible, and simplifying designs assuming it likely to be misleading in principle. Complexity and a large number of actors are, however, needed if we also want to demonstrate, that tacitness is the dominant characteristic of an economy's knowledge base. This we will do later.

Learning-by-doing (Lundberg 1961, Arrow 1962a)[3] is another way of building a case for tacit knowledge, even though this interpretation was not intended by the students of learning-by-doing. Suppose every individual is identical by hereditary competence endowment, but acquires competence through various forms of learning. Their competence will depend on *how* they learn. Suppose instead that they know the same (they have gone to the same school) and take the same job, but that they differ in their *capacity to learn* on the job. Their competence will depend on their initial capacities in that respect. Suppose all individuals are equal in all respects, and have gone to the same school, but then take different jobs. Their ultimate competence will depend on differences in experience from their job careers. With on-the-job learning accepted any heterogeneity on-the-job path will produce the heterogeneity of competence among individuals that limits their capacity to understand each other and, hence, makes part of the economy's knowledge base tacit and incommunicable by coded signals. The message of this book will be that most knowledge that matters for economic performance is of that tacit kind, and has to be communicated ("allocated") by indirect means, through markets and in hierarchies, through on-the-job learning (Eliasson 1994 f).

I.9   THE LIMITS OF REASON

The early economists, including Adam Smith, saw no end to the productivity advance possible to achieve through increased specialization. They were quite content to work with the abstraction of an open system. In Adam Smith's model, saturated markets defined the limits of volume growth of the economy. The marginalist revolution pioneered by Walras, Jevons (and also Menger) in the second half of the 18th century, and the increased use of mathematics in economic analysis, however, required a limited state space within which rational optimizing behavior guaranteed the existence of a unique and stable equilibrium. Powerful mathematical tools limited the intellectual vision of the economist.

The notion of an open versus a closed system, however, is not unique to economics. The old philosophers were discussing the same problem (Gustavsson 1991). It is intellectually uncomfortable to work with open systems. Hume and Locke discussed the world in terms of (1) *memory*, (2) *logics* and (3) *imagination*. Logics and memory were acceptable manifestations of the human mind and allowed a multitude of combinations that defined the perception of the world around us. This is also sufficient to introduce complexity and limits of understanding. Imagination was the rest, whatever it was. Leibnitz, however, accepted no more imagination than all possible combinations of logic and memory (the reducibility presumption).

Kant, however, was willing to go beyond Leibnitz' conclusion and allow imagination to enter as a separate dimension of human awareness.

All this might sound very abstract and academic. But it is not. It marks the dividing line between neoclassical economic theory and what I call the experimentally organized economy, and hence also determines our perception of the firm. It determines the size and accessibility of state space, or the investment opportunity set and the extent to which a full information situation is at all theoretically feasible. To achieve that end for the firm was the ambition of many designers of business information systems.

The classical economic model is based on assumptions that make it possible for each agent to be fully informed at a known cost. In the experimentally organized model, however, each agent will experience what every businessman understands; a limited view of the whole that he or she wants to understand.[4] This situation occurs for several reasons. Heterogeneity of the boundedly rational competence specification of agents is sufficient to create the tacit knowledge that defines such a situation (Eliasson 1990b). Then the situation will arise that I know something that you don't know, that I cannot tell you because you have not got the necessary knowledge and/or experience (*receiver competence*) to figure out what I am telling you.

Under such circumstances there will exist at each point in time a very large number of business opportunities that

- some of us may recognize when we see them tried in the market
- but that cannot be derived from existing facts and theory (logic and memory). Experiments first have to be performed.

This is sufficient to establish the *experimentally organized economy* (EOE) as the only viable theory of economy dynamics.

Business mistakes will then become a normal cost for economic progress in the EOE, and the ability to cope with business mistakes becomes a significant part of agent competence (see more below). Acting upon a hunch based on limited knowledge will be part of the *learning experience* of a firm (Eliasson 1990b). Since the rate of mistaken decisions soon rises out of all bounds, if agents try to speed up learning about the opportunity set, *strongly diminishing returns to learning* prevent at each point in time each agent from coming close to anything looking like a situation of full information. The normal states of operation of an economy will be far below what is technically feasible. The allocation and use of competence and information become the critical concerns of economic analysis. As I will demonstrate in the next chapter this situation corresponds very closely to the mathematical notion of chaos, that may arise out of non-linear representations (models) of the economy.[5]

Unexpected events occur all the time in the experimentally organized economy. To cope with such an environment agents need the intellectual capacity to reorient themselves in the new situation that has arisen. That intellectual capacity has to be present within the top-competent team. Its task is to restaff the organization with people able to cope with the new situation at all levels.

I.10   THE FLORA OF KNOWLEDGE -- A NOTE ON TERMINOLOGY FOR THE BUSINESS INFORMATION SYSTEM

Not until the 1930s and Ludwig Wittgenstein did philosophers and linguists realize that language is the limiting factor of knowledge. The language limits the kind and volume of knowledge that can be transmitted (communicated) on code, as *information*. "How can I tell the taste of coffee to someone who has not tasted coffee?" This limitation has two sides, the *codability* of the message and the receiver *competence* to interpret the coded message. Loosely speaking, information is the codable and communicable part of knowledge (Eliasson 1986b, pp. 24 f).

Non-codability is often referred to as tacit knowledge, being embodied in human beings. *Receiver competence* is often limited by the *complexity* of the message. The abstract concepts just introduced from philosophy and linguistics are the fundamental categories of the practitioners of any *business information system*. With sufficient heterogeneity of business competence to learn, bounded rationality or tacit competence in the above sense can be demonstrated to exist (see above).

If the context is right (if sufficient receiver competence exists), extremely complex messages can be transmitted on simple code. A well formulated question of utmost significance, can often be resolved by a "yes" or a "no".

On the other hand, lacking adequate context, even the most simple message will need extremely complex ("incomprehensible") code to be communicated. One example is that the automation of even simple work processes like "grab" and "lift" in a mechanical workshop needs extremely detailed code, since the receivers of the information -- the robots -- are extremely uneducated. The machine configuration is the context, the receiver competence. The encoding of the work process is a major investment in itself (Eliasson 1980, pp. 235 ff), and the code that guides the machine is almost "unreadable" for ordinary humans. A person, who has already learned to "grab" and to "lift" needs no instructions about how to do it, only what to do. Context will be sufficient.

Another example of complex messages can be taken from the "team" competence in carrying out strategies in American football. The strategies are complex and have to be carried out very fast to prevent decoding by the opposite team. Hence, strategies have to be rehearsed over and over again to be triggered perfectly on a single code word, and implemented, nevertheless, with the individual variation needed to overcome unpredictable local opposition. Such a game sequence of the team can never be coded and learned from an instruction manual. Careful training, however, makes it possible for team members to learn all the individual variation needed to cope with even more individual variation.

Since efficient individual variation in the spontaneous solving of local problems depends on the joint understanding of team members, a unique tacit team competence has to be established.

Similar types of complex communication is needed in warfare, sometimes in science but all the time in high-level business team decision making. In all places specialized languages ("codes", a jargon) develop, and membership in teams is restricted by competence in that language.

A rapid sequence of team decisions in business requires the same internal language development, minimizing the internal team language difficulties associated with translating a complex solution of a problem one-to-one into single valued action of all team members. It is interesting to observe from information systems journals like *Datamation*, how the rapid advance of complex software technology has run into a lack of well defined terminology. Since the technology is only familiar to small groups, and since it has not settled, a seemingly fluent jargon ("flum") has developed that may be perfectly comprehensible to the insiders, but utterly incomprehensible to the outsiders (see for instance O'Connel 1988). The people writing or speaking at that level are not dumb, unrigorous in their thoughts or unclear in their presentation -- they are addressing a specialized, educated circle of readers to which *you* don't belong. The knowledge to use it (the receiver competence) is typically *tacit*. Frontier science is always like this, because most receivers of the information are truly uneducated and will continue to be until the technology has stabilized sufficiently to be generally taught (cf. the proof of "tacit knowledge" in Section I.8 above). This well known situation is illustrated by a comparison (see Eliasson 1989a, p. 40 ff) of mature mechanical engineering industries, knowledge-based pharmaceutical industries and frontier science-based electronics industries. In mature industries the technologically innovative phase is over. Technology can be diffused through intermediaries (consultants, universities etc.). Firms in those markets base their existence on complex organizational competence. It is my conviction that for this very reason, university environments, mentally shaped by their medieval theological traditions of critical scrutiny, educational ambitions and demands on clear (rigorous) presentation will always be the wrong place for innovative activity. "Paralysis by analysis" is a term that I have often met with among business people. True inquiry belongs to the experimentally organized, adventurous business world where you perform by making profits, not by presenting yourself to your colleagues in scientific journals or in lectures.

It is no wonder, then, that the competence to develop high level specialized internal team languages has become a critical business concern. Most often the practitioners are not aware of the nature of this internal language problem (Pelikan 1969, Eliasson 1976a, p. 80 and chapter IV). Nevertheless, the entire budgeting, reporting and control process of a large firm makes up such a special language. Within the field of artificial intelligence, communication (language) systems are being developed which support the endogenous ("through use") expansion of grammar [example; Trillium of Xerox; see Henderson (1986) and interview report].

This overview of the corporate language problem also illustrates the problem of writing an annual report or a prospect of a firm (see Eliasson, U., 1981). The core business problem is not fully understood by the executive team of the company, and even less so by other employees. It is obvious that unsurmountable language difficulties arise when such extreme complexity is to be coded and translated into one language, that is also intelligible to outsiders or laymen. Critical circumstances are simply not communicable because of lack of receiver competence. The language itself often lacks capacity to communicate many facts. The problem is solved through introducing pedagogical designs.

1.   Professional informers may be hired to code the facts of the firm for outsiders.
2.   The code itself (the text) is manipulated to suit the competence of receivers.

The first step is most important. It filters out *what* to present. This selection is influenced by what can be coded and presented. The only guarantee against bias is that top management reads what has been presented. They at least understand what can be understood and tells whether the coded message -- given their way of interpretation -- is unbiased. Comments in business magazines witness the impossibility of achieving full presentational clarity.

Lack of receiver competence is observable all the way down to the interface between information systems producers and users. To push producers out of their hardware mentality to pay attention to software was a very slow process, and a costly one for the producers. The next phase, coping with the complex specification of systems, and the extremely heterogeneous use to which systems may be put has made users more useful to vendors, although their influence has been slow in penetrating strong-minded product development teams (Rothschild 1988).

The presence of tacit knowledge complicates all communication. Economic theory is strongly inclined to assume all knowledge to be codable at a known cost. This is, however, scientifically unacceptable.

The reason is that classical economic theory implicitly assumes, but rarely states, that the economic competence to select (allocate) resources is abundant and costless. The auctioneer/coordinator of Walras and competitive equilibrium theory is a case in point. This assumption is inconsistent with the basic analytical problem of economics, the allocation of scarce resources. As Pelikan (1988a) correctly argues, you cannot then assume the ultimate resource, the competence to allocate resources to be abundant. Anyone who has worked at a research institute or in a business also knows that this particular resource is really what is scarce. Specialists, on the other hand, can usually be hired in the market.[6]

I.11   WHY THIS STUDY?

This book takes a look at the business organization as it in fact operates. It summarizes several earlier studies of mine on decision making in large firms (1976a and 1984c in particular). This time I am also attempting more rigorously to place the empirically observed decision processes of the firm in the context of the economic theory of the firm and the economic theory of markets. What is a market -- or for that reason macro economics -- if not the competitive interaction of all agents in the market? This huge competitive game is best represented by the theory of micro-macro-micro interaction that I have developed elsewhere (see for instance Eliasson 1976b, 1977, 1978, 1985a,b, 1988c, 1990b, 1991a,c). This goes beyond the standard repertoire of economic theory in that it allows the firm to "behave", and set both prices and outputs (Arrow 1959).

To the actors in the business community the standard general equilibrium theory of economics -- and all its static versions of monopolistic competition -- presents a notion of the firm that is totally unrecognizable for everybody that is not properly trained in economics. The alternative intellectual story that is comprehensible to practitioners is what I have already called *the theory of the experimentally organized economy* (EOE). This theory, on the other hand, exhibits properties that are fundamentally different from those of the classical economic model. As I will show in the next chapter the EOE is obtained by slightly and reasonably modifying certain assumptions of the standard general equilibrium model. (Since these assumptions are not always recognized by the economics profession and rarely made explicit in economics texts, my alternative to the classical model might even help understanding the classical model better). This creates, in Chapter II, in a verbal garb, a quite realistic version of the economic environment of a firm, which firm decision makers will recognize. What comes out is a micro, or *organization-based macroeconomic theory* that *should* make both the business administration people and the economists happy, since it merges their two professional fields.

This environmental setting also provides (in Chapter III) *a realistic presentation* (theory) *of the firm as an experimentator*, its success in markets being determined by the qualities of a dominant competence capital (Eliasson 1989a, 1990b).

Chapter IV demonstrates how this orientation of firm decision making is reflected in the organization of its internal information and control system. This chapter is based on interviews, that I have done recently and in the past.

Finally, and very interesting, the last 10 to 20 years have witnessed bold ventures by a couple of dozen computer and electronics firms into the market for *business information systems*, essentially attempting to develop a universal information and intellectual support system for the kind of decisions described in Chapters IV and V. Billions of dollars of corporate research money have been spent, but the product envisioned is not yet in sight. A number of well known firms have failed miserably. Chapters VI and VII tell this story.

NOTES

1.   Menger has also been classified as a marginalist in economic textbooks. His most fundamental contribution, as one of the founders of Austrian economics, however, rests on exactly the contrary position; se below.

2.   See Cohen and Levinthal (1989, 1990) who introduced the related concept of "absorptive capacity".

3.   Or *learning by using* (Rosenberg 1982) or *learning to learn* (Stiglitz 1987b).

4.   The Swedish micro-to-macro model (Eliasson 1977, 1991a) is a simple representation of the experimentally organized economy. Antonov and Trofimov (1993) demonstrate that classical statistical learning methods cannot (within that model) lead to a situation of full information, even when information costs are zero.

5.   See again the previous reference to the Swedish micro-to-macro model which is exactly such a non-linear system with the requisite disorderly properties.

6.   Cf. the discussion on scarcity by Hicks (1932, pp. 124 ff) and Salter (1960, pp. 43-44) and the ridiculous assertion by Fama (1980) that the economic theory of the firm needs no awareness neither of the entrepreneur nor the owners. The services of those "agents" can always be hired in the market. Such an argument can only be cooked up on the assumptions of the static classical full-information model.

II

THE ORGANIZATION OF PRODUCTION, MARKETS AND ADMINISTRATIVE CONTROL SYSTEMS

A General Theory of Innovation and Information, or the Experimentally Organized Economy

The theory of the firm derives its design from the theory of the market environment in which the firm is believed to operate. Most theorizing about the firm, and a significant part of business administration literature have its roots in the classical economic model, a model that when looked at critically doesn't even allow for the existence of a firm. Since the theory of the firm, and the practical management of firms are the main themes of this book, we have to discuss this inconsistency in economic thinking. This chapter introduces a simple micro- or organization-based macro theory, what I call the *Experimentally Organized Economy* (Eliasson 1987, 1988a, 1991c). The experimentally organized economy (the EOE) captures the economic environment of firms, as firm leaders recognize it. I introduce the experimentally organized economy as an alternative to the classical (static) general equilibrium model upon which much thinking on the theory of the firm and firm decision making has been, and still is based. From the classical model only firms that do not belong to this world can be derived. This makes it useless as a theoretical foundation for studying management and information problems of firms. The model of the experimentally organized economy, however, is much more useful in this respect since it captures the relevant realities of firm management life. The model of the EOE is obtained through slightly modifying two or three of the basic assumptions of the classical model. These modifications reflect critical experiences of any high-level firm manager. The general idea is very simple.

It can always be observed that at any level, things can be done in more than one way, most often in many ways. Some solutions are necessarily better than other solutions. The further up and the more complex the decision problem, the larger the number of possible solutions. It is rarely possible to evaluate the solution before it has been tried in the market and it is always impossible to know how large a number of even better, but so far untried solutions that exist. This is the essence of the experimentally organized economy. The economic environment of the firm that now emerges is characterized by so much diversity that it cannot possibly be made transparent to individual actors. The state of full information is never feasible, and therefore neither the state of a static equilibrium. This fundamentally changes the derived characteristics of optimal agent behavior that I will discuss in Chapter III.

II.1   FROM THE CLASSICAL TO THE EXPERIMENTAL ORGANIZATION OF THE ECONOMY

Three assumptions are necessary for the properties of the classical model:

(1) *State space*;
    the opportunity set or the domain over which agents make their choices has to be sufficiently small, or monotonous, to allow complete overview and optimal choice at no, or exactly known and small information costs.
(2) *Behavior*;
    - bounded rationality
    - tacit knowledge
    - intuition
    are not allowed.
(3) *The organization of markets*;
    - atomistic or
    - no, or controlled entry.

These "behavioral assumptions" mean that all knowledge can be treated as communicable, coded information (not tacit), being fully comprehensible, and that all information upon which agents act is also communicable. Modern industrial organization and finance literature discuss asymmetrically distributed information, not heterogeneous competence or knowledge. Information, as I have defined it earlier, is codable or communicable knowledge (see Section I.10).

No innovative, unpredictable entry and exit occur in the classical model, barring stochastic behavior. The number of agents in the market is fixed and known as members of state space, including their behavioral characteristics. The individual actor, the firm, is infinitesimally small (atomistic) and assumed to be fully informed (at no cost) about its interior capacities and about all other relevant characteristics.[1] He or she makes no mistakes. This guarantees that the firm won't carry out unrevealed individual strategies. Hence, the transparency of state space at known information costs becomes a critical assumption of received theory.

No real world actor feels at home among these artificial assumptions, even though -- if university trained -- he has been trained to argue as if.

The model of the experimentally organized economy relaxes these assumptions only slightly, but sufficiently to change the model radically. The behavioral assumption is the critical one. Firms cannot incorporate all information about state space -- and the possible actions of all other actors and innovative entrants -- in their decisions, but rather form a simplified, dated decision model of their perceived economic environments (bounded rationality). I have argued (Eliasson 1992a, p. 23 f) that *bounded rationality means a choice of an equilibrium decision model that makes competitive and single valued decisions possible.* Since the economic environment cannot be characterized by an equilibrium model, the decision model is always more or less biased, leading frequently to significant business mistakes. Such decisions are taken all the time and are the foremost source of variation in economic behavior. The large number of possible, different such decision models is sufficient to preclude that any one of them is exactly correct in its predictions, except by chance. Together all these individual firm models and their consequent decisions make up the reality of the experimentally organized economy. With sufficient entry and exit dynamics of such ex ante equilibrium decision firm models total environmental activity will be sufficiently non-linear to make most individual equilibrium decision models very biased predictors of environmental activity. In the EOE, hence, the local environment of each firm is basically unpredictable. Agents in the market constantly make more or less erroneous decisions based on fragmented and unreliable information, and total economic activity affects the local environments of individual actors in unpredictable ways. The competence of a firm very much mirrors its capacity to cope with this unpredictable environment. Much of the individual, or firm competence base, hence, is tacit and embodied in complex decision structures, including the appropriate choice of decision model for the occasion, meaning that it cannot easily be coded and transmitted to others, at least not at a known cost. Knowledge is transmitted by action, through experimentation in markets. Hence, insider activity or trading is the norm rather than the exception. Finally, decisions can be taken on the basis of much more (tacit) knowledge than is communicable to others ("intuition").

One could say that the assumption of bounded rationality will always become true if state space is made sufficiently large and/or heterogeneous. Tacit knowledge, however, (I think) needs a separate assumption (see below), that also introduces *intuition*.

The "notions" I have put together here -- even though not systematized before as an alternative to the classical economic model -- have appeared in bits and pieces in literature before. The idea of a large state space or an open-ended system, as I mentioned in the previous chapter, has its roots among the early philosophers/economists. The marginalist writers after the 1870s did away with this idea in economics. The unpredictability of the entrepreneur is deeply rooted in the young Schumpeter's (1911) theory of Economic Development, even though the old Schumpeter (1942) was on the verge of giving up the idea, possibly under the influence of neoclassical theorists applying their logic. Schumpeter foresaw the emergence of giant corporations that were able to substitute routine R&D investments and information processing for the creative, unpredictable entrepreneur. The old (1942) Schumpeter can be made right or wrong by shifting your theory between the two sets of assumptions; between those of the classical and those of the experimental model.

Bounded rationality is a concept that Herbert Simon (1955) introduced formally into economics from empirical research in psychology. Simon presented it very much as I want to use it (see Simon 1955) as a choice of an approximate simplified decision model of the firm to make it intellectually possible for the firm to cope with complexity. This notion of bounded rationality has appeared before under different names. The phenomenon was recognized already by Marshall. The notion of tacit knowledge originally came out of psychology, where it had been recognized as an empirical phenomenon long before economists began to think in the same terms (Polanyi 1967). It is still not a welcome notion among economists of the classical school, since it is not compatible with the definition of rationality used there (see Arrow 1986). If accepted and introduced in theory it would shift the classical model in the direction of the EOE.

On the whole the steady accumulation of empirical evidence is pushing heavily in favor of the assumptions of the model of the experimentally organized economy. For me it is sufficient to observe all the time how easily this model is accepted by people from the business or the insiders' world, and how impossible it is to explain to them the idea of the static general equilibrium model.

Let us go through the assumptions again, one by one.

II.2   THE LARGE INVESTMENT OPPORTUNITY SET

Karl Marx, observing the rapid introduction of large scale factory organization of production in the 19th century, projected the trends he observed into the future. He postulated a virtually unlimited physical productivity potential. However, borrowing an old theorem of Adam Smith, he also concluded that the markets would be unable to absorb unlimited *volumes* of physical output. Unlimited concentration of production to a few countries would follow. The same theorem has been applied to explain the internationalization of firms (see Eliasson 1991d). It is the main theme of Keynesian growth theory and, simple as it looks, this "theory" still has some relevance, even though it is so narrow -- so boundedly rational -- as to be mostly wrong.

What Marx forgot, together with most theorists after him, was that the industrial firm is not, and never was a factory for the production of large volumes of homogeneous output. The typical characteristics of industrial output is *product quality*, the creation of which draws the bulk of resources in advanced manufacturing industry (Eliasson 1987). *Allowing for quality of output is synonymous to allowing for virtually unlimited heterogeneity of output.* The unlimited productivity potential of Karl Marx is now replaced by the notion of an unlimited business opportunity set, or an unlimited state space.

Diminishing Returns to Learning Prevent Fully Informed Decisions

Frequent references to conventionally made assumptions are not enough to establish empirical evidence in their favor. However, building the assumptions on more deep, plausible assumptions helps to improve our understanding of the results derived from theory, and to assess their relevance. And the enormous size of state space or the opportunity set is illustrated (in Chapter VII) by reference to what happens in electronics and computer industry and in the markets for biochemical products.

Theoretically it is not nice to assume state space to be unlimited. I want to keep it bounded at each point in time, but sufficiently large to generate all the distinguishing features of the experimentally organized economy. This requires two tricks.

The *first* is the assumption of strongly diminishing returns to learning. If you attempt to speed up learning about the internal opportunities of state space through expanded experimental search, the number of business mistakes (a cost for learning) soon escalates prohibitively. This is the short-term constraint on being fully informed about the existing state space.

The Opportunity Set Grows from Being Exploited -- the Särimner Effect

The *second* trick is to formulate the opportunity set as a set of possibilities, that expands ahead of its exhaustion as a consequence of the successful *learning* that comes with participating in dynamic market competition. This learning process occurs over time and constantly generates new combinatorial possibilities within state space so that it grows in the process.[2] This can be accepted on a priori grounds, or by reference to generalizable examples. A theoretical question to ask is whether the generation of new combinatorial possibilities (the international opportunity set) is faster than the local competence that limits the rate of exploitation of the same state space.

The assumption that *state space expands through its exploitation* is, of course, much more plausible than the contrary assumption that state space is a small enough fixture to be completely transparent. I call my assumption the *Särimner effect* from the Scandinavian viking mythology (see Eliasson 1987, p. 29). The vikings had a pig that they killed and ate for supper every evening, only to see it come back to life next morning to be eaten again for supper. In economics Särimner is a reality. State space may even increase from being exploited. Technological competition in the experimentally organized economy is a forever *positive sum game.*

The Särimner effect generates a *path dependent* economic process with memory. The state achieved at each point in time (call it the state of knowledge) determines the potential of the next step. Even the limited combinatorial possibilities (heterogeneity) of the initial database of the Swedish micro-macro model is sufficient to generate 4×88 quarters of future states that are significantly different and dependent on the development path the model economy takes (Eliasson 1985a, 1991c). This is enough to illustrate the assumption of the vast state space and to make the Särimner effect a plausible reality.

The Limits of Learning

A question of more philosophical interest was whether the rate of expansion of the opportunity set in the very long run equals, or exceeds, its rate of exploitation. If it does, the state of full information is forever beyond the horizon. The experimental organization of the economy is the only viable one, and the classical model is scientifically unsound and misleading. The western intellectual tradition is strongly inclined to reject assumptions that result in such conclusions. If, on the other hand, the rate of expansion is slower than the rate of exploitation, mankind will gradually increase its knowledge of nature, but the dynamics of this learning is economically controlled and may be very slow. The Särimner effect will guarantee that even though all possible development patterns will converge on one and the same pattern in infinity, this state of full information is for the time being sufficiently distant to make it economically completely uninteresting. The experimental organization of the economy is still the optimal one.

Reasoning in terms of the size of the state space may, however, not be necessary to establish the dynamic properties of the experimentally organized economy. A wide class of non-linear models exhibiting sufficient *complexity* can be shown to exhibit all the necessary characteristics of unpredictable, chaotic behavior (Carleson 1991). As has been demonstrated by Day (1982a,b, 1983) even rather simple, traditional economic models exhibit phases of such behavior. Such economic environments evade the learning of agents and prevent the establishing of anything like the standard, full information equilibrium. What is new in the setting of the experimentally organized economy is that such unpredictable behavior can be demonstrated to arise out of the limited, but differently structured capacity of agents to understand an economic environment which is composed of the behavior of all other agents. Such bounded rationality of sufficient variation (diversity) is sufficient to establish a sufficiently large or heterogeneous opportunity set to establish, in turn, the existence of the experimentally organized economy.

The large opportunity set is also a necessary condition for bounded rationality of agents. Hence, necessary and sufficient conditions for the EOE can be demonstrated using only the idea of complexity.

It is again a philosophical question whether such complexity is enough to introduce innovative behavior. Innovative behavior in the limited sense of novelty probably doesn't require more. But do we not normally think of science-based innovations that move the long-term capacity of the world economy as something more deeply founded than a menu of selections lying around, only to be discovered (as in an innovation race)? Perhaps not. What has to be understood is that this kind of innovative activity has a time dimension. Each innovation starts up a cumulative sequence of new capabilities that all depend on what happened earlier, including the learning of all agents. At each point in time "nature" offers a menu of choices, and possible sequences into the future. By making a choice you limit future choices and begin on a path that takes you towards one set of destinations, but not towards other possible sets of destinations (*path dependence*). The degree to which path dependence closes future opportunities is an open empirical question. In a very long time perspective (Eliasson 1983) perhaps all opportunities will nevertheless be open. For most decision makers, however, the time perspectives are much shorter and under those shorter time horizons path dependence is a reality. By adding the time dimensions of all possible sequences, we add to the complexity of the opportunity set.

II.3   TACIT KNOWLEDGE, FREE ENTRY AND TECHNOLOGICAL COMPETITION

Introducing heterogeneity of product quality together with a vast state space is sufficient to demonstrate the existence of tacit, incommunicable knowledge among producers. It is no longer demand -- as with Adam Smith, Karl Marx or Stigler (1951) -- that restricts output, but supply capacity in the form of local, heterogeneous and tacit knowledge, or competence (Eliasson 1990a, b).

This reformulation is sufficient to introduce an economic world, completely different from the one conjured up by the classical model. The setting is now truly Schumpeterian or Austrian. A large number of active and potential players equipped with very heterogeneous local competence, face an immense opportunity set. The commercial outcome of their application of local knowledge cannot be ascertained until they have tried it in the market (the knowledge is tacit). The experimental organization of the economy also requires that potential competitors are free to enter the competitive fray, threatening the existence of incumbents, forcing them to exit (creative destruction) or shape up. The successful, innovative entrepreneur comes up with a new commercial or technical combination that suddenly establishes him, or her as a temporary monopoly in the market -- until somebody comes up with something better. The outcome of this *technological competition* in the experimentally organized economy at the micro -- agent -- level is in principle unpredictable.

A free market is synonymous with free access to the opportunity set, or an unlimited right to establish yourself as a competitor in the market. This requires the absence of artificial regulations or constraints on individual experimentation. There are, of course, technological or physical constraints, e.g. scale, that have to be accepted. However, an important constraint on competition, reducing the profitability of competitive entry is the competitive strength of incumbents. If that strength rests on competence everything is fine. If it rests on accumulated financial power, we have a monopoly "problem". The assumptions of the experimentally organized economy should, however, be sufficient to prevent existing incumbents from being for ever superior, or from accumulating unlimited financial staying power or from taking over entire markets. Part of the prerequisites for that is unregulated ("free") markets everywhere, including the financial market. Under the assumptions of the experimentally organized economy, free raider activity and the free introduction of new credit instruments of the modern U.S. variety is a more effective competition policy for the long run than antitrust policy (see below).

II.4   OPTIMAL SOCIAL ORGANIZATION IN THE EXPERIMENTALLY ORGANIZED ECONOMY

The political implications of the experimentally organized economy obviously are very different from those that can be derived from the "plannable" world that emerges from the classical model. Rather than minimizing slack ("mistakes") the experimental model makes risk averse behavior in firms risky, promotes bold business experiments and treats mistakes as a learning cost. Technological competition among a sufficiently large number of players with local (heterogeneous) competence forces all competitors, and especially the dominant players, to act prematurely, because at least some players will act and a few will succeed, if not by competence so by luck. Firm performance will not be measured by the ability of being right most of the times, but rather by proficiency in learning to be right now and then, and in identifying and correcting mistakes early, something I will elaborate in the next chapter on the firm. In fact, the economically efficient procedure to exploit state space is to have a very large number of experiments in the economy, implying a very large number of both successful experiments and of mistakes (see Eliasson 1991a). The implications for social policy and organization are that Governments can no longer improve economic performance at any level through manipulating certain parameters of the economy, thereby achieving preset targets with some accuracy. This becomes very clear in a model exhibiting the sequential path dependency of an innovation and investment process and the impossibility of considering all the potential long-term implications. Hence, in the process of doing good for its current voters, a Government pursuing extreme short-term policy objectives, like a very low unemployment rate, can gradually, over a generation or so, permanently transfer a once wealthy economy into a relatively poor economy (see Eliasson and Taymaz 1992).

II.5   THE CAPITAL MARKET AND DYNAMIC ECONOMIC COORDINATION -- CLOSING THE SMITH-SCHUMPETER-WICKSELL SYSTEM

The classical economist has always had a problem with the firm. Theoretically it should not exist, and his endeavor to make it come to life (see Section III.17) has been troubled by that contradiction. *The theory of the firm*, as such a theory should be realistically designed, *requires a matching theory of dynamic markets*. Since the classical model is not up to this task, I have designed a crude alternative, the EOE, from which a theory of the firm which meets the specifications of a live firm can be derived.

How to Operate out of Equilibrium?

The Swedish economist Johan Åkerman once (1950) remarked that the four fundamentals of economics ought to be:
(1)   - interdependence
(2)   - welfare
(3)   - process
(4)   - institutions.
As he also noted, modern general equilibrium theory rooted in the Walrasian *equilibrium* tradition was solely concerned with the first two items, studying the consequences for welfare in a static equilibrium setting of interdependent markets. The solution of the coordination problem, leading to a socially and economically efficient equilibrium is achieved through solving a set of equations. For long only models (read equation systems) that have such a (unique) solution have been considered acceptable. Until rather recently the solving of such special models has been assumed costless, thus for a long time removing the concept of *information*

from the concern of economists. In reality the market institutions are agents specialized in coordinating or regulating an economy out of equilibrium (Day 1986a). One of these institutions is Government. Of course, such institutions, accounting for a very large part of total resource use in an economy, cannot be assumed to be costless. In the dynamic setting of the EOE the existence of an equilibrium is not at all guaranteed. On the other hand, the EOE can accommodate live firms as participants (institutions) in the market process. Hence, the classical model is not a very useful conceptual design of the environment in which the economic agents called firms operate. It is misleading. Firms spend the bulk of their resource use on various forms of information processing (Eliasson 1990a, b). Market agents do not face exogenous equilibrium prices or aggregates; they confront each other as rivals. And the organizational design of markets and of their internal hierarchies determine the nature of that confrontation, called competition. The existence of a firm, hence, is a contradiction within the classical model. There, the firm by definition appears as a market imperfection which cannot "behave", and should not be there.

What Bounds an Economy out of Equilibrium? -- the Endogenous Invisible Hand

What controls an economy without central authority? Only one thing is needed to close the experimentally organized economic system. An economic process needs a *control function* to continue. The general equilibrium model needs an exogenous visible hand, the auctioneer, a price controller or the central policy or price maker that places the system in a position where it will remain to everybody's satisfaction; in equilibrium. Such a model is of course very pleasing to the central policy maker, and it is not surprising that the policy community, even in capitalistically organized market economies, has provided ample funding for continued research on that conceptualization of reality. It is more surprising that private business investors have unwittingly acquired the same idea of how things economic work, and that a large part of the profession of economic intellectuals have followed the scent of easy research funding, rather than attempting to understand how an economy works under different regimes.

Anyhow, *Adam Smith* did not want it that way. He wanted his invisible hand to be endogenous. The convexity property of state space that forces fully informed maximizing agents onto an optimal trajectory in the classical model has to be replaced by something that bounds the economic process. We know from observations that activity levels cannot grow indefinitely within bounded time and are almost always positive.

Again, the hierarchical order of the decision processes of the economy gives the answer. Where is the ultimate, bounding influence to be found and how is it exercised?

The Capital Market as the Ultimate Controller

The *first* round of analysis of the classical model traces ultimate control to the capital market and the central political authority, the conventional view. Within the intellectual confines of that model the market economy can never be demonstrated to be superior to the centrally planned economy (Pelikan 1988a, 1992).

In the *second* round of analysis the two contesting power systems of an economy -- the political and the market -- would declare the political authority the winner in the classical economic model and the market system the most probable winner in the experimentally organized economy. This is a more difficult story to tell that rests on the fact that in a democratically organized society also the political system ultimately is competing with all agents in the market for funds. A dictatorial political system might, however, constrain the openness of the markets to such an extent that the experimental process ceases to function. Top down control, similar to that possible in the classical model and in the firm, can then be exercised. Attempts to do that abound in the political system, and most of them have been geared towards the control of capital market processes or the regulating of competitive entry. Such central political control is not a sustainable long-run regime in the experimentally organized economy.

Nevertheless, even so, if exogenous political preferences do not control the directions of change in the economy, what does, and how is this control exercised through the capital market?

Classical theory assigns this control of direction (within the convex set of production plans) to a convex set of consumption preferences. Economies of scale are not allowed by assumption. This does not help when the convex set of production plans -- and possibly also of consumption preferences -- change as a consequence of innovative behavior and the ongoing market allocation of quantities and prices. Successful innovative behavior exhibits itself as a temporary scale economy at the micro level. The control function now has to be what connects the future with today, namely the *interest rate* and *expectations formation*. This introduces the *capital market as the control function of the dynamic process of the experimentally organized economy*. The factors that determine the interest rate also control the macroeconomic growth process. These factors are the expected rates of return among producers (firms) and the rate at which the future is discounted to today among individuals. Both these factors are influenced by the unpredictability of future returns to investment and to saving, and the attitudes to this uncertainty of investors and individuals. Since micro unpredictability characterizes the experimentally organized economy, due to reasons already given, ex ante and ex post returns to both investment and saving will deviate. The realization of inconsistent plans will determine the dynamics of the market process, and a *Wicksellian* (1898) type of disequilibrium will be the typical state in the capital market.

Competence and Competition Set the Limits

With *Schumpeter's* technological competition, new combinations/innovations will move productivity and the growth machinery, making room for advances by competing inefficient producers out of business (exit). The economy will be characterized at each point in time by a distribution of rents (rates of return over the interest rate), the rankings of which do not persist over time (see diagrams below).

The ultimate factor that controls the growth process now turns out to be the set of factors that determines the competence to *innovate* (create new competence), to acquire knowledge (to *learn*), and to face uncertainty (transferring uncertainty into calculable risks, the *entrepreneur*). These factors will be seen in the next chapter to be the determinants of the temporarily controlled monopoly -- the market imperfection -- called a firm.

At the macro-market level control is exercised through innovative (technological) competition limiting the earnings power of incumbent firms by reducing the economic value of their competence capital, without reducing the *productivity capacity* of the same competence capital. The nature of this competence creation, however, can only be revealed by taking a closer look at the business organization itself. This, by the way, is also the only way of understanding the contribution of the firm to economic growth, the potential of various forms of organization of the market economy and the importance of differently designed information technologies used by business organizations.

Having established the existence of an experimentally organized economy, rather than a potentially plannable and controllable economic system, we have to deal with a very different concept of knowledge than before; the decision problem is no longer restricted to the gathering of information in order to be fully informed. Information is not well defined in the experimentally organized model and only partially accessible by analytical methods (Eliasson 1994b). "Access to information" will be seen to mean access to people with competence as much as to data. (See further Chapters III and V).

II.6   THE THREE AXIOMS OF KNOWLEDGE (BEHAVIOR)
    -- PROVING THE EXISTENCE OF TACIT KNOWLEDGE
    -- EXCURSUS ON THEORY

The information content of the same coded message changes as a consequence of its use. We are concerned with more or less tacit knowledge shaped and interpreted by the humans that use it. Let me introduce the next chapter by going through this again.

The Three Axioms of Knowledge

To understand the limited information processing capacity of individual agents and of all agents together, I introduce the three axioms of knowledge.

(1) *Complexity* makes decisions *boundedly rational* in the sense of Day (1993) and of Simon (1955).

(2) *Embodiment* makes knowledge a partly *tacit* property in the sense of Polanyi (1967).

(3) *Intuition* allows decisions to be based on more information than can be communicated (see Eliasson 1990b).

Together these three axioms establish the existence of *transactions costs* and prevent the opportunity set from being immediately exploited.[3]

Bounded rationality keeps individuals or teams at work, searching in small corners of the opportunity set, employing the local knowledge capital they possess.

"Tacit knowledge" limits the scope of synergizing knowledge through team formation, since people have to cooperate to form a team. If cooperation is explicit (non-tacit), as it is, for instance, in an automated factory, information processing is coded and transaction costs can be estimated. If complexity and demands on flexibility mean that operating instructions cannot be coded, more informal means of communication are needed for a team operation, like special languages (Pelikan 1969), proxy variables and informal rules (Eliasson 1976a) etc. This is exactly the point made in signaling theory (Akerlof 1970, Spence 1973 etc.).

The Limits of Analytical Methods

The concept of "tacit" knowledge by definition refers to a relationship of more than two people, implying limited communication. Tacit knowledge is always present when human competence is heterogeneous and/or unevenly distributed, meaning that some messages cannot be received by others, because they do not possess the required receiver competence. Chapter I defined general education as a means of increasing the part of total knowledge capital that is not tacit. In what follows I will argue the same thing about modern information technology.

Axiom (3) introducing *intuition* enhances the capacity for problem solving of the individual beyond what he can communicate to others, but prevents critical, complex knowledge from being communicated to others.

A key problem of this study, hence, is to find out whether modern information technology will ease the restrictions associated with each axiom, i.e. with

- expanding the ability to deal with complexity (calculation, *analysis*)
- separating knowledge, as information from human beings (codability, *presentation*)
- increasing awareness (*transparency*).

As long as the use of tacit knowledge cannot be reduced to insignificance, the optimal information system of firms will include a critical non-analytical element, access to information being synonymous with access to people.

It is important in this context to observe that this means that no universal information system exists. The internal information system of a firm, as well as the theory of the firm or of the economy, will always be an ad hoc intellectual structure, designed to deal approximately with a certain set of decision or policy problems. One such ad hoc factor is *tradition*.

The Impact of Tradition on Modes of Decision Making

Documented practice on the mode of management exhibits a strong influence of business literature based on the classical economic model and the theory of planning. This was typically so in the 1960s and early 1970s. A shift towards the experimental mode of behavior came out of the crisis experience of the 1970s (Eliasson 1976a, 1984c). Normative academic literature, however, has taken a long time to catch up. What is today called technological management is based on even stronger (implicit) assumptions about what can be learned about state space than was assumed in the "long range planning" exercises so popular in the 1960s. The purpose still is to feed the firm information system with reliable external forecasts. As we learned in the economically disorderly 1970s, this task is not meaningful in the experimentally organized economy. Hence, planning was thrown out, and attention refocused towards achieving reliable internal *information systems* that made the firm transparent and allowed decentralization of operations through improved profit control (Eliasson 1976a; Eliasson, Fries, Jagrén and Oxelheim 1984), supported by the analytical competence to identify mistakes early, and effectively correct mistakes (*flexibility*).

Not even the ambition to enhance flow efficiency through improved overview (information efficiency) has been very apparent from my discussions with information, budgeting and control people over the last couple of decades. Learning during the 1970s has clearly influenced the organization of firms during the 1980s.

II.7 EMPIRICAL EVIDENCE ON THE EXPERIMENTALLY ORGANIZED ECONOMY

Evidence on the hypothesis of the experimentally organized economy vs. the classical model will always have to be indirect. The assumptions can never be proven right or wrong. The assumptions are, however, so reasonable that the only defense for the classical model is that its very special assumptions do not distort analysis and do not matter for the applications to which it has been put. On that score I would propose to get the classical model removed from industrial organization theory, from the theory of the firm, and as a foundation of macro economics.

To document the experimentally organized economy the previous, very abstract presentation has to be reformulated in more observable categories. This is most effectively done in terms of the Swedish micro-based macro model, in which macroeconomic growth is driven by technological competition fuelled by innovative behavior of firms, including innovative entry.

A Generalized Salter Curve Analysis of Innovative Behavior and Enforced Competition

Competition takes place among live agents in markets, called business firms. The existence of a firm is based on its competence to generate organizational synergies, needed to earn a rent above production and financing costs. To explain how the firm captures its rent both a theory of the firm and a theory of the market environment in which the firm is supposed to operate are required. The deep problem in economics is that the characteristics of the market needed to explain firm behavior is totally dependent on the dynamics of all business agents. Mainstream economic theory has no live firms and, thus, offers very little in the form of a useful theory of the market to explain the dynamics of firm behavior. Dynamic micro-macro theory is needed, embodying an explicit representation of competition as a dynamic process. This process does not necessarily converge to an equilibrium determined outside the economic system. The direction of change of the macro economy depends on the micro structures developing along the way, and on how competing agents react to, and change them. This is the theory of the market.

A market, or the entire economy can at each point in time be represented by a distribution of potential performance characteristics, like the rates of return over the interest rate ($\bar{\varepsilon}$) in Figure II.1A. These types of distributions -- especially if presented as productivity rankings of establishments (Figure II.1B) -- are often referred to as Salter (1960) curves. Each firm is represented in this curve by a ranking on the vertical axis (the columns in Figures II.1A, B), the width of the column measuring the size of the firm in percent of all other firms. Figure II.1A shows that even though the firm in the model has increased its rate of return between 1983 and 1990 it has lost in ranking. Figure II.1B shows the same firms' labor productivity position. Finally, Figure II.1C shows where, underneath its own productivity frontier, the firm was operating to position itself on the productivity and rate of return rankings of the market. This is still actual ex post performance 1982 and (simulated) 1991. The dynamics of markets, on the other hand, is controlled by the potential ex ante set of distributions that capture the planned action of all other firms, including new entry.

Figure II.1   Salter curve structures illustrating the dynamics of the Swedish micro-to-macro model

Figure II.1A   Rate of return distributions in Swedish manufacturing industry, 1983 and 1990

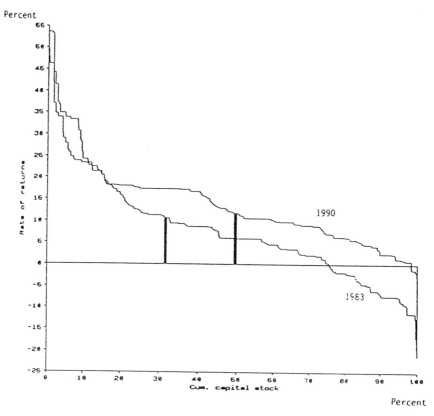

Note: The rate of return measure (= $\bar{\varepsilon}$) is the nominal rate of return on total capital over the nominal interest on industrial loans.

Figure II.1B *Labor productivity distributions in Swedish manufacturing, 1983 and 1990*

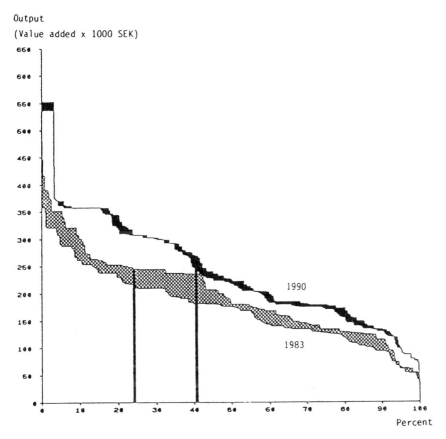

Output
(Value added x 1000 SEK)

Percent

There is still another set of Salter curves that tell how *each firm sees itself positioned relative to other firms*. The real world of the experimentally organized economy, as well as its model approximation, the Swedish micro-to-macro model, shows large *divergences between actual and perceived positions*.

The ex ante distributions tell the potential for the firm to outbid all other firms in wages, or in paying a higher interest rate.

Learning about one's competitive situation -- in reality or in theory -- occurs in different dimensions. Prices offered in the market tell something about how other firms -- notably the best firms -- view their competitive situation. Competition, production, hiring, etc. can also be directly observed. The firm, finally, learns directly itself, when it enters the market. The critical learning experience to observe in this context occurs when firms observe that competitors can do better. Firm management then knows that this can be done and that it had better improve in order not to be pushed down, right along the Salter distribution, and, perhaps, out.

Similarly, when the firm finds itself at the top, or close to the top, it knows that a whole lot of "closely inferior" firms feel threatened, and are taking action to better their positions through innovation or imitative learning.

Figure II.1C   The productivity frontier of one firm, first quarter 1983

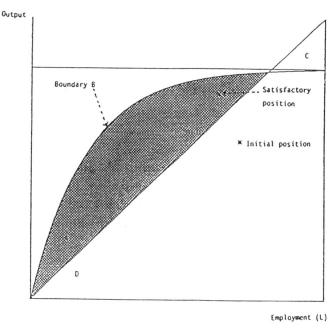

Note: Boundary B represents the upper output level per unit of labor input. The straight diagonal corresponds to the minimum labor productivity levels compatible with the minimum targeted profit margin, given expected wages and prices. This targeted profit margin has been derived from a targeted rate of return.

Source: Eliasson (1991a).

The conclusion is that if potential Salter distributions are sufficiently steep and if all firms know it, firms -- and especially the top left-hand group -- will feel sufficiently threatened to actively aim for improving their positions on the Salter curve through innovation. If such innovative activity, notably through innovative entry in markets, is freely allowed, necessary conditions for maintaining sufficiently steep Salter distributions to move the entire economy through a selfperpetuated competitive process have been established (Eliasson 1985a, 1991a,b). These conditions become both necessary and sufficient if the opportunity set is sufficiently large. This also establishes the link between dynamic competition through the Schumpeterian (1911) entrepreneur and innovative entry, argued by Smith (1776) to be the critical factor behind economic growth, that perpetuates a disequilibrium economic process type Wicksell (1898) -- the SSW connection (Eliasson 1992b). A sufficiently large and heterogeneous state space, boundedly rational behavior on the part of agents, and sufficiently free innovative entry are the small modifications of the classical model that create the experimentally organized economy.

The Very Large Productivity Potential

The Swedish micro-to-macro (M-M) model features firms or divisions as well defined decision units operating in dynamic markets. Figures II.1 show that very large productivity gains are potentially possible through a recombination of factors, especially if the bad performers can be forced to shut down. This is so even though no new entry or no new investment in the best firms occur. Carlsson (1991) also demonstrated that the by far largest productivity improvements in the short and medium term were achieved through such reallocations. The structure of the opportunity set of the micro-macro economy, represented down to the level of resolution of the firm or the division is sufficient to create the virtually non-transparent business opportunity set of the EOE (see Eliasson 1991a). Predictability is for all practical purposes removed. The theoretical point I want to make, however, is that if we allow for similar reallocations also within firms and divisions taking the analysis down to the very fine level where allocation and technical decisions are made, the number of possible combinations within firms and also between firms expands without limit, as does the productivity potential. Predictability vanishes at the micro level. As a consequence the notion of a macro productivity frontier cannot be upheld. There is either no way of defining the macro production function or, if you do, the agents will always be operating *very far below* it, being dependent upon their temporary location in a dynamic process coordinated by endogenous prices. This in turn means that price signaling, as shown by Antonov and Trofimov (1993) will never be able to disclose any efficient equilibrium or convergence trajectory of the model. We can also learn from this analysis, that if there are no social problems, or political constraints relating to the reallocation process, the potential for productivity improvements in an economy is enormous.

The Swedish Micro-to-Macro (M-M) model, hence, exhibits all principally important features of the EOE. Dynamic competition as described above determines entry and exit and hence the selection processes that create a path-dependent evolution, and non-stationary behavior that prevents classical learning. This is so even though the M-M model for all practical purposes is deterministic. If you have the code of the M-M model, you can of course predict through a deterministic simulation. But without access to the code you cannot learn the structure of the model [to perform that prediction from observing the output from a large number of simulations (see further Eliasson 1994a, p. 146)]. The seemingly erratic behavior exhibited by the model economy like major macro collapses that occur out of the blue (Eliasson 1983, 1984b, 1991a) all originate in the endogenous changes of the Salter distributions, characteristics that are impossible to reproduce in a predictable way by known estimable modeling techniques. This is sufficient to rule out classical learning in the experimental setting of the M-M model, as shown by the learning experiments of Antonov and Trofimov (1993). Forcing individual firms to use a neoclassical or a Keynesian learning model to search their way into the complex MOSES Salter landscape means imposing too simplistic intelligence structures on firms. It narrows their minds such that they are not capable of exploiting the rich business opportunities offered in the MOSES environment. The efficient long-run procedure from a macroeconomic point of view is to allow each firm to search *the opportunity set of MOSES* according to its own mind. This close to random, experimental procedure increases the failure rate, but it also makes some firms capture opportunities that were closed to them in the narrow, enforced scenarios restricting them to preset search mechanisms. The wider search proves superior for macroeconomic performance.

I could also add the amusing experience we have had over the many years of modeling work. If you sit down at the computer and attempt to correct unexpected, disruptive and "socially undesirable macro behavior" by using its almost full assortment of traditional policy parameters, you tend to create more and stronger disruptive macro behavior of the same kind at some later period (Eliasson 1985a, pp. 78 ff).

The M-M model is a highly simplistic dynamical systems representation of the real market economy. Even though individual mechanisms are traditional and can be understood partially, the dynamics of the evolving system prevents classical learning. Reality, of course, requires that much more complexity be coped with.

Innovative Entry is the Key to Macro Dynamics

The critical understanding of markets, hence, comes with understanding the nature of competitive, innovative entry and the dynamic market process that innovative entry keeps in motion. This understanding requires a broad definition of innovative entry, from the launching of a new product, via the establishment of a new company to the merger of two large companies, with the purpose of improving long-run profit performance.

Experience would suggest that small firms are superior to large firms as innovators, even though the consensus is not 100 percent (cf the contrary conclusions of Holmström 1993 and Granstrand and Sjölander 1993). The large firms, however, together spend significantly more on R&D than do small firms. New entry is not always in the form of new firm entry. It can occur through the establishment of a new business activity within a large firm or, through the introduction of a new product. As I said, the merger of two large firms occasions market effects similar to those of new entry (Eliasson 1991b).

The rôle of small firms and new entry therefore should be seen in the context of the following three observations:

1) The direct macroeconomic effects will be very slow in coming (Eliasson 1991b, 1993c). Empirical evidence shows very small effects even after a 15-year period. Simulations on the Swedish micro-to-macro model show a significant direct macroeconomic influence only after some 20-30 years.

2) New entry in a broad sense preserves structural diversity, making faster growth feasible (Eliasson 1984b, 1991b). Even if entrants are on the average no better than incumbents, the spread in performance among them is larger. Since only the best survive in the long run, viable entry and exit preserve diversity of structure.

Above all, however,
3) new innovative entry in a broad sense serves as a competitive force to shake up incumbents and move the market from Ricardian to Schumpeterian type competition.

Hence, understanding competition requires understanding the forces that drive new entry, and this is not easy. With the average new entrant being rather somewhat inferior to the average incumbent -- if performance is measured by labor productivity or the rate of return (Granstrand 1986, pp. 295-310) -- but the spread in performance being much wider, most new entrants will soon fail and exit.

The Swedish micro-to-macro model (Eliasson 1977, pp. 5 ff., 1978, pp. 52ff) embodies the type of competition that is generated by new entry and exit in the EOE. Such competition occurs in the "broad-based Salter (1960) landscape of firms" described above, depicting the distribution of productivities or rates of return over the firm population. Entering firms are represented by a "smaller such Salter distribution" with a much wider spread, disrupting the balance on the margin in the tail end of incumbent firms, where the marginally worst producer just covers wage costs.

Marginal incumbents exit and new product and factor prices are established at levels where most of the new entrants will soon perish and exit.

Many large incumbents will, however, be shaken by the remaining supreme entrants and be forced to shape up their competitive performance in order not to lose market share, which presumably corresponds to the size of their invested capacity to produce.

In the very long run the remaining, superior new entrants will begin to exercise a direct influence at the macro level. Performance characteristics after a 30-year simulation shows the upper left, "supreme" corner of the Salter distribution to be occupied by the new, now old entrants (Eliasson 1991b).

As most analytical results, this one is, however, obvious from the assumptions I have made. The critical issue is to understand why firms enter the market in large numbers despite being inferior, and do it repeatedly.

Such phenomena cannot be explained within the static, full information general equilibrium model, and not within an asymmetric information version of the efficient market theory, so popular in financial economics. It fits, however, nicely into the EOE. Under the assumptions of the EOE the entrants perform an experiment, the outcome of which cannot be assessed until it has been tested. The EOE has to possess a sufficiently large number of such potentially competent and optimistic entrants or experimentators for the growth process to occur.

The four change mechanisms of economic growth

The *intensity of competition* depends on the spread in the capacities of business organizations to generate synergies, or scale economies, or rents, or productivity. A ranking of such capacities is made up, not only of existing firms, but also of what every firm expects existing firms to be capable of doing, like the consequences for market competition of investment, of exit and of not yet existing firms, that may come into existence (entry). The combined "carrots and whips" of markets make up the incentives and the dynamics of the macro economy.

Economic growth is created by the live agents of the market that enter to compete with existing firms, or respond to competition through building and exploiting their organizational competence, or exit if they fail. As I will demonstrate below (see also Eliasson, 1993b, 1995a) the four mechanisms of Table II.1 are sufficient to explain economic growth.

Each mechanism operates in different time dimensions. Innovative entry takes very long to exhibit direct effects on output and employment, but affects competition in markets directly, and thus forces incumbent firms to reorganize, rationalize or exit. New, innovative entry, hence, is the driving force in the economic growth process, and Adam Smith (1776) was very right in putting prime emphasis on the importance of entry as the moving force behind national economic wealth and for the maintenance of competition, forcing contraction or exit among low performers, thus releasing resources at reasonable costs for expanding industries.

Table II.1 is a stylized version of a growth process as it occurs among an endogenously varying number of well defined firms.[4] It represents four different *investment categories*, the last one a disinvestment. In reality this process, of course, occurs at a much finer level of resolution exhibiting also break ups and recombinations of firms. The very fact that such fragmentation and recombinations of existing firms also impair existing, internal firm information systems (see already Eliasson 1976a) is of particular interest in this study.

Behind business success lies some form of competence and my whole story will be about the way the business agents called firms build and apply that competence to succeed in dynamic, competitive markets. An important part of that competence, in turn, lies in the firm's managerial capacity in understanding itself and its relations to its market environments. Much of that competence should be reflected in the information system of the firm, the concern of this study. Only large firms, however, employ formalized and objectively observable information systems. For that reason most of our empirical concern will be with very large firms and their internal information, control and decision systems, i.e. with growth mechanisms (2), (3) and (4) in Table II.1. This, however, does not mean that we disregard the importance for the competitive environment of the entry mechanisms. As it happens, Swedish industry has exhibited excellent performance under mechanisms (2) and (3), but extremely bad performance under (1) (see Braunerhjelm 1993a,b).

Table II.1   The four mechanisms of economic growth

---

1.   Innovative entry
2.   Reorganization of existing firms
3.   Rationalization of existing firms
4.   Competitive exit (the bankruptcy institution)

Sources: Eliasson (1993b, 1995a).

The firm growth mechanisms of the economy shown in Table II.1 represent different time dimensions. The experimentally organized economy is dominated in the long run by the selection mechanisms: entry, reorganization and exit. The classical model only recognizes operations management, i.e. (3). If selection mechanisms can be demonstrated in the micro-macro model (see Eliasson 1991a,b, 1993c) to be important for macroeconomic behavior, like growth, the existence of that endogenous process has been demonstrated. Until evidence of some other observable growth mechanism has been demonstrated, it should be understood as the preferred explanation. While there is no evidence to reject the experimental model, no convincing empirical analyses support the classical model.[5] In fact, testing the classical model in its neoclassical "growth version" including the so-called "new growth theory" of Romer (1986) and Lucas (1988) is only weak evidence for an alternative. Since the new growth theory can be derived as a very special case of the experimental selection model such macro econometrics *also* supports the experimental model. Choosing one in favor of the other requires that we look for empirical evidence at a more basic, assumptional level. Let me report some results from IUI research.

Unpredictability in the Swedish Micro-to-Macro Model

The Swedish micro-to-macro model is a model of the experimentally organized economy. It features path dependence through selection mechanisms (exit, entry) with paths that differ depending upon the setting of certain parameters that regulate the speeds of market arbitrage (Eliasson 1983, 1984b, 1991a). This, for instance, means that long run simulations featuring more or less of, or no, entry, everything else the same will generate very different industrial structures over longer periods (Eliasson 1991a), and thus also different local environments for each firm at each point in time, and different competitive processes at each point in time even though the rules of the market (the arbitrage parameters) may be the same. To uncover the nature (the code) of these growth processes the initial state and the regime parameters have to be estimated. This is not possible. The process, once stated, has few repetitive patterns (is not stationary). Hence, the local environment of each firm is not learnable except by chance, or the learning of some "proxy pattern" that can be interpreted with some accuracy, at least temporarily. In principle the Swedish micro-macro model thus exhibits features that resembles real life. Knowing the code the model can be tuned such that certain pattern characteristics of the real world can be generated. This is, however, no test of the realism of the model, since it may be possible to generate similar path characteristics using other parameter settings. Nevertheless, this illustrates the problem of limited insight into the opportunity set of each individual actor, something that is made even more clear, considering the correct interpretation of expectations models firms use in the model and in reality (Eliasson 1976a, 1985a). It is, therefore, even more interesting to see that limiting the choice in the use of information in the model means a significant deterioration in the long run macro-economic performance of the model economy (Antonov and Trofimov 1993).

This intractability of the EOE becomes even more intriguing if we think in terms of the allocation of human-based competence, that at all levels requires a superior competence to be efficiently allocated. The experimental organization of markets is the only way to take decisions down to the level where the competence to make the best allocation decisions resides. For the reason just stated, however, nobody will ever know whether the best decision was arrived at, only that a centrally imposed decision would probably have produced a worse outcome.

Following a Sample of Firms for Some 60 Years

That the rather rapid elimination of firms typical of the experimentally organized economy, is also a feature of life, is illustrated in Jagrén (1986, 1988). A random sample of some 150 firms from a register in 1922 had been reduced to 22 autonomous firms by the early 1980s. Most of the remaining firms, furthermore, had remained small. Two firms of the sample, however, exhibited remarkable performance generating a total output growth of the remaining cohort of firms somewhat faster than total industrial output in Sweden for the same period.

On the whole, however, the EOE would predict any random sample of some 100 firms and up, to generate over some 50 to 100 years a total output growth (of the remaining firms) somewhat slower than growth in total manufacturing output, allowing for the additional influence of entry. The composition of the "cohort" of firms should, however, be similar; one or two expansive firms accounting for most of the growth.

Not Even Very Large Firms Live For Ever

The duration of Swedish *Stora* (the world's oldest joint-stock company, see Figure II.2) as an autonomous company, is the objective of most firms, large and small. Very few firms reach such age. A large firm usually has a longer power due to its larger accumulated financial resources. A large firm, thereby, should not have to be wiped out by a temporary market adversity, if it quickly adjusts costs downward. Facing such temporarily bad conditions in the late sixties Boeing thus saved itself through cutting employment from 150 thousand to just above 30 thousand over three years. But also large firms eventually die or dwindle into insignificance, at enormous costs in the form of capital value destruction, if badly managed. Any cohort of firms chosen at random (as indicated by Jagrén 1988, 1993) will eventually be emptied. It is only surprising that so many of the old firms from the late 19th century still remain as dominant manufacturing firms in Sweden (see Table II.2).

Figure II.2   The share of Swedish manufacturing output of *Stora* 1340-1988
-- company turnover in percent of total manufacturing and mining
production

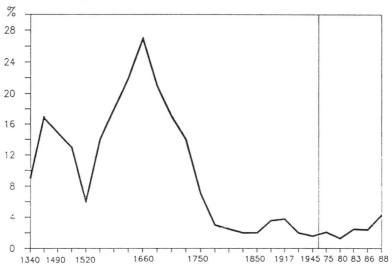

Source: MOSES Database, Research Report No. 40, 1992, IUI, Stockholm, p. 94.

Figure II.3   Survival rates in a sample of firms
-- number of employees, 1925 and 1980

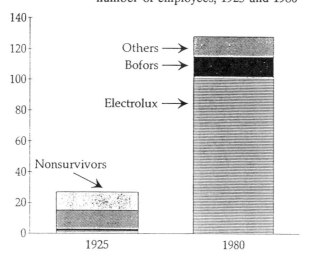

Source: Jagrén (1988).

Table II.2 **The very old, large Swedish firms**
Changes in the ranking order over 50 years -- firms ranked by size of Swedish employment

Company	Number of employees thousand 1945	1983	1990	Rank 1988[a] by exports	market value	Rank by number of employees 1945	1983	1990	Year of establish-ment
Volvo	*	57.1	50.7	1	1	*	1	1	1926
ASEA[1]	23.2	37.2	32.7	3	2	1	2	2	1883
Procordia	-	*	29.2	27	10	-	*	3	1970[b]
Electrolux	-	30.4	27.6	7	3	*	5	4	1910
Ericsson	9.8	32.7	26.6	12	9	3	3	5	1876
Stora	7.5	8.1	22.1	4	5	6	14	6	1288
Saab-Scania	*	32.2	20.5	2	8	*	4	7	1937/1891
Nobel	9.2	(9.9)	14.8	6	14	4[2]	9	8	(1873)
Trelleborg	*	(8.1)	13.4	11	13	*	13[3]	9	1925[b]
SSAB	*	14.1	11.5	13	-	*	7	10	(1978)
SCA	6.5	9.8	10.7	8	4	17	10	11	1929[b]
Sandvik	5.9	10.9	10.5	9	7	14	8	12	1862
MoDo	*	*	10.0	5	18	*	*	13	1873
FFV	-	7.9	7.4	26	-	-	15	14	1943
Esselte	*	*	6.8	*	*	*	-	15	1933
Svenska varv	*	17.0	5.7	*	*	*	6	-	(1977)
SKF	8.5	8.2	5.0	22	12	5	11	*	1907
Arla	-	8.2	6.1	-	-	-	12	*	(1975)[b]
Uddeholm	9.5					2	-	-	1668
Fagersta	6.4					8	-	-	17th cent.
Swedish Match	6.2					10	*	x	1917
Gränges	6.2					11	x	x	1896
Götaverken	5.8					12	-	-	1841
Huskvarna Vapenfabrik	5.8					13	x	x	17th cent.
Hellefors Bruk	5.3	-	-			15	-	-	1639

[a] In Day, Eliasson and Wihlborg (1993, pp. xv f).
[b] The year the firm was founded through a merger of other firms.
1) Merged in 1989 with Brown Bovery into ABB
2) Earlier Bofors
3) Earlier Boliden
* Outside list
x Acquired by other firm

Source: See Introduction by Gunnar Eliasson to R.H. Day, G. Eliasson and C. Wihlborg (eds.), *The Markets for Innovation, Ownership and Control*, IUI, Stockholm and North-Holland, Amsterdam; and Jagrén, L., 1993, "De dominerande företagen"; in *Den långa vägen* (The long road), IUI, Stockholm.

Table II.3   The ten largest Swedish manufacturing corporations
                              accounted for

	1965	1970	1978	1986	1990
Percent of					
Swedish goods export	19	25	31	37	34
Foreign Swedish employment	78	73	69	75	85
Manufacturing employment in Sweden - direct	16	19	24	31	27
- incl. also indirect employment in subcontractors	-	-	31	-	-
Total manufacturing R&D	-	-	**44**	**74**	**72**

Source: Eliasson, G., 1991, The International Firm: A Vehicle for overcoming barriers to trade and a global intelligence organization, diffusing the Notion of a Nation; in L. Mattsson and B. Stymne (eds.), *Corporate and Industry Strategies for Europe*, Elsevier Science Publishers B.V., 1991, *MOSES Database*, IUI 1992, and updatings from 1990 IUI survey of Swedish multinational firms.

The additional feature of, for instance, Swedish industry, however, is its extreme dependence on a small group of very large international firms, some of them very old (see Table II.3). Concentration in that respect has increased over the years, making some observers believe that the old Schumpeter proposition might come true.

The question, hence, has two dimensions; (1) the time perspective and (2) what do we mean by a firm?

The firms we observe now as dominant have been filtered out over centuries, the largest and currently most successful ones belonging to the late 19th and early 20th century. The older firms, still belonging to the group of large firms, have exhibited less glamorous performance recently, many of them disappearing in the wake of the oil crises of the 1970s.

The interesting question, therefore, is not whether they will all stay for ever -- they won't -- but where the candidates ready to move up are. If you think you can find them, fine, that supports the theory of the EOE. If you see none, the evidence is even stronger, and if in fact there are none, this is a possible outcome for a country in the EOE.

It is, however, not correct to "test" for the EOE by looking at the current population of firms. Any large surviving firm from the past century, has been near bankruptcy more than two times. What we now observe is a varied mix of earlier independent firms that has been formed through mergers, acquisitions and divestments over their history. As a rule the firm retains some structure from the past, most notably its product and market orientation. The combinatorial complexity between firms and within firms that closer historic scrutiny reveals is exactly the prediction of the theory of the EOE. No agent called a firm can live a stable inner life for long if it wants to survive, and this observation carries significant consequences for the design of business information systems.

Which Firms are Innovative?

The, perhaps, best support for the experimentally organized economy is found in the Chronicle (of Chapter VII) that identifies the critical events in the development of a new information product and of new firms.

The Chronicle illustrates the following:

(1) New ideas/technologies are (practically) always first implemented on an industrial scale in new firms (minicomputers, PCs, workstations etc.).

(2) Old, large firms sometimes have resources and inhouse technology (competence) to catch up. IBM has been the supreme performer in that game for a very long time.

(3) Old, large firms, however, often are aware of what should be done, but are -- even after enormous investments -- normally unable to implement radically new technology on an industrial scale. Internal, intellectual resistance to radical change is one reason. Even after many costly attempts IBM has not learned telecommunications technology. AT&T has not yet learned commercial computer technology.

(4) The results of the large R&D expenditures in large firms to get out of old technologies are not infrequently picked up by other, newly started firms. IBM did not understand the Xerox copier. The PC was developed by the Xerox Palo Alto Research Center but was commercialized by Jobs who started Apple. The new office information technology that everybody was

aiming for at the beginning of the 1980s, after billions of R&D dollars lost in large firms, may very well be put together into a product by a new outsider. Even though IBM seems to have understood where IT markets were heading in principle in the late 1980s, it was incapable of realizing its understanding in industrial practice.

(5)   New successes within large firms are often entirely accidental, and the result of the development being removed from CHQ conservative controls. The PC of IBM and the minicomputer success of IBM in its Rochester division are examples.

The size of state space has been one important characteristic of the experimentally organized economy. For the following chapters we should remember that the information system of a firm determines how far into state space it can reach; both in the sense of making state space transparent and (most important) avoiding getting lost. This task is not an analytical problem in the sense of interpreting coded information. It will be seen much more as the problem of organizing people with competence into efficient teams, making their experimental business hypotheses better designed and focused and the organization more alert and capable of spotting both successes and mistakes faster.

NOTES

1.   The reader should remember for the final chapters that "transparency of the organization" was the ambition of the new business information systems to be discussed in Chapters IV and V.

2.   As pointed out by a careful reader of an early manuscript, its exploitation also eliminates other possibilities and blocks certain exploratory paths. Development becomes *path dependent*.

3.   Earlier in this chapter I simply assumed the opportunity set to be large enough to make all information tacit, in the sense of being filtered through a special interpretation model of a human being or a firm, i.e., all agents are boundedly rational.

4.   for instance in the Swedish micro-to-macro model MOSES. See Eliasson (1977, 1991a).

5.   The experimental model includes the neoclassical growth model in "the new growth theory" as a special case. The new growth theory excludes the alternative micro versions. Most easily demonstrated is the selection bias. Empirical results based on the classical model, that reject its predictions will go unreported more often than results that do not reject the hypothesis tested.

III

THE FIRM AS AN EXPERIMENTAL MACHINE -- ITS DECISION PROBLEM

In contrast to the classical model, the model of the experimentally organized economy is well supported by empirical evidence. Particularly convincing evidence is that top level CHQ departments of firms are organized as if the EOE is the market environment in which they operate. This chapter will illustrate how. Above all, business firms have by now all but abandoned the notion of a plannable, potentially full information economy, implicit in management practice of the 1960s, and closed down their strategic or long-range forecasting and planning departments. This development could be seen coming already by the mid-1970s, in the wake of the crisis years. The more biased towards planning machines the less successful the firms were in weathering the 1970s (Eliasson 1976a, 1984c).

An interesting observation is the extent to which many business leaders unknowingly accepted the conclusions voiced by the economics profession during several postwar decades in organizing their own business towards a stronger belief in centralist planning, a belief that would not have been sustained after a more careful checking of the assumptions upon which such advice was based. Advice on the merits of formal planning was frequently articulated both by business theorists and by consultants as well as by well-known representatives of the business community. Such advice was clearly reflected in the formal planning routines of big corporations in the 1960s. An interesting *question* is to what extent these formal planning routines influenced actual decisions and behavior (see Eliasson 1976a, Chapter X).

The internal life of a business organization is characterized by several conflicting modes of behavior, representing different interests. Many of these internal conflicts split the firm into groups of people in charge of different tasks, notably those responsible, on the one hand, for the long-term survival of the firm and those responsible for day-to-day operations. Whether representing vested interests of groups of people, different evaluations of a complex situation, or responsibilities defined by top level management, this fragmentation of internal firm life is unavoidable and has to be understood when studying its decision processes. Internal conflicts are both codified and solved by the authority hierarchy of the firm's internal organization. This organization coordinates people, orients the focus of individuals and defines the internal allocation of human competences. This is one reason why *organizational change* is the method of solving major business problems of a firm. It *determines how the total competence base of the firm is allocated*. Organizational change also changes the internal power structure of a firm and the internal hierarchy of objectives. Thus, the existing "physical" structure of the business organization, even though complex, may be described. There is, however, a virtually unlimited number of alternative ways to reconfigure a business organization to achieve higher productivity, and the way chosen determines the ways it manages to focus the competence of its hierarchy of teams of people on the right tasks. As we will find in the empirical section, the information support of that task has to be made the critical part of the business information system.

The life of a real firm, hence, is characterized by two contradictory modes of behavior:

(1) the need to come up with a common sense of direction among all employees and

(2) the awareness that the direction chosen may be completely wrong and that the course may have to be corrected.

These conflicting modes determine the competence specifications of a business organization. Typically, the groups of people embodying the different modes of behavior are organizationally separated within the firm.

III.1 THE COMPETENCE SPECIFICATION OF A BUSINESS ORGANIZATION

The experimentally organized economy forces the firm to be organized as an *experimental machine*.

First, technological competition constantly downgrades the economic value of competence or knowledge capital of firms. The prime task of top level corporate management is to organize its human capital through recruitment, replacement and internal education to steadily upgrade its competence base. A theory of the firm that fails to recognize how its *top-competent team*, or *hierarchy of competent teams*, controls and reallocates the assets of the firm including its own competence capital (see below) will thoroughly misrepresent the behavior of both firms and markets. As we have already shown, this misrepresentation has long been the state of the art. The experience is that it is more difficult and takes more time to adjust obsolescent competence capital (embodied in people) to the requirements of new market situations, than it is to change other assets on the balance sheet. The reason is that *it requires competence to change the competence capital*, and that this was usually missing in the first place when a firm encounters big problems. Hence, the solution normally has to be to change the key people of the organization, those who make the top-level decisions, notably on recruitment and restaffing. Obviously this is no simple task, since it requires competence of an even higher order, this time of the owners of the firm. Failure, consequently, is typical.

Second, technological competition among a large number of firms in global markets, facing a virtually unlimited number of more or less well defined investment opportunities pushes firm management to take action long before they confidently know what steps to take. *The guiding management principle in the experimentally organized economy* is, that *if you have an idea that you consider good you had better realize it as a business very soon, because if it is good, as you believe, a competitor might otherwise do it before you, and beat you.* Hence, *it is risky for top-level management to exhibit risk aversion.* Firm management, therefore, faces two kinds of risks of failure.
- *First order risk*; of making a mistake by being too early.
- *Second order risk*; of being beaten by a competitor for being too late.

When this is rephrased in terms of the EOE the meaning of risk aversion changes character. I will return to this below.

Classical economic theory implies (Pelikan 1986b) that microeconomic decisions

(1) *never build* on contradictory, or erroneous information,
(2) *never require* creative work, or "new combinations",
(3) *never lead* to mistakes and
(4) *never allow* "tacit" knowledge associated with people, or groups of people, to play a rôle.

The experimental model of the economy reverses these four assumptions. Real firms, after a brief experience of advice from the professors of academia (Eliasson 1976a) have organized themselves along entirely contrasting lines, making mistakes a natural consequence of the ongoing business, and a learning cost to be carried in the books, not to be eliminated, not even to be minimized. The competence specification of the firm is given on stylized form in Table III.1.

The sense of direction element (item 1 in Table III.1) is imperative. Without it coordinated action cannot be achieved. Technically it requires two decisions;

(A)   *choice of a decision model* that directs the firm into the future in an ex-ante unbiased way, i.e. the business idea has to be right in principle
(B)   choice of a decision model that can be solved uniquely to guide downstream decisions

Table III.1 Competence specification of the experimentally organized firm

Orientation
1. Sense of direction (business intuition)
2. Risk willing

Selection
3. Efficient identification of mistakes
4. Effective correction of mistakes

Operation
5. Efficient coordination
6. Efficient learning feedback to (1)

Source: Eliasson (1990b).

This is where the contradiction emerges. There is no equilibrium model that maps a path dependent, experimentally organized economy in an unbiased way. Hence, any decision model chosen to orient the firm will only be temporarily right, and possibly wrong from the beginning. But it, nevertheless, has to be imposed on the organization as *the* business solution that everyone shall follow. It cannot be a disequilibrium decision model or a model with many solutions. The orientation to be effectively implemented has to be unique. It has to be an ex-ante equilibrium model (see Eliasson 1992a, p. 23 f). In terms of the general presentation in Chapter II the large size of state space or the business opportunity set and boundedly rational agents force firms to take such partly misconceived decisions prematurely, on the basis of not revealed competence (tacit knowledge, intuition).

A risk averse (item 2 in Table III.1) high-level corporate team as it is revealed under item 1 is a sign of incompetence. However, what may look to the outsider as a highly uncertain situation, may in fact be a controlled and computable risk situation -- as perceived -- by the corporate decision makers under item 1. Whether the risks are really controlled or not depends in turn on the quality of the "sense of direction" (item 1). Good such quality makes the firm generate an above normal rate of successful experiments.

The critical competence items (3 and 4 in Table III.1), however, refer to the ability to spot the successful experiments and to identify mistakes early, and correct them immediately. As I will demonstrate later, the identification and correction items are clearly observable in the design of firm information systems. A theory of the firm that fails to incorporate items 3 and 4 is simply scientifically faulty.

A few side remarks are at place here. *First*, the competence specification of a firm of Table III.1 makes the public (nationalized) firm an inefficient organizational solution by definition. A politically guided business enterprise may do all right on item 1 (sense of direction), item 2 (risk willingness) and item 3 (identification of mistakes) -- at least one can formulate no general prior argument to the contrary. But the politically controlled business firm will always be incompetent in speedy correction of mistakes. The political decision process simply is not designed for correcting mistakes, and should not be (see Eliasson 1990b).

Second, and relating to the management of competence in an organization; the lesson of the above summary table is never to organize internal executive careers on the basis of uninterrupted success stories. At the top level, mistakes become very large and costly to correct. A top-level management team without experience in correcting mistakes, and solving an organizational crisis situation, will impose an excessively costly, sometimes destructive, first learning experience on the entire firm, if they get their first lesson at that level. In fact, to the extent that a theory of the experimentally organized economy is empirically relevant, an active career to the top of a large business organization -- where this argument carries momentum -- is unlikely not to be interrupted now and then by a mistake or a crisis experience. If not, it is because of sheer, unlikely "luck", or risk-averse behavior, the latter disqualifying the candidate from top-level positions.

III.2   THE MAIN FUNCTIONS OF A BUSINESS ORGANIZATION

A business organization is constantly facing a number of tasks, all relating to the information taxonomy of Table I.1 in Chapter I. A minimum number of tasks have been listed in Table III.2. The taxonomy of Table III.2 allows us to formulate a theory of the firm as a knowledge-based, profit-oriented financial decision system (next section), and to design a statistical measurement system for the same firm (also next chapter).

The main empirical fact to establish here is that within the hierarchy of the manufacturing firm a number of service production activities are carried out that aim at enhancing the quality of output. As will be demonstrated in the next chapter the costs associated with this service production dominate over direct costs and labor input in goods production. Remove item 11 in Table III.2, and a service firm has been defined. At the level of Table III.2 one obviously cannot distinguish between a public and a privately operated organization. The taxonomy of the table is very general.

In the next chapter considerable space will be devoted to giving Table III.2 a quantitative content. This chapter will focus on the representation of the firm as a decision system and its internal business categories (activities), as they should figure in a theory of the firm.

Table III.2   Main operational tasks of a manufacturing firm

Selection (*identification* of business ideas and local competence by top competent team)
1) Choice of market, product, technology
2) Entry, exit, recombination
3) Career filter

Creation of new knowledge (innovation)
4) Innovative
5) Internal reorganization

Coordination
6) Investment bank portfolio management
7) Risk management
8) Product development and promotion
9) Commercial bank (cash management)
10) Insurance
11) Materials processing
12) Purchasing
13) Marketing and distribution

Learning
14) Education, knowledge accumulation and knowledge transfer
15) Welfare (unintended income redistribution)

The Hierarchy as a Conduit of Information and Authority

Figure III.1 is a simple, a common, but still a quite realistic representation of the management hierarchy (and its tasks) of any organization. It partially maps into the categorization of Table III.2. The three decision levels are clearly distinguishable in the organization of any large corporation.

The bottom level defines the operational activities. There things are being done. Efficiency upgrading is called rationalization of individual production sequences. (We are now at the finest level of work specialization where "scale economies in the small" are achieved.)

The middle management level specializes in coordinating these various (given) work sequences. Efficient coordination includes both (1) the achievement of overall flow efficiency, (2) the efficient stimulation of these rationalization efforts, and (3) the efficient allocation of investment funds on the various, given activities.

Figure III.1   Levels of decision making within a business organization

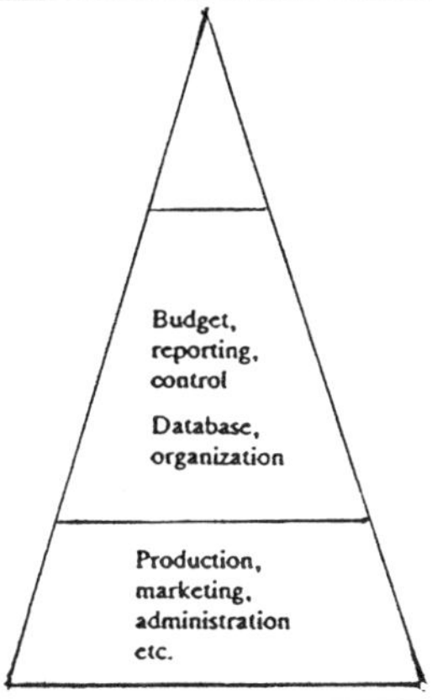

	Decisions Type	Taken by and where	Answers question	Competence creation
	1. **Strategic, selection (affecting structures)**	CEO Board owners	What?	*Selection* Varied career Ability to solve problems
Budget, reporting, control Database, organization	2. **Tactical, control, (inform, coordinate and enforce)**	CHQ middle manage-ment	In which order?	*Education* College and university Analytical training Expertise
Production, marketing, administration etc.	3. **Operational (produce and rationalize)**	Locally (workers)	How?	*Training* Vocational skills

Source: Eliasson, G., *The Firm and Financial Markets in the Swedish Micro-to-Macro Model*, IUI, Stockholm 1985, p. 14.

The coordination task of a large firm has been systematized and formalized in internal managements procedures and is best represented by the *budgeting process*. This process is predominantly a matter of communicating information by way of proxies from bottom up and from top down ("targets") in the organization (Eliasson 1976a). The main task of middle management is to act as intermediators in this internal communication process; to make top corporate targets operational, understandable and enforceable at local levels, and to signal upwards when performance is off targets. The -- to a large extent -- codable nature of this information processing, however, also makes the coordination task a prime target of rationalization. (The business information system partly has that aim. See next two chapters.)

Efficient Information Transfer Requires a Stable Internal Language

The key element of an efficient coordination function is a reliable language, through which signals can be transmitted, that translates profit targets as close as one-to-one as possible into operational instructions. This special language for internal communication will always be based on proxies, learned by firm management through experience. The reliability of the language will depend critically on the stability of internal operating structures on which the taxonomies of the databases are built. Such operating structures, in turn, relate the firm to the business environment, or the opportunity set. It includes choice of products, technologies, markets and internal organization. The operating structure of a firm is a very dated thing, since its operating domain, a subset of state space, may suddenly change, because of changes in market conditions. This change, in turn, affects the reliability of the internal language that supports coordination of the firm and helps identify and correct mistakes.

The extension of budgeting into long-term budgeting or planning in the late 1960s, however, based as it was on the static notion of a plannable economy, totally missed this point of top strategic management decisions.[1] My conclusion (see Eliasson 1976a) was that this -- with many exceptions of course -- was more a reflection of voluminous, articulate authorship from the academic and the business press and speeches from business representatives, than of a real mode of thinking among top-level decision makers. One should, however, not at all exclude the possibility that excessive articulation of how to make decisions, if left unopposed by the turn of real events eventually will affect actual decision making.

Internally Disturbing, Innovative Organizational Change has to be Decided by Teams Organizationally Separated from Routine Management

Top management handles *innovative organizational decisions* at the corporate level. We can establish as a fact of business life that firms, operating in a free market environment that have attained a long life have also been successful at this level.

At this level business strategies are chosen. Innovative organizational change will always change the underlying operational structures -- this is the main point of organizational change -- and, hence, affect negatively the reliability of the internal communication language specialized for effective coordination (Eliasson 1976a). This establishes a direct conflict between the upper and middle management levels, that cannot be solved through consensus type interaction. The middle management hierarchy wants to keep the operating structure of the organization unchanged. Effective control and enforcement of their operating targets depend on efficient internal communication. They will, hence, represent a conservative, structure-preserving mode, which opposes top level pressure for change. The conflict is always solved through keeping the two types of decision teams organizationally separate (Eliasson 1976a, Thorngren 1970). The top-competent team and/or the dominant owners should always be authorized to change the organization of the firm at its discretion, and will also take responsibility for the consequences for the value of the firm.

There is an important "tactical" phase (Ledin 1988) concerned with the implementation of strategies conceived at the top, into the corporate hierarchy. Since this is really the critical phase of the strategic task, a fourth tactical level should be inserted in the pyramid in Figure III.1.

III.3   KNOWLEDGE AS A SCALE FACTOR

Many studies have recognized the presence of economies of scale associated with one particular form of knowledge investment, namely R&D spending. R&D investment often needs large production volumes for costs to be recovered. The discussion of scale effects associated with technological development has mostly been phrased in terms of expanding markets through internationalization, i.e. through direct foreign investment in production.

The modern firm, however, is mostly concerned with customized product development for specialist markets. Since product development is becoming increasingly costly, an international marketing organization is needed to reach, inform and convince the right customers, and a very large number of such customers. Hence, marketing may be considered a form of product development. Strong synergy (scale) effects result from combining extensive R&D spending with large investments in international marketing. In fact, a proper balance between these two intangible capital items seems to be a necessary complement to a satisfactory return on hardware process investments, the only type of capital normally activated in the accounts of firms (Eliasson 1986b, 1990a,b, 1992a). In addition, a global marketing organization that allows the firm to implement and to cash in immediately on new innovations, rather than sell licenses, or be imitated or cloned, appears to be the best protection from competition, if the firm is technologically competitive to begin with (Eliasson 1986c). However, huge administered hierarchies, displaying orderly, "equilibrium" internal behavior appear not to be the best habitats for innovative behavior. To capture the complexity of this activity mathematically remains a distant hope for theorists. It has, however, to be integrated in the ordering of the business organization, and the way it is done in each case decides the long-run fate of the organization.

A *production function* is defined to describe the relation between inputs and outputs. Production analysis in economics conventionally approaches this relationship at a high level of aggregation. Here the theoretically unclear nature of aggregate capital has been a major problem, and the main reason for criticizing the notion of an aggregate production function. Another equally important point of criticism concerns aggregation itself. Since reorganization of the production system is the major source of productivity advance in a firm, there will simply not exist a stable relationship at the firm or division level between aggregate inputs and outputs. Hence, firm management never uses concepts like aggregate production functions in their internal information system. They have access to the internal structural information they need. Since this organizational information disappears with aggregation they do not find such descriptive methods useful (see Eliasson 1976a). If machine capital cannot be quantified at the firm or division level, how could that be done with such a diverse input as knowledge capital? This capital is, nevertheless, there. It is maintained and upgraded at great expense, not in the least through learning by mistakes. How should it be represented in the quantitative framework of a firm information system?

First, we have the actual process application of certain types of knowledge. The *upgrading* of quality of products through R&D spending was introduced as a separate factor of production already by Nadiri (1978). We do the same for marketing capital.[2] However, the *general organizing and innovative know-how (organization)* is still not accounted for. And this knowledge should operate directly as a leverage, or scale factor on total factor productivity. Let me try, provisionally, to introduce this factor into the information system by way of a standard production function. We are still thinking of the production function as a choice of technology.

Mathematical Excursus

Suppose,[3] that the production function for a firm

$$Q = F(k_i, K, x_i) \qquad\qquad\qquad (III.1)$$

is concave as a function of measured factor inputs k_i and x_i for any fixed value of K. K is the *level of general knowledge* which improves the productivity of all other factors. K is a capital good with an increasing marginal product. (As long as there are strong diminishing returns in the activities that create K, the static general equilibrium model will have a finite solution).

Let us assume that measured factor inputs are:
k_1 = Machinery and equipment capital
k_2 = Product-oriented R&D capital
k_3 = Marketing capital
x_1 = Labor input, standard hours, allocated to the various capital items, $i = 1, 2, 3$.

K is now the general, unmeasured knowledge base of the firm that is accumulated as part of the ongoing production process. In so far as some "tacit knowledge" has been compensated in the form of wages to other factors x_i, K incorporates the general organizing knowledge needed to organize all other factors into a team, a firm. K has thereby been defined as the recipient of residual profits when all other factors have been paid. This is a capital input traditionally associated with the risk taking of owners, but it can as well be associated with all knowledge (competence) inputs of the owners (Eliasson 1990b). In so far as top level managers hold stock in the company, they get paid two ways for their competence input; in the form of salaries and in the form of dividends and capital gains on the company stock, if their competence contributions generate excess profits.

The main point here is that the competence capital K generates increasing returns to all other factors of production of the company, but that it is a scarce resource whose *production occurs at diminishing returns*. The K factor input does not depreciate from use, as do other factor inputs, only in economic value relative to knowledge in other firms.

Let me first show that K, in fact, has the "scale" or "leverage" properties we have postulated. To do that -- following Romer (1986) -- assume F ( ) to be homogeneous of degree one as a function of (k_i, x_i) when K is constant. This is an insignificant further restriction. Given that, for any $\phi > 1$.

$$Q = F(\phi k_i, \phi K, \phi x_i) > F(\phi k_i, K, \phi x_i) = \phi F( ) \tag{III.1B}$$

F now exhibits increasing returns to scale in K. In the growth process of the firm, K is the know-how created, say from organizational learning that can be exploited by increasing the size of the firm.

Example:

The proof I have given has been in terms of the traditional, static production function defined for a firm or business unit. It has been demonstrated that a particular kind of "infrastructure" capital K in a firm, call it top-management competence, can be imposed on the organization in the same "mathematical" fashion as a scale economy that influences productivity characteristics of a large steel plant. This competence capital will determine the rents earned by the firm. A good example of such competence is the reorganization of a firm to be able to cope with a new market environment [item (2) in Table II.1]. We can use the term economies of scale for this, although economies of *scope* may be a better word. Mathematically (in terms of III.1 or 1B) there is no difference.[4] Even this term, however, is not the right one, since we are talking about an *organizational learning* process that creates a higher level of general competence (K) embodied as a form of infrastructure in the organization and its people.

If both traditional economies of scale and unspecified embodied knowledge accumulation are present, the two cannot be theoretically and econometrically separated. And if the tacit knowledge capital -- whatever it is -- is perfectly correlated with "scale", a prior scale formulation will reinterpret improvements in organizational competence as originating because of scale and vice versa. The acquisitions of Zanussi (Italy) and White Consolidated Industries (U.S.) by Swedish Electrolux provide a good illustration. Obviously the acquisitions enlarged the scale of Electrolux in physical terms. There should be mechanical scale benefits to exploit. However, the success of Electrolux over the years has to do with more than that in the sense that top management in other firms doing exactly the same thing would not necessarily have created the same successful results, because they lacked the particular experience the Electrolux management team had obtained over the years. Even though one can give several examples of pure, physical economies of scale with economic implications (e.g. the natural laws controlling electricity transmission, see Smith 1966), the notion of scale becomes the wrong concept if the exploitation of economies of scale requires technology, i.e. receiver knowledge that is not always present. The question, then, is how to represent the dominant competence input in the production process mathematically. The above production function representation, borrowed from Romer (1986), is a step in the right direction, but it does not take us out of the static neoclassical world, since it does not explain the accumulation of competence. This has to be done simultaneously with the explanation of production, if competence, or knowledge capital, is "tacit" and "learned" through participation in production. Then dynamics is created and a "path-dependent" economic process to which we turn in the next section.

III.4   THE DEPRECIATION OF KNOWLEDGE

Before going on we have to recognize that the standard assumption that knowledge does not depreciate may be wrong. Traditional investments in knowledge accumulate as brick laying on a solid foundation of well established knowledge (the truth). Hence, no obsolescence, or redundancy, occurs. If the value of that knowledge changes the neoclassical tradition attributes this to a relative price change of a well defined capital item. This is, however, wrong at any level of aggregation above that where the price change occurs.[5] Therefore, all aggregated capital has to be depreciated economically. Much of existing know-how will, furthermore, be redundant in a few years. At best human beings who have not retooled intellectually will be displaced. Then, their knowledge has to be written off, both in terms of economic value and "physically", as a factor of production. This is so except, perhaps, in two senses. *First*, the neoclassical proposition is that knowledge, removed from production should be considered a form of exit caused by a relative price change. If economic value comes back, it can be switched on, and the knowledge services rendered would be unaffected by the age of the knowledge. This is a terminological twist designed to save the neoclassical features of the production model. Romer (1986), hence, needs this assumption. But it requires that the physical properties of knowledge can be separated from the economic ones which we have just concluded to be theoretically impossible. *Second*, the prior accumulation of knowledge may somehow be an input in the accumulation of new knowledge. So without the past, the existing state of knowledge would be lower. Knowledge accumulation is "path dependent". This means two things. You cannot recreate the current state of know-how in an *organization* (a firm) in another firm, by simply sending in "experts" ("tacitness" prevails). Even if you need the past to upgrade competence you may have to eliminate the past from actual production because in the production process old knowledge may exercise negative effects. It is, furthermore, a well-known fact that teams of people that have been unable to upgrade their state of knowledge may block the upgrading of the general state of knowledge in an organization. The solving of this dilemma is one of the major challenges of top management in any business organization.

III.5   THE CREATION OF DOMINANT KNOWLEDGE

Business and technological competence resides at all levels in the competent team hierarchy. It is embodied in human beings and it moves and is upgraded through "on-the-job learning" as human beings change their location in the corporate team structure. Hence, the organization of human mobility, internal labor markets and careers is the most important (and most neglected) area of corporate management. The standard management view, that comes out of economic theory, is that you buy a package of ready-made talent and competence when you hire a person. You pay him accordingly. You may even think that you are paying him his marginal productivity contribution to your operation.[6] When he leaves you, you have to hire an identical replacement at a transactions cost.

First of all the value of individual competence contributions always depends critically on the team context in which they are allocated. If you hire the wrong person or allocate him inefficiently, you get less than potential value out of him. *Second*, the new employee almost always upgrades his competence to some extent in the environment where he/she is placed. To some extent this creates a team specific competence with a small alternative value outside the team, to some extent it is more general. This means that "your" employees to some extent are hostages to your organization, and that you get more value out of them, than alternative employers would. You know the value of your competent employee better than external employers. As a consequence you will (probably) pay him more than alternative employers, to keep them from hiring him, and he or she will still create additional (surplus) value in your business. Hence, you should not have to worry about investing in his human capital upgrading -- if you believe in his competence -- since you will always know his potential better than any external employer. However, you do not have to pay him his full marginal value wage, only up to the alternative wage the less informed bidder is willing to pay, and some more.

As a consequence, a competent employer or owner will always earn a satisfactory return from managing his team efficiently, because he should always be able to afford to pay the members of this team more than alternative bidders, and nevertheless earn a good margin. This human managerial competence includes selecting the right people, i.e. those who perform well in production and can be upgraded through investment.

This competence includes organizing lower-level management to bring the right vocational skills into the firm (see Figure III.1). It includes bringing the right middle-level managers in to handle the recruitment of lower-level managers and so on. The economic value of lower-level work, however, critically depends on the vision and choices of the top competent team -- what markets to be in, which product, which technology etc. to adopt.

Most important of all, hence, the dominant competence base of the business organization only survives in the longer run if an efficient career system exists that filters people out of the middle hierarchies for career -- on-the-job learning promotions, that bring only the best to the top. Their internal career system always has to be complemented with an entry function bringing fresh talent in from the outside, if only to introduce competition and reduce the sense of security that would otherwise prevail among the career candidates. In most firms, however, the total career organization is run in a very unsystematic, ad hoc manner.

The dominant, top-level organizational competence is defined by the ability to manage team competence accumulation and earn a long-run return on such human competence investments. Thus, competence resides ultimately at the top executive level of the firm and possibly among a group of participating dominant owners. Each firm applies its "self taught" organizational technology, and different countries engage different organizational traditions, that have emerged, out of their cultural and legal traditions. One would, hence, expect this ultimate organizational competence to capture a "rent" somewhere in the compensation system of the economy. For the dominant owner or owner manager the solution is easy. The value of this competence contribution is returned to him through capital gains on his share in the business. By owning a large share of the business he signals (to outside suppliers of finance) confidence in his own competence to run the business, or in selecting the right people to do it for him.

III.6   SELECTION OF THE TEAM

The selection of the top team capable of further downstream competence selection and internal competence upgrading to satisfy financial targets, hence, is the prime top management task of a business organization. Since the top "team talent" is always tacit, modeling this process will have to be made in terms of experimental self-organization and organizational learning. *First* of all efficient organizational learning occurs through the allocation and the learning of corporate officers in the career system. Such learning requires significant delegated decision making and, hence, as well a central information and control system that makes owners and the top people allow lower level career people to exhibit their talent. *Second*, there is the critical task of selecting and trying out compensation or *incentive schemes* that stimulate and force everybody to efficiently work for the ultimate financial goals of owners. Such schemes will have to mobilize the talent of the entire organization, not only some of it. Recent literature has discussed a number of such compensation schemes, many of them being phrased in terms of so-called "tournaments", that are in principle structured as the career organization of a firm, notably in presenting the winner, the leader, or the superstar (Rosen 1981) who takes most of the prize. I will pay considerable attention below to these human competence management and compensation problems, since the ways they are organized and solved are reflected in the internal information and control systems of firms.

III.7   A STYLIZED CAREER MODEL OF THE FIRM

Most empirical evidence suggests that human competence is undervalued in the labor market, and that low-quality staff is overpaid (Eliasson 1992c, 1994f). The higher the levels of competence involved the more pronounced this under-valuation. The reason is the limited capacity of the external market to assess the value of heterogenous human capital!

With human capital being the dominant performance determining capital of a business this places formidable demands on the top competent team of a firm ultimately responsible for the recruiting of talent, the inhouse upgrading of competence and the firing of incompetence.

Two observations should be made here. *First*, the ability to recruit talent and to develop competence depends positively on the talent and competence of those responsible for recruiting, who are in addition unlikely to hire people above "their own level". *Second*, there are narrow limits to compensate people within an organization for their superior competence contributions (Eliasson 1990b, 1992c, Chapters 5 and 6, particularly Section 6.9). Hence, which is always the case at a workplace, superior competence tends to be very undervalued while low-end talent and competence, if allowed to stay gets paid much above the economic value of its contribution. The often mentioned rationale for this practice is the workplace social tension that would otherwise arise and disturb work, and the difficulties and frustrations associated with a constant negotiating of individual wages based on competence assessments or observed performance.

The endogenous organizational response to this at all levels is as straightforward, as it is typical of the construction workers teams of the building trade, notably in Sweden, that negotiated contracts for large jobs and, hence, operated very much as firms (Eliasson 1992c, p.115). The team rejects and pushes out members that perform below average, but also tends to reject performers far above the team average, who, if accepted, often leave when seeing that they will not get better paid than close, underperforming (compared to them) team members.

Human-based organizational competence being the dominant and decisive capital input in a firm makes those selection processes extremely important to consider. The firm learns organizationally through upgrading the composition of its team hierarchy. *It is more important for top level management to force out low performers at the low-competence end, than it is to attempt to staff the top with the very best.* The reason is, of course, that such deliberate efforts will more often fail than succeed because of the difficulty of the task. It is more rational and remunerable for the business to use its interior competence (through organizational incentive designs) to prevent low-level competence to exert any influence on top level recruiting decisions. Above all, it is absolutely fundamental to prevent the low-end competence of the business to advance upwards in the team hierarchy. This can all be handled by organizational incentive designs. What is more difficult is for the top competent team of the business organization not so well endowed with top-ranking human capital to staff itself with the best talent in the market. Hence, the board and dominant owners play an important rôle as an external force and as a competence input on the recruiting side, but the failure rate is high.

On the basis of this stylized selection model some very interesting conclusions on firm behavior can be drawn.

Teams that exhibit internally diverse but (by members' own judgment) equal competence tend to be formed. Between teams (read firms), however, a wide dispersion of competence can be observed. The internal dynamics of team member quality selection determines the success of the firm and the ability of the top level team recruiters to steadily hire above-average quality new members, and push out low-end quality. It decides whether the firm will improve its position in the market game or vice versa. With this stylized selection model in mind one can see that a firm organization is normally inclined to embark on the easy way of steady decline by letting in below-average members and gradually reducing the upper-end capacity to hire top level management competence. It is also easy to see that in such a situation owners' best choice is to replace the entire top level team, even though that involves other, not negligible risks.

This simple story or model could be further complicated by taking diversity of competence demand in different markets and other difficult things into account. But the principal conclusions would remain the same, and that was my point. The second point is that if this stylized human capital based firm model captures something important of business firm behavior it has strong implications for how a business information system should be designed. As we shall see, we will have strong empirical evidence supporting our so far theoretical conclusions, as they can be derived from the assumptions of the experimentally organized economy.

III.8   THE VALUATION AND COMPENSATION OF DOMINANT INDUSTRIAL COMPETENCE

We have demonstrated how a dominant corporate competence capital can influence productivity and output and how such competence can be accumulated and organized within the firm. Since this competence, whether it resides in individuals or groups, is largely tacit, it cannot be coded and coordinated centrally through explicit planning. The hierarchy of competent teams that makes up the firm organization (Eliasson 1990b) has to be reined in and made to perform through some decentralized, organizational method. This method includes an *authority* hierarchy, assigning responsibilities, and an incentive system. The *incentive system* and the assignment of responsibilities together incorporate major elements of the tacit organizational competence of the firm. It makes the firm behave coherently as a financially defined system that earns a satisfactory return to (all the) assets invested.

We concluded already in the previous chapter that the value of the assets of any agent operating in an experimentally organized economy is constantly at peril, because of unpredictable (technological) competition from other actors. Protection of economic values requires constant initiative and action.

The competence capital residing in the firm, furthermore, has no value if not put into action. Since the market environment of a firm is genuinely uncertain, the total competence capital of the firm hierarchy depends ultimately on the competence of the top people to overcome their aversion to uncertainty, i.e. on the ability of the competent team of the firm to convert uncertainty into what *they* consider subjectively computable risks. The ability to do so defines one side of their ultimate competence. The other side is their "bounded intellectual ability" to create subjective order out of their complex *business environment*. I have called this *business intuition* in Table III.1. In one sense this intuition and belief in one's own competence is the very foundation of the firm (Eliasson 1990b).

The results of the ultimate organizational competence of the firm accrue to the contributors in the form of higher work compensation (salaries) and to the owners in the form of higher profits. Current and future (discounted) profits represent the value of the firm. This value is currently determined in the markets for ownership and control (the stock market).

It is obvious from what I have said above that conflicting valuation standards based on diverse knowledge endowments will be applied. The market agents will push low-performing managements to do something, through refusing to supply new risk finance, through lowering their valuation of the firm and/or through financing takeover action of (hostile) raiders. In this capacity the market for ownership and control performs the ultimate allocation function for top-level management competence (Eliasson 1990b). It is, thus, ultimately critical that the agents in this market also possess competence to perform that function. The only way to make sure that competent players operate in the market for control is to make sure that the markets are open to competition for anyone who wants to enter.

Since top level management competition is tacit and hardly communicable at all, the owners of a large corporation will never pay the top competent team their full marginal contribution. The value of this contribution, furthermore, may ex post be in the range of several millions, or even billions of dollars. Hence, good top level management will always be underpaid and bad management overpaid. The way to deal with this compensation (incentive) dilemma is for top management to become owners, and profit and risk sharers in their own business. There are numerous such bonus and profit sharing arrangements in use in the industrial world. The compensation can be tied to profit performance (a bonus) or to the valuation of current and future profits in the market (ownership).

In the very long run, all future profits will eventually be realized and accrue to owners. In any intermediate term the possibilities for the top management team to cash in their compensation, depends on the competence of the market specialists to evaluate the firm. While the lower level people are hostages to their organization, the top people become hostages to the stock market, or rather the competence of stock market agents to understand how good they are. The ultimate solution to this dilemma is *to create a deep and competent market for corporate control.* Paradoxically this obvious conclusion runs counter to most policies directed towards the capital market in the postwar industrial world, a highly topical issue considering the way the political establishments in the West look at innovative capital markets, insiders, and hostile raiding activity.

One could say that a member of the top competent team that does not dare, or is unwilling to buy stock against their own competence, which they can evaluate as true insiders, should not have been promoted into the top competent team. There are, however, two hitches. *First* of all the valuation of the firm depends not only on "fundamentals" but also on the competence of market agents to understand and evaluate the competence of the team in charge. If stock market agents are unprofessional and not very competent such risk taking on the part of the top competent team, becomes detrimental to firm performance. The top managers might even opt for short-term arrangements and try to manipulate the market. The insider problem, however, has very little to do with insider action. If there is a problem it means that there is a lack of professional and competent traders in the stock market. Insiders should be there to make market valuations more informed.

The *second* problem has to do with market myopia, and the push on the corporate top level team to go for immediate profits at the expense of more risky but potentially very profitable long-term investments (see next section or the measurement of firm performance). While corporate CEOs complain about demands to show steady quarterly improvements in earnings, the market enthusiasts say, this is just their way of hiding incompetence. There is no scientific answer to this dilemma, since the issues at stake are the possibilities or the competence to evaluate the future profit stream of a business. There is also only one answer; a professional and competent market requires a sufficiently large number of actors to make sure that at least one understands roughly what is going on and is willing to come up with the financing needed for the top "believing" competent team to take their operation private on a long-term contract. This is a pro-market answer and it tells that the junk bond market is an ingenious device that will improve the long-term performance of an economy.

III.9   OBJECTIVES OF THE MARKET AND INCENTIVES OF THE TOP COMPETENT TEAM

The financially oriented business organization that we have introduced is best characterized by its financially defined objectives, and its internal financial information system (statistical accounts) and monolitically controlled by a dominant competence capital vested in its top executive team or a concentrated ownership base or both (Eliasson 1990b). The competent owners aim for earning a satisfactory long-term return on their assets, above the going market interest rate. In doing that the top competent team is responsible only to itself, having invested equity, and to the capital market, that may also have contributed equity or supplied other forms of financing. This conceptualization of the firm is a satisfactory base, both for *theorizing* about the *firm in the market and for designing its information/control system*. Such an information system geared to the performance measures used by top managers and market traders can be mathematically derived from the internal accounts of the firm. Some internal information is only available to insiders, leaving outsiders with less information. Even for the insiders critical "information" often will be no more than guesses about the future. We will go through these accounts in what follows.

The top competent team of the firm is primarily interested in earning as high a return to its assets as possible above the going market rate, for now and for the long-term future. This "economic fundamental", the return to investment over the interest rate, we call $\bar{\varepsilon}$.

$$\bar{\varepsilon} = R^N - i \tag{III.2}$$

where R is the rate of return to assets, N stands for the nominal (N) return to assets, and i is the going market interest rate.

The future flow of these returns to investment can either be distributed as dividends, or reinvested in the firm. Over an infinite horizon we can disregard the terminal value of the firm. Its present value (today) VA can therefore be expressed in two ways, as the present value of all expected future dividends:

$$VA = \int_0^\infty DIV \cdot e^{-\delta_1 u} du \tag{III.3}$$

where δ_1 is the discount factor, or the market interest plus a suitable risk factor. DIV is the dividend.

At each point in time the present value VB of a firm can also be expressed in terms of its future expected profit flow, i.e. as:

$$VB = V_0 \int_0^\infty e^{(R^N - \delta_2)u} du \tag{III.3B}$$

where V_0 is the *initial value*, after dividends have been distributed for the period. [Expression (III.3B) implies no external financing and/or that no dividends are distributed and/or that dividends are reinvested at the same return as the *discount rate* δ_2].

Apparently, in both cases, the value of the firm depends on judgmental factors (expected profits or dividends, and the discount factor). The insider might know a bit more about future profits than the outsider, and the outsider might be inclined to express himself in terms of dividends, using formula (III.3). On the whole, the market should be replete with different judgments, but those willing or allowed to pay most for the share will determine the price (= MV).

While the top competent team is interested in making both VA and VB as large as possible, it is also interested in -- together with all other share owners in the market -- what value MV the market will put on the shares of the firm. The top competent team is really interested in boosting VB through raising R^N for ever. Since it holds confidence in itself it won't put the δ factor much higher than the market interest rate i. The top competent team should know best. And the task of the market specialists is to access the same future profit stream. Being outsiders, however, they cannot assess this income stream with the same confidence as the insider team. Hence, their risk or discount factor will be larger than that for the insiders: $\delta_1 > \delta_2$.

The outsiders may also consider themselves incapable of predicting the income stream of the firm and, hence, rely on proxies, like past dividends, i.e. they use formula (III.3), again applying a significantly higher discount rate δ_1 than the owners. This is the reason why economies that cannot develop viable venture capital markets will rarely prosper for long. A venture capitalist distinguishes himself by being more like an insider than an outsider contributor of funds, thus daring to enter new ventures with a lower risk premium in his discount factor than other providers of risk capital. The venture capitalist may know more about the firm and its management than the market, but the true venture capitalist is also a competent person in his or her own right in the business he or she invests in.

Very much like the outside employer who doesn't know the full value of a competent employee in another company, the competent team won't get properly evaluated by the market. Hence, to the extent possible, the team wants to pass on its confidence to the outside market agents. The most efficient way to do so is to buy a large and significant stake in their own company. This is important for the top competent team since its compensation is partly based on how fast the value of its stock increases. And if they believe very strongly in their competence, they want that value to increase a lot so that they can borrow against their stock and buy more stock, and so on.

This said, we have established that the top competent team has an interest in seeing to it that several goal variables are as large as possible, like $\bar{\varepsilon}$, VA, VB, MV. Some of them reflect the long term better than others.

Let us now introduce *the effective rate of a return (ER) of a company:*

$$ER = \frac{\Delta MV}{MV} + \frac{DIV}{MV} \tag{III.4}$$

and

$$\bar{\bar{\varepsilon}} = ER - i \tag{III.5}$$

The more efficient the market specialists in evaluating the fundamental profit streams of the firm the closer

$$\frac{\Delta VA}{VA} + \frac{DIV}{VA}$$

$$\frac{\Delta VB}{VB} + \frac{DIV}{VB}$$

$$\frac{\Delta MV}{MV} + \frac{DIV}{MV}$$

and also the average over time of

$$(\bar{\varepsilon}, \bar{\bar{\varepsilon}})$$

In an efficient stock market arbitrage should see to it that VAR ($\bar{\bar{\varepsilon}}$) is not much larger than VAR($\bar{\varepsilon}$).

It is interesting to note from Figure III.2 that the opposite holds. This being the case one wonders what it means for real economic performance if the top management team is more concerned with boosting $\bar{\bar{\varepsilon}}$ than $\bar{\varepsilon}$. If the $\bar{\bar{\varepsilon}}$ are constantly trailing the $\bar{\varepsilon}$ it means that the firm has made bad investments, or that the stock market agents are undervaluing the stock. Hence, owners cannot cash in the value they think they have created through sales of stock.

For owners and/or the top competent team aiming for the very long term this may not matter, except if they need additional external funding through stock issues or through borrowing. In the latter case the valuation of the firm may mean something for how much they can borrow and for what interest rate they have to pay. Depending upon which goal variables they look at and try to influence, the real consequences for the firm will differ.

Figure III.2   **Excess returns to capital ($\bar{\varepsilon}$) and effective rates of return ($\bar{\bar{\varepsilon}}$)**
-- Swedish manufacturing 1951-1988

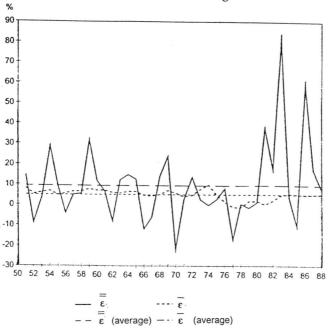

Source: MOSES Database, Research Report No. 40, IUI, Stockholm 19, p. 125.

II.10   THE VALUE OF OWNERSHIP

The property rights institution is the very foundation of a market economy. It defines the right to *manage*, to *assess the rents* of and to *trade in the assets owned*. The property rights institution is a set of laws and conventions that regulate these rights. This right is not an obvious right. It took a long time for it to be established in the late 18th century in Great Britain and in the U.S. It is absent in a large part of the world. It has been frequently tampered with by socialist regimes in the industrial nations, that owed their wealth to its previous existence (North and Thomas 1973).

The most difficult property right of all to establish is the ownership to future rents from entrepreneurial investment activity today (Eliasson 1993a), as embodied in VA, VB or MV in the previous section. Ownership contracts to such intangible wealth are also difficult to define legally, but this ownership is the very foundation of the capitalist system. The trading of these entitlements to future rents constitutes the foundation of the stock market. The extent of tradability allowed   determines how well MV compares with the other measures. The relationship between MV and VA or VB normally influences the incentives of managers, especially if hired on performance related contracts, and definitely the wealth of owners. Hence, the incentive system of a business is determined through the compensation contracts of managers by the property rights associated with the value of the business:

- who *manages* the assets?
- who *accesses* the profits of these assets?
- how easily are they *traded* in markets?

The tradability of the stock is probably most important. The public and private firm differ a lot in that respect. Undeveloped stock markets, like in the formerly planned economies, put less value on performance related compensation contracts than the same contracts in a sophisticated U.S. stock market. The owners can arrange their assets or relinquish control to hired hands. They can access the profits, but may have to do it through their hired hands. But they can also do it through selling their assets. What they then capture as their rents depends on

(a)   the values accumulated in the firm in the form of hoarded or expected profits as expressed by (III.3B).
(b)   how the market agents evaluate the same assets as expressed by MV.

With this definition the capital market becomes the dominant *disciplinary force*, *investment allocator* and *incentive factor* under the capitalist market order. It becomes no little task for the financial system to make sure that the capital market is governed by competent traders. In order to understand this we have to discuss how the values owned by the capitalists are influenced by the profits generated within the business organization. The next section does that mathematically.

III.11   THE FIRM AS A LOCUS OF FINANCIAL OBJECTIVES

I first formulate the profit targeting and profit monitoring formulae used for both production and investment decisions. These guide the firm in its gradient search for a rate of return in excess of the market loan rate ($= \bar{\varepsilon}$), a performance the market hopefully will observe and reflect in a correspondingly higher effective return on the stock over and above the interest rate ($\bar{\varepsilon}$).

Defining the rate of return

To derive the *control function* (cf. Section II.5) we begin by decomposing total costs (TC) of a business firm over a one year planning horizon, into:

$$TC = wL + (i + \rho - \frac{\Delta p^k}{p^k}) p^k \cdot \overline{K} \tag{III.6}$$

w	= wage cost per unit of L
L	= units of labor input
i	= interest rate
K	= replacement value of capital stock.[7]
ρ	= depreciation factor on K = $p^k \cdot K$
$\underline{p}^k$	= capital goods price, market or cost
$\overline{K}$	= units of capital installed (deflated K)

Normally the various factors (L, $\overline{K}$) *within* a firm can be combined differently, and still achieve the same total output. This multiplicity of outcomes increases with the level of disaggregation. Depending upon the nature of this allocation the firm experiences higher or lower capital and labor productivities, as defined and measured below. In what follows we investigate the capital labor mix as it is achieved through the dynamic market allocation of resources *among* firms.

Firm sales ($S = p^* \cdot S$) over total costs generate surplus revenue, ε, or profit:

$$\varepsilon = p^* \cdot \overline{S} - TC \tag{III.7}$$

where $\bar{S}$ is the deflated value of S and p* the deflator. The nominal rate of return on capital $(= R^N)$ in excess of the nominal loan rate:

$$\bar{\varepsilon} = \frac{\varepsilon}{K} = R^N - i \qquad \text{(III.8)}$$

or

$$R^N = \frac{\varepsilon + i\,k}{K} \qquad \text{(III.8B)}$$

$$R^N = \frac{\Delta K}{K} + \frac{DIV}{K} \qquad \text{(III.9)}$$

In this formal presentation K has been valued at current reproduction costs, meaning that ε/K expresses a real excess return over the loan rate, but that i is a nominal interest rate.

The top competent team controls the firm by applying targets on R^{EN}, the nominal return on equity capital $(= E)$. This is the same as to say that they apply profit targets in terms of ε. Thus, we have established a direct connection between the goal (target) structure of the firm and its operating characteristics in terms of its various cost items. These connections, as we shall see, are systematically put to use in the internal control systems of firms.

The reader should now note that the competence input of the top competent team is not represented in the cost accounts, except salaries paid to the members of the competent team. Let us assume, for simplicity, that all other factor inputs are controlled by the top competent team and are represented and paid at a rate corresponding to their marginal contribution (perfect markets assumed). The residual profit ε, hence, includes the extra value, over their recorded compensation, created by the competent team, either because it has hired factors cheaply, combined them innovatively and productively, or chosen the right products for the right market. To some extent the ε depends on luck, to some extent on competence in terms of Table III.1. The accounting point I want to make is that the return to the unrecorded competence input of the top competent team is reflected in ε. It reflects whether the firm is an above-average or a below-average performer. If the ε stays negative for a long period it becomes perfectly warranted to speak about a negative competence input.

The ε is what makes total costs (TC) equal to the value of output $(S = p^*\bar{S})$ in (III.7).

The Control Function of the Firm

Using (III.6, 7 and 8) the fundamental control function of the firm can be derived as:

$$R^{EN} = M \cdot \alpha - \rho + \frac{\Delta p^{k}}{p^{k}} + \bar{\varepsilon} \cdot \phi = R^{N} + \bar{\varepsilon} \cdot \phi \tag{III.10}$$

$$\underbrace{}_{I} \quad \underbrace{}_{II} \quad \underbrace{}_{III} \quad \underbrace{}_{IV}$$

$$M = 1 - \frac{w}{p^{*}} \cdot \frac{1}{\beta} \tag{III.11}$$

where

M	=	the gross profit margin, i.e. value added less wage costs in percent of S
R^{EN}	=	$(p^{*}\bar{S} - TC)/E$ the nominal return to net worth (E = K − debt)
ρ	=	rate of economic depreciation
α	=	$\bar{S}/K$
β	=	S/L
φ	=	Debt/E = (K − E)/E
ε	=	$(R^{N} - i)K$
E	=	equity or net worth, valued according to the same principle[8] as K
θ̂	=	the rate of dividend (DIV) pay out of equity (= E)

(III.10) can also be rewritten as

$$R^{EN} = \frac{\Delta E}{E} + \theta \tag{III.10B}$$

where

$\hat{\theta}$ = DIV/E. The reader should observe the analogy between (III.4) and (III.10B). I will refer to this in discussing the valuation of capital in Section III.12.

The Organization and the Separable Additive Targeting System

As we will discuss further below the control function (III.10) represents a linear organizational breakdown of the accounts of the firm that corresponds to a real departmental break down in most firms of some size (Eliasson 1976a, pp. 244 ff). Item I [in equation (III.10) above] measures the contribution to profitability from the operating departments. They can, in turn, (see below) be broken down into operating profit centers. Item (II) is an accounting item, including depreciation charges on capital account. One can say that this is a pure book keeping entry of little economic significance. And it is often treated as such in the internal accounts by firms. The cost of capital is, however, really the most critical item in the firm profit targeting system, since it determines the definition of the targeted rate of return and, hence, very much influences the investment decision of firms. We will return to this problem below.

Item (III) represents here [in equation (III.10)] capital gains on capital account. In a more generally represented asset specification of the firm balance sheet item (III) would, however, pick up all capital gains accruing to the firm and, hence, very much represent, through its representation in the internal accounting/information system, the way firms look at capital. This "view" in turn is typically reflected in the corresponding organizational structure of the firm. Item (IV), finally, represents the contribution to the rate of return on equity of the financing department of the firm. This control function easily generalizes to include all input deliveries (the purchasing department), taxes etc. The control system can be organized mathematically to stay linear for easy interpretation (see Eliasson 1976a, p. 191 f). This is also the way such control systems have been designed in real firms and they correspond to the view discussed here (see next chapter), that firms have to organize themselves such that they can view both the world around themselves and their interior (the controller) as consistent equilibrium systems (Eliasson 1992a, pp. 23-24).

Apparently equation (III.10), or more elaborate versions, defines a *control*, a *responsibility* and an *incentive* hierarchy by which the top competent team can delegate various activities, measure and control their contributions to overall objectives and apply a suitable compensation scheme for good performance.

This delegation/organization grid is also very explicit in identifying contributions to top corporate objectives ($\bar{\varepsilon}$) from selecting the right product, or the right market price environment to operate in, or in achieving high process efficiency (α, β), or in managing assets efficiently etc.

Apparently an erratic price development in markets, a disturbed price system (e.g. through political action), and regulations concerning access to financing etc. -- that all affect top corporate objectives -- can detract top corporate attention from focusing on these objectives that also contribute to economic growth and social welfare. We will, therefore, elaborate the relationship between profits and productivity further.

The standard theory of the firm treats the firm as a machine that can adjust itself to a given price system that varies physical inputs to obtain the output that maximizes profits, given the technical constraints of a production function. As can be seen from the above presentation, and as will become even more clear from the presentation of the real firm in the following chapter, this physical production function linking, for instance, $(L, \overline{K})$ in (III.6) with $\overline{S}$ in (III.7) is not well defined. It is defined at each point in time through the adjustments in $(L, \overline{K}, \overline{S})$ being made within the organization in response to pressure brought from above to increase $\bar{\varepsilon}$ to meet targeted $\bar{\varepsilon}$ in (III.10). Since targeted $\bar{\varepsilon}$, once set through a combination of external market pressures imposed through $\bar{\varepsilon}$ in (III.5) and internal administrative pressure imposed through (III.2) and (III.7) both the organization of the firm hierarchy and the organization of the capital (stock) market influence targeted firm performance. This also illustrates that it matters which internal controls dominate, be it the internal hierarchy as in the Japanese system, or internal market controls as in the German industrial bank organization or the external market as in the U.S. system. The relative merits of these different organizational forms for establishing a desired trade off between the long and the short term, and in effectively valuing the firm, will be discussed below.

III.12   THE VALUATION OF CAPITAL

The above discussion illustrates the problem of appropriately measuring capital. *First*, one has to decide on the purpose of such measurements; for production analysis, for corporate cost control or for trading the assets in the market. *Second*, there is no principal difference between measured production capital ("machines") and other assets. The differences in method of quantification used are strongly conditioned by tradition, which determines what we see. Those who argue that intangible capital cannot be measured and should not be measured are really saying that capital should not be measured at all, and theoretically they do have a point. Anyone who sets up a balance sheet for a biotech company should, however, attempt to get some quantitative estimate on the value of intangible capital. For both categories of capital there are at least three different ways to define and to measure capital.

(1)   *Cumulative investment (accounting method)*. Deduct assumed depreciation and correct for inflation. This method makes it necessary to *define investment* empirically (i.e. to separate out investment from total costs) and to make meaningful assumptions about depreciation rates. The nature and the quality of data are determined by this definition and the assumptions. This is the most common method in economic analysis. This definition is used in the (III.10) rate of return measure.

(2)   *Compute present value* of future expected profits using (III.3B). The reliability of this *insider valuation* method depends on the competence to assess the future earnings potential of the firm. Different people know different things. One would expect insiders to know best, and thus, if allowed

to trade for profit, would be the best supporters of unbiased values. To obtain unbiased estimates profit expectations (forecasts) have to be correct in expectation. Apparently the rationality of this method depends on which model of the economy you are thinking in terms of; the classical model or the model of the experimentally organized economy. In the latter unbiased earnings forecasts of individual firms are not possible in principle.

(3) Use the *assessments of the stock market (external proxy valuation)*. Here the valuation is left to external experts that may use any of the two methods above. The quality of the assessments depends again on the competence of the experts of the market to make forecasts of profits or dividends. The quality of this valuation depends on how open the markets for valuation are, i.e. which, and how many actors that are allowed to trade. This capital measure gives us the effective rate of return in (III.4).

Two things should be observed in this context. *First*, all measures rest on subjective evaluations, be it either depreciation rates, earnings forecasts or risk assessments. There is no universal and objective computation method, except by arbitrary agreement; that we decide to do it this way. A complete valuation *should* be based on a model of how these valuations *should* be done or a model of *how* these valuations take place; in the firm or in the market. My argument in (1990b) was that external experts will always be inferior to insiders, and not very reliable. Hence, if you want to improve the state of information in the stock market you should let insiders trade for profit. But the value of the firm to a buyer of its stock does not only depend on how much information on the firm the buyer has. The buyer may be able to add to the value through contributing competence or being able to realize a new business combination. In this market for mergers and acquisitions a different kind of information or knowledge is at play. Similarly, not even the first accounting method is entirely objective in its use of information. The rate of depreciation assumed depends on the alternative use to which the equipment can be put and the extent to which information on such alternative uses is available. Hence, depreciation rates depend, indeed, on the existence of secondary trading (markets) in used equipment or assets. This moves the accounting method closer to the third market valuation method, since the stock market is a market for secondary trading in corporate assets. You trade in all (incorporated) assets of the firm, not only in individual items.

Second, therefore, all three (or at least the second and third) methods essentially address the problem of valuing the total capital of a firm. Total capital includes all items of capital that contribute to the earnings of the entire firm. This apparently establishes a relationship between profits and productivity. We talk about capital values, not volumes, and the same capital contributes both to output (the *production function*) and to profit (the *profit function*).

It is obvious, concluding this argument, that the principles by which capital is measured are critical for the quality of the internal information system of the firm, and that efficient external markets in corporate assets contribute to the information support of and the control of internal business decisions. To bar insiders from trading for profits in external markets, thus, does not contribute to efficient and informed business decisions.

Summarizing on this controversial issue: one could, of course, use all three valuation principles and hope that they will bracket the true value of capital. This would, however, again be the wrong conclusion to draw. In the experimentally organized economy there exists no such thing as the true (read "equilibrium") value of capital corresponding to a fully informed decision. One might, however, say that the accounting method ($= 1$) as used internally by firms expecting to stay profitable in business[9] will produce the highest capital values, while the outsider market valuation ($= 3$) will produce the lowest values because of lack of information on or knowledge about the business and because of high discount factors ($= \delta_1$ in equation III.3).

For firm management it is always important to determine how to allocate scarce investment resources on various investment categories, by profit center and/or by type (machines, marketing, R&D etc.). This allocation determines total profitability and productivity of the firm. Hence, a production function including all categories of capital should reveal (provided quality of output is properly measured and part of output) the relative contribution of various capital categories to output. Similarly, a profit function including the same capital items, can be used to determine their relative contribution to the rate of return. This would be one method of dividing up total capital value of the firm on the various categories. Paradoxically, this way of looking at the problem suggests that the production function analysis might be much more subjected to bias than the profit function analysis, since the former requires that output be properly measured statistically, i.e. including quality change. The profit function analysis, on the other hand, does not require that, only that we know the specification of the production function and that the market is reasonably informed and has evaluated, through higher or lower prices, the quality of output (see Eliasson 1976a, pp. 296 ff; Mellander 1993). I venture to say that this may be the reason why the concept of a production function is never used within firms, while profit or cost functions appear frequently.

In static equilibrium we know that these difficulties disappear and the three valuation methods coincide, as in the classical model. In the experimentally organized economy, however, these conditions are never satisfied, the three measures differ and one does not even know whether they bracket the truth, since the true capital value is not well defined (see also Eliasson 1992a, pp. 49 ff).

This universal state of imperfection is well recognized -- as we shall see -- in the internal information systems of firms.

III.13 PROFITS AND PRODUCTIVITY CHANGE

The organization of a firm and its internal statistical information system are both designed to link -- as directly (one-to-one) as possible -- numerically specified top corporate objectives with interior performance characteristics, down to the finest detail that can be reliably and meaningfully measured. To my experience, however, it is rarely so that anybody in the business organization is explicitly aware of the theoretical relationships controlling the internal number system, that also defines each account in the context of corporate objectives. Neither seem these theoretical systems to be taught very profoundly at universities or business schools. This is all the more puzzling since the number systems are, in fact, used in firms, often inconsistently but very elaborately and intensely. They do influence major decisions and a theoretically, consistent accounting superstructure to account for these relationships exists, which is also fairly easy to represent mathematically. It rests soundly on the foundations of double-entry bookkeeping. Carrying the mathematical exercise through to the very end, as we will now do, also takes us right into the mess of capital theory, and the inconsistencies that prevail there. The general arbitrariness of any economic measurement system reveals itself. This is also an extremely useful piece of insight to be aware of for those who use these number systems in their daily working life. So before we look at what economic theory has offered in this context (end of this chapter) and how firm information systems really look (next chapter) I will try to show how the information system -- the special quantitative language for internal communication -- of the firm depends on the organization of the firm. I will introduce the unavoidable conflict between systems performance and the state of information of the system. More specifically I will show how the information system of the firm gets disturbed by *organizational change, even though organizational change is the critical factor behind productivity advance* that maintains or increases rates of return to assets, and that such productivity advance remaining after all measured factor inputs have been accounted for, can ultimately be associated with the unmeasured inputs of top level competence in the firm, called K in (III.1).

The more productive and profitable the firm the less reliable the control system, or the specialized language that represents the relationships between lower level performance characteristics and top level corporate profit objectives. Rephrased somewhat, *the more profitable the firm, the faster internal organizational change and the more difficult it is for top management to control the internal activities of the firm, notably costs.*

III.14 PRODUCTIVITY CHANGE THROUGH ORGANIZATIONAL CHANGE -- INTERIOR PRODUCTIVITY PERFORMANCE

Corporate Headquarter (CHQ) and division heads interact through principal-agent contracts formulated in terms of ε (Eliasson 1976a). Division heads are pressed to deliver as large a surplus ε (after "agency costs", Jensen and Meckling 1976, 1979) as possible.

Operations are controlled from division head level through targets on measures on M. CHQ can influence division contributions to corporate ε through the capital allocation process. Division management can influence its contribution through α and $\overline{S}/L$ in (III.10) via the investment decision and through operations control.

Using the taxonomy of the cost accounts we can now aggregate upwards to a goal formulation of the entire corporation, a description of its organization (functions) and an allocation of responsibilities. Observe, however, that this aggregation assumes prices to be given (exogenous).

III.15   PROFIT MARGINS AND PRODUCTIVITY

This section is slightly technical and has all been explained verbally above. It can be skipped by the fast reader, but the math is the deep structure of the business information system.

A Breakdown of the Profit Accounts

Equation (III.11) shows the profit margin M to be a price weighted labor productivity measure. The willingness of the division head and of management to pay higher wages depends on how well rate of return targets have been met. This, in turn, depends (inter alia) on how high labor productivity is compared to wages. Hence, we would expect the pair (the real wage level and labor productivity; w/P^*, $\overline{S}/L$) to increase reasonably parallel over time so as to stabilize the contributions of ε to CHQ. w is the wage and p^* the sales or output deflator.

Combining (III.6) and (III.8) we obtain:

$$\frac{\varepsilon}{K} = M \cdot \alpha - (i + \rho - \frac{\Delta p^K}{p^K}) \tag{III.12}$$

where

$$M = 1 - \frac{w}{p^*} \cdot \frac{1}{\overline{S}/L} - \frac{p^I}{p^*} \cdot \frac{1}{\overline{S}/I} \tag{III:13}$$

$\overline{S}/L$ is a proxy for firm labor productivity
$\overline{S}/I$ is a factor (I) use coefficient.

This formula can be generalized to all other input categories:

$$M = 1 - \sum_j \frac{w_i}{p^*} \cdot \frac{1}{\overline{S}/L_j} - \sum_j \frac{p^i}{p^*} \cdot \frac{1}{\overline{S}/I_j} \tag{III.14}$$

where j stands for the division or firm. Apparently we now have the beginning of the formula for growth accounting used by Denison (1967). The whole problem is to what extent included factors are properly priced (Jorgenson and Griliches 1967) or whether additional factors (like tacit knowledge) have been accounted for.

The Virtually Unlimited Ways to Reorganize Production for Improved Efficiency

For example, the profit margin can be high because of higher labor productivity (high $\overline{S}/L$), or low wages (w), or missing cost items. Costs for capital inputs obviously is one such missing item.

We are, however, not interested in estimating production functions, but in designing the appropriate profit and cost control system for top level management. If lower level factors are underpriced we attribute the profit consequence of this to top level competence inputs. Hence, as we will see, the productivity contribution of these cheap factors by prior design appear as contributions of the top competent team, or rather as consequences of its ability to find and select suitably priced factor inputs.

Production of a division, given capacity utilization and prices, can now be described as a bundle of *factor use coefficients* (productivity coefficients). When these coefficients are weighted together with the relative price of this factor we obtain the profit margin M, which is a *real* profit variable.

If you dig sufficiently deep into the accounts of a firm each factor use coefficient can be given a well defined operational content. The cost accounts of the firm also describe what is going on at a level of very fine detail. It is nevertheless important to understand, that however fine the detail, the taxonomy corresponds to *a given technology*. The finer the detail, the larger the number of combinations (process solutions) within that technology that can be captured with the measurement system. If *sufficiently fine there should always be -- at given relative prices -- at least one different combination that yields a higher aggregate productivity and, hence, a higher margin. Furthermore, each shift in relative prices means that a new combination will give higher aggregate margins.*

Choices of new such allocations of factors is a major top level management task and the outcome shows its organizational competence. Such choices change the coefficients of the productivity measures. These coefficients define the "technological or productivity memory of the firm".

Normally such recombinations within *a given technology* are associated with investment and new risks. But we can report on a number of reorganizations that have yielded higher productivity at no or minor investment spending (the so-called Horndal effect, or embodied technological change, see Lundberg 1961, Arrow 1962a, Eliasson 1980). The Horndal effect appears to have been attributable to reorganizations of production, mostly to reduced final product variation in the workshop (Vinell 1992).

Connecting Rates of Return and Total Factor Productivity Advance

Competence coordination and monitoring is a matter of managing people with competence to maintain or improve profitability. Here we will mathematically relate total factor productivity change to the rate of return (R^N), or more specifically, to the rate of return above the interest rate ($\bar{\varepsilon}$), and show how both the use of different price deflators and organizational change disturb this relationship. This amounts to a comparison of *profit* function analysis and *production* function analysis.

In this section I link the "unmeasurable knowledge" or innovative competence to firm objectives (profits) and the creation of economic value over and above the value of resources put in (total factor productivity growth = DTFP)[10] I will do this mathematically in terms of the information and monitoring system of a firm as it appears in the Swedish Micro-to-Macro (M-M) model. The task is to establish a relation between the competence rents (= epsila), firm total productivity change (DTFP) and growth in output (DQ).

In doing so I cut right through the dynamics of competition discussed in the previous chapter. I exclude the endogenous growth mechanisms of the macro economy by assuming perfect competition and making ex ante equal to ex post. No organizational change can occur. All agents are assumed to be price takers. Let me, furthermore, assume for simplicity that the only measured inputs needed to produce output (Q) are labor (= L) and capital (= K). DX stands for the rate of change in X.

$\bar{\varepsilon}$ in (III.2) is the difference between the rate of return on total assets (R^N) and the interest rate (r) paid by the firm. $\bar{\varepsilon}$ can be positive or negative. But a firm will not survive long with a negative $\bar{\varepsilon}$. Compare (III.6) and (III.7) with (III.10) and you will see that ($i + \bar{\varepsilon}$) is the equilibrium price for capital services that exhausts total value (= pQ) product when R^N = i and $\bar{\varepsilon}$ = 0.

$\bar{\varepsilon}$ > 0 [in (III.8)] arises -- as suggested by McKenzie (1959) -- as a consequence of unmeasured (or not measurable) capital, not included in K. This asset has a time dimension in the sense that returns may come with a delay. Even if the $\bar{\varepsilon}$ is negative the corresponding asset, hence, might very well have a large positive present value. Part of this time dimension can be interpreted as a risk factor that demands a reward (a risk premium).

To the extent $\bar{\varepsilon}$ measures value created by a not measured capital input it must have something to do with economic growth. I, therefore, prove (see appendix to this chapter) the following relationship:

$$DQ = s_1DL + s_2D\overline{K} + \Delta\varepsilon/pQ \qquad (III.15)$$

s_1 and s_2 measure labor and capital income shares respectively. Apparently $\Delta\varepsilon = 0$ when these shares exhaust total value added.

A whole lot of technologies are compatible with constant income shares s_1 and s_2, the most well-known being the power function (so-called Cobb-Douglas) specification.

After differentiation the entire class of functions:

$$Q = CL^{s1}K^{s2}T \qquad (III.16)$$

becomes (III.15), where T is a shift factor, usually assumed to represent exogenous disembodied technical change.

Apparently from (III.15) and (III.16) total factor productivity change becomes:

$$DTFP = DT = \Delta\varepsilon/pQ \qquad (III.17)$$

under the assumption of Cobb-Douglas technology. This is enough for my purpose. I have demonstrated -- for one particular production technology -- that the estimated [on specification (III.16)] shift factor (DTFP) picks up a host of economic influences related to the allocation of resources and the exercising of competence within the firm. As a consequence the return to that unmeasured capital -- that I have labeled $\bar{\varepsilon}$ -- also shows up in the "technical shift factor". This competence input -- by definition -- also includes the ability to deal with uncertainty (successfully taking on business risks). Hence, the interpretation of $\bar{\varepsilon}$ in the modern theory of finance becomes part of this more general formulation.

III.16 WHAT DOES IT MEAN TO BE RATIONAL?

Rational thinking was the philosophical foundation of the time of enlightenment. The philosophical problem then became to decide what should be meant by being rational. The firm is typically defined in normative economic theory as a rational decision maker. One has difficulties thinking about a "theory of the irrational firm". One would expect such rational behavior to be reflected in the demand for information of top management as reflected in the information systems of firms. Hence, in a book like this the concept of rationality has to be addressed, and it leads naturally over to the final section of this chapter on the theory of the firm.

To be rational requires that one is *consistent* in one's decisions, and selects the best ex ante option (*optimization*), given available information. This can be prevented by two things:
-    knowledge may be lacking,
-    the decision situation may be too complex.

Both circumstances may make the ex post outcome differ from the ex ante evaluation. Hence, rationality also requires that ex post error correction be part of the ex ante decision. The weight given to that error correction in the ex ante decision determines the decision maker's attitude to risks. In assessing the rationality of an individual two qualities should be recognized, namely that:
1. more complex information can be taken into account in a decision than can be presented or communicated,
2. when complexity becomes too large, simplification is resorted to.

The mind picks a simplified model representation of the world in order to be able to come to a conclusion (*bounded rationality*).

Once the second problem is recognized, the *choice of model* becomes the important decision, which embodies all the other requirements, including the competence of the individual to cope with its environment. The more choices matter the more of information handling in society will be *tacit* and non-communicable.

Classical economic analysis for a long time did not recognize that these particular factors made a situation of full information and a universal equilibrium state unfeasible operating points of an economic system. An alternative version of such equilibrium thinking is the rational expectations (RE) or efficient market theory. In their general and verbal forms these theories postulate that agents will eventually learn about the parameters of the model that generate the data constituting their economic environment and position themselves around the exogenous equilibrium in a stochastic manner. Modern learning theory excels in such analysis, but a RE equilibrium requires very nice properties of the model of the economic environment (stationarity etc.) or a different world than ours.[11] Such theory, even though it dominates modern finance theory, has little to do with the economic environment firms have to cope with.

For a century or so philosophers and linguistics have discussed the possibility of bringing logical thinking higher and higher up into complex and judgmental decision contexts, i.e. increasing awareness, making the decision explicit, transparent and communicable. This ambition was taken over by the designers of business information systems.

Artificial intelligence (for an explanation see Chronicle) represents part of this ambition. The interesting question is whether artificial intelligence increases the *explicitness* and awareness of the decision process in handling a given problem or whether it makes it possible to handle more complexity irrespective of whether more or less explicitness is achieved -- or both.

On this score we can make two distinctions. Does artificial intelligence support in decision making

- make it possible to handle more complexity, mimicking the way ones brain works or
- does it make it possible to handle the problem differently, more straightforwardly or better, by redefining the problem?

Doing it differently may be one way of coping with complexity.

The above principal presentation of a decision problem illustrates how a firm should be organized to learn through experimental, trial and error activity in markets. Under such circumstances it becomes important to identify mistakes early! Hence, early identification of business mistakes becomes a key purpose of well designed corporate information systems and a technology to allow delegation without losing central control. Efficient central capacity to identify lower level mistakes makes the organization less risk averse.

In addressing the problem of whether firms behave rationally or not, what they *know* has to be determined. That being said, however, we also have to incorporate in our analysis the decision of firms to acquire (at a cost) more knowledge or information and so on. This rapidly leads to an infinite regress that makes optimization impossible.

Among the classical economists (Arrow 1986) rationality often had the limited meaning of preferring more to less. Agents that climbed hills of profits or utility were then perfectly rational, a rationality definition that easily lends itself to a dynamic interpretation. John Stuart Mill, *(Principles of Economics*, Ch. 4 1909 ed.) had a definition of rationality less typical of the "modern" economist when he argued that custom, not competition ruled the world. Such thinking is returning in the more recent analysis of economic behavior of researchers influenced by psychology and institutional considerations. Thus Tversky and Kahneman (1986) argue that the deviations of actual behavior of firms and individuals from the normative economic model "are too widespread to be ignored, too systematic to be dismissed as random errors, and too fundamental to be accommodated by relaxing the normative system". They conclude that normative analyses and their descriptive method cannot be reconciled: their descriptive theory of risky choice, called *prospect theory*, includes two phases; one of framing and editing, and one of evaluation. This is again very similar to one of Simon's (1959) formulations of bounded rationality, namely as a choice of personal model, through which the economic environment can be interpreted. In this setting (Eliasson 1992b) the choice of interpretation model or the editing phase becomes the dominant part of the decision process. One could say that the economic environment is framed and edited such that optimization can be performed; the latter being the trivial task, compared to the first choice process.

The editing process is not part of standard economic modelling. If heterogeneous choice mechanisms are part of rational behavior, Arrow (1986) points out, neoclassical equilibrium analysis breaks down, something that already Knight (1921, pp. 76-79) had pointed out. However, rationality is not necessary for a theory of the economy, Arrow continues. The combination of rationality, incomplete markets and equilibrium often leads to very weak conclusions, or technically, to a continuum of equilibria. This is exactly, Arrow points out, what modern game theory has experienced. One solution (according to Arrow) would be to recognize that limits on rationality will reduce the number of equilibria, or change the concept of equilibrium (or the solution, decision) that has become standard in economic theory (see Eliasson 1985a). I would add (Eliasson 1992b) that this modeling experience of game theorists unavoidably leads to an increased need for empirical specification to be able to choose the empirical, relevant specification, the model, out of a very large number of possibilities. It would mean accepting Simon's (1955, 1957a, Chapters 14-15) concept of bounded rationality and the necessity to make choice of model or frame of mind part of economic theory. Then, individual or firm rationality to the outsider becomes dependent on this individual frame of mind, or competence, which precludes any universal definition of rationality, an observation that effectively should remove the neoclassical model from the analysis of firm behavior.

Once this intellectual step has been allowed, the theory of the firm suddenly requires that the choice of model also be explained. Since the number of choices are virtually unlimited there is no way to do that except through sequential or evolutionary learning. This introduces, as we have already concluded, structural path dependence in the economic system.

III.17   THE THEORY AND THE REALITY OF THE FIRM

Literature offers many *images* of the firm. Its *contours* are rarely well defined. Business administration literature is solely concerned with various aspects of the firm. In some important branches of economics, on the other hand, the firm doesn't even exist. General equilibrium theory, and in particular in its pure forms, has no place for the entity called a firm. Literature, hence, is very fragmented. The notion of a firm that behaves, reorganizes itself and interacts explicitly with markets, is still to be worked out. The various bits and pieces of theory being circulated, however, are not unimportant. Some ideas of economic theory have significantly influenced the theory of business administration, notably economic planning that has, in turn, influenced business practice, with sometimes devastating results.

The Firm and the Market

As said before, the theory of the firm, as well as the real firm must depend on the theoretical or real market context in which it is supposed to operate. Thus, (*first*) an information system of a firm -- our object of inquiry -- has to be built around some notion (theory) of what the firm is and how it relates to its market environment. The image of the firm of the academic world thus significantly depends on the theoretical market context into which it is supposed to be placed. Since economic theory, and "modern" mainstream theory in particular, has always had a problem with modeling the market, the theoretical notions of the firm abound. Hence, theories of the firm are leading an uncomfortable life in the neighborhood of mainstream economic micro theory. *Second*, the market environment of each firm is the total dynamics of all other firms, each firm acting upon expectations about what their competitors will do. Hence, the common assumption, to make a firm play against a *given* market environment, the extreme case being the price taking firm, is the wrong foundation to begin with for theorizing about the firm. This is a problem of major proportions if you want to construct macro theory around models of firm behavior in markets. It has, therefore, been important for me to create, for this book, an alternative to the general equilibrium model of economics -- to serve as a "habitat" for firms that are more similar to the firms of the real world whose information and decision systems are studied in this book. This is part of the service the EOE does to us. In particular, the EOE presents a live background of the real dynamics of markets in which firms compete.

There is also a *third* aspect of the EOE to consider. An explicit and reasonably well formulated, known market environment lends intellectual strength to the concept of a firm that can be derived from it. Concepts of the firm without such foundation in a market context will inevitably be labeled ad hoc. The bad fate of the so-called managerial or behavioral theories of the firm (see below), including many relevant and observable properties of the real firm lacking in standard economic theory, to a significant degree can be explained by the lack of an intellectual context from which these properties could be derived as rational devices to cope with a competitive market environment. It is, therefore, interesting to observe how modern information theory is gradually revising the theory of dynamic but imperfect markets, thereby giving rise to a renaissance of old corporate financial models, that incorporate many relevant features that appeared ad hoc in earlier, perfect information financial economics, but now suddenly have a logical foundation (see below).

A final (*fourth*) observation to make, therefore, is that if you don't want to exclude, by prior assumption, internal *organizational change* of the firm as a significant factor behind firm formation and growth, and hence of macroeconomic growth, you also have to model the dynamics of market institutions explicitly, and "institutional substitutability" between the market and the internal economies of firms. *The firm changes its internal structures through reorganization in response to a changing competitive situation in markets*, i.e. in the badly defined intersection between the firm as a hierarchy and markets. It is very much a concern for this study to make this internal dynamics of the firm part of the theory of the firm and to understand both (1) how existing information systems support such change and/or (2) how such information systems can be improved in the same respect. This is why I spent several pages on creating a new theoretical market framework -- the EOE -- that would serve as a reference both to describe the real firm and its internal control and information system and to discuss the many theories of the firm.

Since different authors approach the theory of the firm very differently, the dividing line is between those who want to stay in touch with mainstream economics, and those who don't care. My ambition is to represent a business organization which important characteristics are well supported by empirical evidence and to stage it in a dynamic market environment. My preference for organizing this brief overview, hence, becomes to look at the *firm as a competent* team and a *learning organization* and *on how competence and learning should be conceptualized in the experimentally organized economy*. This means that the firm becomes a superstructure of organized human talent specialized in organizing and using the physical means at their disposal (capital etc.) to achieve financial objectives. The choices open to firm management in organizing people to achieve financial objectives are enormous. Hence, the theoretical representation of the firm as a physical production machine is misleading. In reporting on what other theorizers have done and what purpose their models have been designed to serve I will keep this new theoretical reference in mind.

Experiments, Uncertainty and Risktaking

The experimentally organized economy features the firm as an experimental machine, that has to take decisions prematurely and always has to be prepared to handle small or major business mistakes. Hence, risk and uncertainty, to use the terminology of Frank Knight (1921), is a key factor in business life, and -- as I have emphasized -- a standard cost for economic growth. Risks are *dealt with very differently in economic theory*. Modern finance theory has a stochastic, rational expectations-based version of general equilibrium theory, which does not recognize the distinction between uncertainty and risk. This distinction returns, however, and becomes necessary in the experimentally organized economy.

Two other dimensions of risktaking are also interesting in this context, namely the contrary positions taken in modern finance theory and industrial organization (IO)-based labor market theory. While finance theory concludes that firms should not be engaged in risk diversification, but unload risks on specialized and more efficient markets for risks, labor market theory emphasizes the firm as a social institution, that makes a business of insuring its employees from the vagaries of market life. While the original criticism of the "modern" finance theoreticians (Miller, Modigliani, Markowitz and Sharpe) is equally valid for the labor market analysis of Lazear (1981), Solow (1990), and others, the position of finance theorists can in turn be criticized on empirical grounds. Do perfect separable markets for risks really exist? If there are significant *synergies* associated with combining manufacturing production and risk finance (like in the venture capital market) the answer is no, and the pure M-M-M-Sharpe position collapses. What should firm management do if its employees demand insurance protection from the firm, and pay handsomely for the protection in the form of lower wages? Production of goods and services and social insurance becomes a joint production activity.

Firm Dynamics, Competition and Macro Behavior

Agent behavior (rivalry, dynamic competition) is the main force behind macroeconomic behavior. Firm dynamics so to speak is the core of the macroeconomy, and dynamics is created as firms enjoy economies of scale from merging internally different markets, notably the real and financial markets, through their organization.

General equilibrium analysis has problems with (1) externalities, (2) increasing returns to scale and (3) producers that are not price takers (Debreu 1959). The problems that arise concern (a) the standard assumption of profit maximization, (b) existence of equilibrium and (c) the rationality of marginal cost pricing (Cornet 1988). These are all "features" that we associate with the firm as it appears both in literature and reality. A large part of reasoning about production, allocation and (even) economic growth, again typical activities associated with the firm, has been formulated within the general equilibrium model. Hence, in addressing the theory of the firm we are (by definition) addressing a general inconsistency of the mainstream intellectual structure of economics. Nevertheless, both the firm of mainstream theory and that of the popular planning models of the 1960s, or, for that reason, much of down-to-earth business planning literature (Eliasson 1976a) relates -- it is interesting to note -- to the classical model.

This problem has not gone unnoticed. It has, however, not been addressed as a consistency problem. And many attempts have been made to resolve it partially, among the first being Arrow and Hurwicz (1958) and most importantly Shubik (1959, 1960, 1975), using game theory. Arrow (1959, 1986 and other references) can be interpreted as pessimistic observations that the problem still remains to be solved.

The Business Problem as Part of Theory

Studying the firm means studying the *internal economy* of a hierarchy of people. We then have to pay attention to (1) the structure of *information processing* within the hierarchy (observation, communication, computation), and (2) the *structure of authority* which sets the rules of the internal players (Radner 1986a,b). There is, however, an important distinction to be made between information processing in the firm as a pure analytical system, and *information processing through people*. This distinction becomes important to the extent tacit knowledge is important for internal communication. As I have already observed I will take the relative tilting of internal information systems in firms towards, on the one hand, analytical tasks such as comprehensive planning or automated production and, on the other hand, towards coordination through competent people as an indication of the relevance of the concept of tacit knowledge. To this should be added the *objective (goal)* structure and the *compensation* of competence providers or the *incentive* system (Eliasson 1990b). These four structures (see Table III.3), or the hierarchy, define the *rule system* or the *jurisdiction* that controls decision making within the firm, and (as long as the firm lasts) does it better than the market.

The design and coordination of these four dimensions of *the internal economy of the firm constitute management solutions ("competence") to achieve synergies (economies of scale) from integrating the financial and real dimensions of economic activity to earn a monopoly rent in the financial market.*

The internal economy of the firm solves coordination problems that can also be solved in the markets for finance and in the labor market. The firm, thus, exists and earns its rent in the intersection of markets in Figure III.3. The rationale for its existence is the capacity of the organization (the hierarchy of competent people) to do it better than the market (Coase 1937). I will elaborate these propositions in the following chapters.

Table III.3   The firm as a local jurisdiction (rule system)

---

(1) Objective (goal) structure
(2) Structure of information processing
(3) Structure of authority
(4) Reward (incentive) system

Figure III.3   The firm in the markets

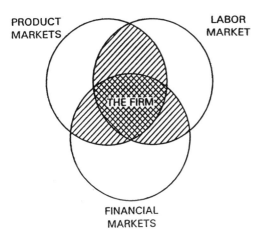

Source: Eliasson (1989c).

The power of the intellectual heritage is enormous. For several centuries economics did not acknowledge the rationality of thinking about "the firm". The empirical existence of the phenomenon apparently did not influence the "thinkers". The early literature did not recognize the firm as a viable decision entity operating in dynamic markets. The reason probably was that the firm as a juridical entity, a finance contract, in these days was not well defined. The discussion was in terms of branches, technologies or -- at best -- the representative firm of Marshall. Marshall was, however, only concerned with being able to aggregate systematically. It is easy to see how this essentially static concept carries over to modern micro theory, modern aggregation analysis, and how the hardware notion of the firm as a factory has established itself in the thinking of economists.

The early thinkers were also concerned with ethics. The "joint stock company" that Adam Smith studied was a financial privilege or a monopoly, with no wealth creating capacity. Adam Smith formulated, through his theory of the division of labor, the rationale for the existence of the firm as a production organization. He was worried about the potential for that firm to grow beyond bounds, to leave a dominant monopolist, a concern later voiced by many, e.g. Joseph Schumpeter (1942). To counter such negative effects Adam Smith emphasized the need for viable competition through free innovative entry. The free entry clause and the entering agents are what I emphasize as the viable force in the EOE. It took, however, until Coase (1937) for the firm to appear in economic literature as a production organization, enjoying scale economies minimizing transactions costs through the hierarchy and contributing to the wealth of nations. The firm as a competent team, earning a rent within a financially defined organization belongs to the last few years only.

The classical economists, who were concerned with the sources of economic growth never recognized the presence of firms in the growth process (Arrow 1971). The neoclassical economists were not interested in economic growth, but in distributional problems, and built a structure of thought that -- at least to begin with -- was not compatible with the existence of a live firm.

The firm exists on its capacity ("competence") to create synergies by solving organizational problems more efficiently than markets. Essentially similar tasks are being performed in the market and within the internal economies of firms. I will give examples from both the financial markets and the labor market below, thereby suggesting some intriguing interaction between the theory of the firm, on the one hand, and financial and labor market theory, on the other.

The capacity to create such synergies from integrating markets rests on the competence residing in the firm to organize competent people in efficient teams (Eliasson 1990b). As I have argued in Sections III.6, 7 and 8 the central business problem of a firm, hence, is to prevent this team from being staffed by incompetent people; particularly at the top level. Top level people set the competence standards of all lower level people in the firm, and control the hiring process. This is basically an organizational problem, i.e. about the design of the filter that selects, allocates and upgrades the people of the organization and determines the non-convexity upon which the firm earns its rent. This organizational problem has yet to be recognized in the economic theory of the firm. The organizational problem, furthermore, blurs the distinction between the firm and the market, which complicates economic analysis.

Theoretically there are two ways of looking at the firm or the business enterprise:

(1) *as* a part of some other phenomenon, e.g. explaining macroeconomic growth. This is the economist's perception of the firm,
(2) *as* an entity to be controlled; the management or business administration approach.

The *economist's* approach (1) requires the *context* (the market environment) to be part of the analysis. Until recently the economist has abstracted from the organizational problem, and at best looked at the firm as a price taker in an anonymous, atomistic market (see below).

Business administration literature takes the environment as externally given but more diversified than a price system and studies the ways the firm adjusts to this environment (old corporate finance theory, the theory of organization etc.). The two sets of literature represent two different intellectual worlds.

Different Images of a Firm -- a Systematic Overview

An emerging awareness of the interaction between hierarchies and markets (coming logically out of the notion of the experimentally organized economy) is forcing the two approaches to the theory of the firm to reluctantly interact. The necessity of that intellectual merger for understanding the firm is the main hypothesis of this section. I will organize my presentation of the history of doctrines -- or the theory of the firm -- accordingly.

There is an additional empirical reason for this. The firm of this book, or at least the important firm concept of this book has to be intellectually compatible with the fact that survival capacity in the experimentally organized economy originates in interior firm organizational change, defining a separate approach to the theory of the firm, leading up to a need for an organizationally based theory of mergers and acquisitions. The firm does not exist "on the same grounds" for more than a limited time period. As a consequence the following types of principal questions have been raised in literature:

(1) Why does a firm exist (*existence*)?
(2) How, and why does it come into existence (*entry, exit, competition*)?
(3) How does it behave and grow (firm *dynamics*)?
(4) How long does a firm live (*survival*)?

Literature deals with these problems in principally different ways. I can discern several strands of literature:

Economic *micro* theory: Places the firm in a macroeconomic context.

Financial economics: Does either corporate financial modeling (old fashioned), principal agent control and incentive analysis, or questions need of a separate theory of the firm.

Business administration: Studies the management and control problems of the
                            internal economics of the corporation (firm) in a *given*
                            economic environment.

As I will show, *all three fields, despite their disparate objectives, have influenced
each other*. Within the field of economics a "methodological fragmentation",
hence, emerges.

We have:
  a) The early literature on the firm of classical economics; industry studies,
      market organization and competition but no explicit decision unit called
      a firm.
  b) The firm in the neoclassical, static general equilibrium environment; why
      does a firm exist?
  c) *Behavior*; bounded rationality and the behavioral and managerial theories
      of the firm; maximizing vs. satisfying.
  d) Dynamics; why does a firm enter, compete and grow, or fail.
  e) The efficient market story.
  f) Competence; the labor market connection.

As a consequence of all the various notions of the firm, it appears (in theory)
in different shapes and forms:

Existence: Why?

-   as a *production function* and price taker in standard micro production theory.
    Economies of scale pose problems in the static general equilibrium setting,

-   in classical economics, as an "industry" or as a Marshallian "*representative
    firm*",

-   as an *administrative system* (a hierarchy) à la Coase (1937) or Williamson
    (1975) that beats the markets in minimizing coordination costs on the margin,

-   as a *contract* between a multitude of parties designed to minimize transactions
    costs [see, e.g., Holmstrom and Tirole (1989), and also Cyert and March
    (1963)],

-   as a *price setting "market imperfection"* of the neoclassical model (Arrow
    1959),

-   as a *workteam* à la Alchian and Demsetz (1972) or Marschak and Radner
    (1972),

- as an efficient *collective action* à la Arrow (1974, p. 33) when the price system fails, that restricts scope of action to achieve simplified objectives,

- as the *principal* in charge of *agents* (Ross 1973),

- as an *efficient converter* of uncertainty into computable and manageable risks à la Knight (1921),

- as a *competent team* à la Eliasson (1990b).

Dynamics; entry, firm growth

- as an *innovator/entrepreneur* à la Schumpeter (1911) who saw a new combination as the setting up of a new firm (*entry*),

- as a *mover of dynamic market competition* à la Smith (1776), Clark (1887) etc. (entry/exit),

- as a *disequilibrium system* à la Penrose (1957) that is growing through continuously exploiting internal economies of scale through removing bottle necks (cf. division of labor and economies of scale),

- as a *biological system* -- a lifecycle theory of the firm (Boulding 1950, p. 34, Alchian 1950, Winter 1964 etc.; perhaps even Marshall),[12]

- as a *"machine"*, a *"biological system"*, a *"culture"*, a *"political power game"* etc. depending upon what you are interested in (Morgan 1986),

- as an *"experimental learning machine"* (Eliasson 1990b).

Hence, there are many theoretical reasons for the establishment and the existence of firms. They can all, however, be summarized by the *financial objectives aimed for*. By decomposing the profit variable into its constituent parts different theories about how profits are aimed for and are achieved can be identified. It is, therefore, both conventional and empirically relevant to introduce (in terms of the rent ε) the separable additive targeting or control function (III.10). This business rent is constantly sought after by the firm, and to the extent the firm succeeds it represents a *capital market imperfection*, based on a merge between its real and financial dimensions.

This sketchy presentation of the still ongoing evolution of a theory of the firm has a well defined purpose, namely to derive (out of literature) a firm that might resemble the real firm presented in this book. I will, hence, focus the rest of this section on how the relevant behavioral characteristics of the real firm are reflected in the theoretical firm, the purpose being to highlight the characteristics of internal firm life that are important for the organization of its internal information, decision and control system. In this sense this is a biased or selective presentation with a purpose. In doing so I will focus on the firm as

a)   *a* converter of uncertainty into computable risks,
b)   *a* manager of risks in financial markets,
c)   *a* boundedly rational organization and the optimal managerial span,
d)   *a* behaving, rather than existing agent,
e)   *a* competent team and an organizational learner,
f)   *an* experimental machine.

This overview will, in fact, be seen to lead right up to the notion of the firm of this book as an *experimental* machine, aiming for *financially* defined *objectives*, using a uniquely specified *competence* capital to succeed or fail.

a)   A converter of uncertainty into computable risks – the Knight (1921) proposition

I attribute the perhaps most sophisticated formulation of the existence problem to Knight (1921). He makes the competence to convert *uncertainty into computable or manageable* risks the rationale for the existence of the firm. Knight can be interpreted[13] as having argued that agents act *as if* they perceive subjective probabilities about the outcomes of uncertain decisions. Uncertainty then arises in situations when the insurance market fails. In this sense (LeRoy and Singell 1987) Knight can be said to have been very modern and to have anticipated modern IO literature. He can perhaps be said to be even more modern, since this conceptualization of subjective probability is a particular expression of competence, or bounded rationality. This notion is directly compatible with the ex ante version of efficient market theory, firm management being confident in their "insurance business", viewing all departures from their computed expected values as insurable risks. Particular problems arise, however, in a dynamical systems market context, where the realization of ex ante perceptions is not a predictable process. Here Keynes (1921) is more up-to-date in recognizing Knight's distinction by arguing that agents do not stop acting if they cannot form subjective probabilities. [Also cf Keynes (1936, p. 214) and compare with (1921)].

Logically, Knight (1921, p. 251) considered business decisions as uninsurable. "Business insurance markets" would fail because of *moral hazard*, and the business incentive system would be adversely affected. This clearly anticipates the idea of the firm, the entrepreneur as an experimental machine operating in a non-predictable, non-stationary environment. This notion is not compatible with rational expectations and efficient market theory (my observation). This is, however, not the general reading of Knight. Hicks (1979, p. 107) reads the efficient market into Knight. Schumpeter (1954) understandably did not: As Stigler (see LeRoy and Singell 1987) points out, Knight's book was not very consistently written, containing ideas that were not fully thought through. It should be observed, however, (LeRoy and Singell 1987, p. 405) that Knight discussed matters of economics that now belong to the core of economic analysis, that it took the profession "another 50 years" to be "substantially improved on".

The firm as a manager of risks in fact permeates (as we shall see), all three dimensions, and the critical empirical problem is whether separable, perfect markets for risks exist, as has become a standard assumption of finance theory.

Earlier in this chapter I summarized the competence endowment of a firm by the six characteristics of Table III.1. The ability to *sense the direction* [item (1) in Table III.1] *better than the market at large* reduces the uncertainty that the firm is experiencing compared to outside market analysts, and allows it to act faster and more daringly. What the outsider may regard as non-calculable uncertainty, the executive team converts into an appreciable risk situation (a hypothesis, an experimental design) on which it acts. This conversion, however, is entirely subjective. Each actor imposes a simplified personal (subjective) theory on all the "facts" to achieve *subjective order* out of an immensely complex business situation. Such boundedly rational behavior (Simon 1955 and Day 1971) is necessary to be able to act, to carry out the experiment. "Bounded rationality", hence, incorporates *important management technology, namely the competence to choose the right "theory" through which to filter the facts, to evaluate the business situation.* No outsider can make the same "conversion" except by proxy, i.e. by evaluating the team which has set up the business experiment. (Hence, outsiders will perceive risk neutral -- or even risk averse -- behavior on the part of the top executive team, as riskwilling).

Making the competence to transform "uncertainty" into "computable" or "insurable" risks (Eliasson 1985a, p. 315) the rationale for the existence of the firm is most adequately credited to Knight (1921).[14] In Knight (1921) computable risks could be handled in the insurance market. The entrepreneur is not concerned with insurance or risk taking (Schumpeter 1954, p. 556) but with uncertainty, which by definition corresponds to a local "tacit" competence to put the business on a rational, computable footing. He has chosen his "view", his theory, and *faces uncertainty associated with choice of model, a "subjectively computable risk".*

As a byproduct of this discussion choice of appropriate decision model for the occasion becomes the mechanism through which diversity is entered into economic behavior.

b) *The firm as a manager of financial risks*

The theory of finance of the 1950s and the 1960s was largely represented by financial modeling of the firm in terms of its budgeting process, reflecting rules of thumb to evaluate, e.g. risks in firms or by markets. This entire body of ad hoc theory, related to the managerial theory of the firm was dealt a devastating blow by a series of articles in the late 1950s and the early 1960s. Modern *financial economics*, originating in the three controversial articles of Markowitz (1952), Modigliani and Miller (1958) and Sharpe (1964), is a different, anti-Knight animal. It embodies the notion of efficient and separable markets for money and for computable risks. It allows for no distinction between risk and uncertainty, and the two concepts are used synonymously in finance literature. This is correct under the assumptions of the static general equilibrium model, or its stochastic version, the rational expectations-based efficient market theory. In this model there is really no place for owners or entrepreneurs, whose services can be rented in perfect markets (Fama 1980). In fact, and for the same reasons neither can a firm exist in this model. The efficient market story, however, allows us to discuss the rôle of markets in the management of risks. Financial markets operate as *disciplinary agents* on the firm's financial targets, but also as *suppliers* of the means to acquire *resources*. The problem is that the assumptions used allow only infinitesimal entities and quantities which makes the discussion too artificial in our context of the real firm.

The separability assumption introduced by the Modigliani, Miller, Markowitz and Sharpe putsch carried a lot of further intellectual consequences. The firm should not engage in risk diversification, because it was less competent to do this than specialists in the markets for risks. However, if there were synergy effects associated with merging risks and finance, which is exactly what the Knight proposition presumes, the whole idea collapses.

When, in fact, business ventures are highly complex and uncertainty should be expected to prevail, such separable markets do not form spontaneously. They are either merged in the internal financial markets of large firms or in industrial bank groups. Hybrid organizations between a firm and a market can be formed, as in the venture markets, which is the market that most typically violates the assumptions of the efficient market.

More recently the notion of asymmetric information on different sides in the market and modern signaling theory have allowed market imperfections to reenter the theory of finance. In fact Miller himself (see Miller and Rock 1985) and a few others have been instrumental in occasioning this revision and of bringing back the old proxies for risk exposure in the balance sheet etc. This time, however, observed rules of thumb are being based on a rational foundation. Hence, the firm becomes visible in financial markets.

c) Bounded rationality, financial markets and the optimal managerial span of control

Economic literature takes for granted that rational firms are concerned with profits, notably with maximizing profits. It is, therefore, natural to begin studying the firm as a financially defined (profit) oriented entity, defined by its financial objectives and its information system vis-à-vis the capital market (Eliasson 1976a, Chapter XI). Old *corporate finance* literature emphasized financial management of the firm. The managerial theory of the firm of the 1960s attempted to model observed behavior of the firm and gradually (notably through Simon 1957b etc.) became interested in the optimal size of the firm or the optimal span of managerial control. Modern finance theory has a similar problem when emphasizing the anonymous financial market as a disciplining force. The two approaches represent two distinct traditions. Simon and others (see below) studied the efficiency characteristics of internal management control. Finance theory assumes that efficient markets make firms efficient. To understand how firms behave, reorganize and perform one would, however, have to study the efficiency characteristics of imperfect internal firm management operating in imperfect financial markets. This is the logical, but difficult course to follow after Coase (1937).

Using the idea of Figure III.3, placing the firm as a hierarchy in the intersection of markets, we can observe that the external *financial markets* and the *firm (internally)* perform essentially the same three types of tasks.

These three tasks (functions) are performed in varying proportions in all firms. The balance between the three tasks is usually associated with particular dynamics, in which organizational change is the vehicle for firm growth, and by this observation also macroeconomic growth. There still exists, however, a semi-statically oriented literature on

- centralized vs. decentralized hierarchies
- industrial bank organization
- internal information equilibrium to coordinate hierarchies.

Table III.4   Three types of financial functions performed internally in the firm and externally in markets

	The firm	The financial market
(a) Holding Transactions Money (Production)	Liquidity Management	Classical Banking
(b) Investment Allocation	Investment Finance	Capital Market
(c) Entrepreneurship Innovation	Venture Financing	Stock Market

They are all versions of the old Coase (1937) proposition that can be extended to the question of the optimal span of control of an organization or of a hierarchy. The span of control discussion treats vertical and horizontal markets differently. Horizontal control is in general much more difficult than vertical control. In both cases the problem of bounded rationality arises, meaning limited understanding, or transparency of the decision situation. In both cases the information problem is approached in reality (see the following chapter) through the organization of the firm and its information system, a fact that is to some extent reflected in the theoretical discussion. These are the internal information and control problems. The external information problems, also featuring bounded rationality come next.

The optimal managerial span of control

This question was first addressed by Simon (1957b), studying the size distribution of firms and asking; what is the optimal span of control in a firm? This literature has come back recently in terms of the administrative technology of internal coordination through hierarchies and "transactions costs" economics (Williamson 1964, 1975, 1981; see also Camacho 1988, 1991 and others).

A common proposition under this heading combines the division of labor with Coase (1937) and bounded rationality. Division of labor creates an internal productivity potential that is checked by rising coordination costs (with size) due to bounded rationality (Camacho and White 1981, Camacho 1988). The determination of optimal firm size depends critically on the existence of an *indivisibility* (Camacho and Persky 1988). Camacho's and Persky's conclusion is that with a sufficiently complex coordination problem, and boundedly rational managers, coordination of the team has to be solved through a hierarchy. There exist an optimal division of work.

Economies of scale (or scope) is of course the covering term for the potential of forming a hierarchy (or firm) that beats the market in coordination. A whole lot of suggestions appear in literature:

- The divisional organization of the firm, that began to appear in the 1920s in the U.S. has been heralded by Williamson (1981, p. 1555, 1986, p. 151f) as the "most significant organizational innovation of the twentieth century".

- Complementaries in products and transactions costs activated through vertical organization (Williamson 1975, Ch. 5).

- Similar complementaries (synergies) activated in internalizing "the supply of knowhow and other inputs common to two or more production processes" (Teece 1980).

Managerial synergies

While Alchian and Demsetz (1972) and Marschak and Radner (1972) explained the existence of the firm or the team in terms of Coasian (1937) *positive team-synergies*, Monsen and Downs (1965), unaware of Coase, had already used Coasian reasoning to discuss the possibility of *negative synergies* (dysfunctions) in the form of large corporate bureaucracies, internal information biases, risk aversion, managerial waste etc. While Alchian and Demsetz (1972) forgot negative synergies altogether, Monsen and Downs (1965), in good tradition, forgot positive synergies altogether, and came out with altogether negative conclusions on big business.

This discussion postdates the analysis of *weak diseconomies* of scale begun by Simon (1957b) with a model of executive compensation and addressing the *optimal span of control* in organizations. It also relates to the task of the business executive (formulated already by Barnard 1938) to organize people in teams that effectively coordinate economic activities.

Simon's notion of a limited *effective managerial span of attention and control* that limits the size of the firm was further elaborated by Simon under the name of bounded rationality, a concept that has reluctantly entered economic analysis recently.

Marris and Mueller (1980) also distinguish between the static and the growth-oriented managerial theory of the firm. This distinction more clearly shows the lack of context and ad hocness of this theory. The *static* version represented by Baumol, Williamson, and Cyert and March is said to be concerned with the size of the firm (= sales), size being the ultimate objective of management, while growth in sales is the ultimate aim of growth-oriented businesses, a notion proposed by Baumol and Williamson. Profits, under this heading, serve as a constraint, rather than as an objective. In Manne (1965, 1966), and Jensen and Meckling (1976), the market for corporate control is argued to serve the same disciplinary function.

Integration versus subcontracting

One particular problem of internal control is vertical integration. Lewis and Sappington (1991) study the choice between subcontracting out and vertical integration and the boundaries of the firm. This choice is affected by the better control of own production activities, partly compensating for the possible lower costs of a subcontractor. In general, cost-reducing technological change makes it more profitable for the firm to produce the input itself, as is the case for technological change which requires more highly skilled labor. The reason is (p. 893) that more advanced equipment, that requires more skilled labor, raises capital costs, but also raises innate labor productivity throughout the organization, thus making more internal provision profitable.

Hart and Moore (1990) address a similar problem, developing a theory of the *optimal assignment of assets* to understand the boundaries of the firm. The key is how the contract between owner and operator specifies the control of assets and the distribution of rents. One choice is between employing people to do a job or employing a subcontractor. When the production or investment task becomes very specific and detailed it becomes impossible to write long-term contracts about how rents should be divided up. It becomes easier to internalize production. This controls opportunistic behavior, but incentives are negatively affected. Another benefit of integration is that the firm then can fire workers it does not want selectively, whereas non-integration requires that the entire firm is "fired".

d) Behavioral and managerial theories of the firm

The notion of *boundedly rational behavior*, formulated and introduced into economics by Simon (1955) marks the advent of the managerial or behavioral theory of the firm. It was partly conceived as a rationale for an alternative to the profit-maximizing assumption of neoclassical economics, namely *satisfying* behavior, and it did not fail to provoke heated intellectual debate.

Neoclassical economics dug in with the assumption of "perfect" or "fully" informed and rational decision making, well into the 1970s. The controversy about satisfying vs. optimizing behavior, hence, evolved into a long history (see Machlup 1967, Friedman 1953; for a survey see Eliasson 1976a, pp. 249 ff) and remains unresolved in the sense that there has been no general agreement on a common way of looking at the problem. Day (1967) argued that maximizing was a special case of satisfying. As I concluded before (Eliasson 1976a, p. 257) the Friedman (1953) proposition is false in the EOE, i.e. that all firms must be profit maximizing, because only profit-maximizing firms will survive in the long run, i.e. in equilibrium. In the real world of the EOE imperfectly managed firms compete in imperfect markets. There are better ways of managing most firms, and when they have learned to be better the conditions for profit maximizing will have changed. There is no way to determine the characteristics of the efficient market and the profit maximizing firm, if this behavior can be defined, might very well be a bad performer. Static equilibrium is not a feasible operating point in the EOE and, most important, profit maximization has no meaning beyond the trivial observation that firms do their best, given what they think they know, in a market where everything depends on what everybody expects everybody else to do.

The core of the controversy concerns the possibility of achieving a state of full information in which management is fully informed about the internal capacities of the firm and its external environment. Technically the debate was about the possibility of maximizing profits. This debate has now more or less ceased as the notions of imperfect, asymmetrically informed or failing markets have gained acceptance.

Since "bounded rationality" is currently creeping into mainstream economics through the back door under the name of "asymmetric information" a few comments are in place. The idea of bounded rationality that I have used throughout this text, is that of a "choice of interpretation model" to organize your facts and thoughts to reach a personal understanding of the whole to be capable of reaching a decision. Simon (1959) expresses this as follows; "the economic actor (the firm) acts on and responds to the subjective environment that he perceives". We have to know something about his "perceptual and cognitive processes" to understand what he is doing. This choice of your personally restricted vision to be able to cope with environmental complexity is of course not unique to economics. Psychologists have long been aware of this mode of thinking. The concept can be found in Simon (1945, *Administrative Behavior*, 1957 ed., pp. 39-41) under the name of "limited rationality". March and Simon (1958) use the term (section 6.6) "the bounds of rationality".

The person who has pushed the concept of "bounded rationality" most intensively is Williamson (see 1970, p. 21, and 1975, p. 4). Williamson even refers to Coase (1937) as implicitly having recognized the phenomenon of bounded rationality. As I suggested above, Knight's (1944) proposition that firms conceive of their environment such that it makes computable sense to them ex ante is also an instance of bounded rationality that is closely related to entrepreneurial and business competence.

e)   The firm as a competent team and organizational learner

Financial economics emphasizes classical competition, i.e. the end result of competition (= efficiency), and hence tends to reduce the significance of the firm and its behavior. A particular result is the negative conclusions on risk diversion through diversification implicit in the Markowitz-Modigliani-Miller-Sharpe propositions.

The firm as an insurance provider

An exactly contrary development of thinking is currently taking place within labor market economics and the economics of internal labor markets, where the notion of the firm as an insurance provider is emerging. Several strands of thinking can be observed in literature.

A natural inclination among labor market economists has been a political bias towards the social side of the labor market process.[15]

As in financial economics we can also view the firm emerging in labor market economics as providing essentially the same services as the market, the rationality for its existence being its superior cost efficiency in providing these, namely

   (a) employment insurance
   (b) allocation of competence (selection, hiring)
   (c) competence upgrading in the firm as a learning organization.

Lazear (1981) coming out of labor market economics and its particular problems provides a sketch of the firm as an insurance provider to risk avert labor. Rosen (1972) discusses on-the-job learning in the firm, and Aoki (1986) the best organizational design to facilitate internal learning. The organization of the internal allocation of people (the assignment problem) enters in Sah and Stiglitz (1985), Ricart i Costa (1988) and in a tournament setting in Lazear and Rosen (1981). None of these articles are really concerned with the theory of the firm, but a labor market version of the theory of the firm emerges if you emphasize the synergy capacity associated with the formation of competent teams (Eliasson 1990b).

The classical model required diminishing or constant returns on all factors. The classical economists had a problem with the contrary indications of empirical observations. To resolve this dilemma Knight (1944) suggested that competence or knowledge is "the only possible offsetting effect" to that "natural tendency to diminishing returns". The classical model also assumed that the wage was equal to the marginal productivity of labor. Also this assumption was contradicted by observations, and total product failed to be exhausted by factor payments as it should be in equilibrium. Here McKenzie (1959) suggested that the residual product value remaining after all factors had been paid had been created by an invisible knowledge capital that was being compensated this way. It is thus -- at the firm level -- very natural to interpret this residual profit as the return to superior organizing knowledge residing in the top competent team (including dominant owners) of the firm (Eliasson 1990b).

The competence explanation provides a direct link into labor theory (Eliasson 1992b,c) that I will pursue here to establish the temporary competence monopoly as the rationale for the existence of the firm in terms of its financial objectives (Eliasson 1991e).

The firm as a learning organization

Establishing the firm as a competent team, superimposed on top of a physically defined organization of machines and labor hours leads right up to the appealing conclusion that the long-term success of a firm depends on its ability to organize its career system (filter), to upgrade the tacit knowledge base of its top competent team, very much as suggested in Section III.7. This team sets the direction of the firm, and mobilizes and directs lower level competence. The selection of this team is largely self-organized, but the dominant owners play a critical role, either as raiders in the market, if the corporate officers manage to form a closed shop -- as is often the case in the U.S. -- or through competence contributions via a varied, informal interaction with the CEO, which is more typical of Swedish groups. Hence, *the firm learns* (see Section III.6) *as an organization through recruiting, restaffing and training its employees, and through reorganizing*. The knowledge of how to organize a firm as an efficient learning entity is "tacit". It is no surprise that so little empirical literature on this exists. Those who know do not write articles.

In the last few years, however, organizational learning has been intensively discussed in literature and the problem has been to give this typically tacit knowledge visible analytical forms. Aoki's (1986) model is particularly useful for our attempts to link education and internal training, via firm organization to the performance characteristics of the firm. Aoki distinguishes between the centralized American A-type organization, and the Japanese J-type organization, that builds on the ability of workers to relate to the whole organization, thereby acquiring competence to solve local problems, that would otherwise require other specialists, and to discover new possibilities, an individual capacity that is systematically built through self-motivated learning by doing and job rotation.

The A-type organization, on the other hand, requires specialists in coordination (managers) and significant, central administrative efforts for monitoring and control. Specialization, furthermore, means a standardization of tasks, and that markets for standardized specialties exist. This may increase labor mobility between firms, but means that the integration of specialties in production becomes another, higher level specialty, and so on.

The J-type organization, on the other hand, makes coordination an organic part of the whole, requiring fewer specialist coordinators (managers), since each worker has acquired a capacity and a motivation to relate himself to the whole. This mutual understanding of the members of the firm, a culture, becomes the result of the systematic training of individuals. It takes a long time to develop and therefore requires life time employment contracts.

Aoki (1986) especially emphasizes the capacity of the J-type organization to efficiently communicate internally, which means that it doesn't need the elaborate A-type organization with well defined responsibilities and decision hierarchies and a preoccupation with shirking problems. The J-form is self-monitoring and difficult to represent on organizational charts. It is not exactly known centrally how decisions are taken and executed and responsibilities exercised. The J-type organization takes well care of its workers and gives them useful training and a firm-related work experience. Workers, however, become hostages of the firm which equips them with a non-tradable knowledge capital.

An interesting question is which firm organization that is most innovative, the J-type or the A-type. About this we can only speculate, but theory provides a strong argument.

The A-type organization is capable of forcing change top down on the firm when the situation demands it, "specialist" top management forcing a new combination of specialists on the organization.

The J-type organization does not possess this top level reorganization specialist group. The organization has been trained to selforganize, which requires that changes be small to avoid destroying the self-organizing capacity of its experimentally developed internal signaling system (see Eliasson 1976a, 1992b,c). Hence, there will be nothing ready to put in its place if the old system fails. Hence, the J-type organization will probably be conservative and difficult to innovate radically.

f) The firm as an experimental machine

The more competitive the market setting, the more critical the filter that selects the competent team at the top that can take early and fast action on a sense of direction that is relatively better than that of other teams. In this sense *the firm is setting up and enacting subjectively controlled experiments, based on hypotheses about opportunities in the market*.[16] Each agent (competitor or market analyst) is an outsider in this game. Each individual actor may nevertheless act *as if* he appreciates his environment as a learnable, estimable process by imposing his personal interpretation. Hence, the agents can optimize on their perceptions of their environment even if the economy is experimentally organized. Behaving as if the economic environment is predictable in order to be able to optimize in a mathematical sense will, however, normally mean that you are making an error. Rational learners will, hence, eventually learn that they won't be right in expectation (Day 1975).

Confidence in the decision model chosen and a willingness to act (prematurely) on its predictions are conditioned by the ability of the competent team to cope with mistakes, early and reliable identification of mistakes and effective correction of mistakes [type (3) and (4) of the competences identified in Table III.1]. Firm management now faces a narrow and well defined analytical problem, that is more in line with the "decision theory" one learns at school. This is the management activity most easily observed by outsiders. Hence, it is also fairly well described in literature, however, not from the point of view of the purpose presented here. Finally, if the experiment has been checked and cleared for the market, an entirely new information technology clicks in, designed for efficient flow operation [item (5) in Table III.1] of the organization and increased preparedness for future innovative, experimental and possibly disastrous action [learning feedback, item (6)]. This specification of competences will be seen to be reflected quite clearly in the organizing of information and control systems in firms.

The early analogy of the firm as an *experimental machine* is the *biological theory of the firm*, an entity that survives on the basis of particular competence characteristics, including its ability to learn to reorganize internally to cope with change.

It appeals to the economists' mind to see the firm as a life cycle story. Already Marshall (*Principles of Economics*, 1920 ed., pp. 286-287) used the analogy of a bee that was born, grew and eventually lost in vigor with age. Boulding (1950) came back to it, as did Alchian (1950). And even though Penrose (1952) expressed severe criticism and doubts, the analogy surfaced again in Winter's (1964) thesis at Yale. A political version of the biological story of the firm is the concentration debate and the worry that a few monopolists would eventually take over the markets. Schumpeter (1942) was here, as were Marris (1971a,b, 1972) and Marris and Mueller (1980). Mueller (1977, 1986a, 1990) was particularly worried about the "permanence of profits". In this intellectual dispute I think Winter comes out right. Penrose's argument is that there is no principal common factor between a biological system and a firm, since firms tend to live very long lives. This, however, is wrong. Most firms die very soon, or get acquired by other firms. Some firms grow suspiciously old (see e.g. Figure II.2, and the oldest joint stock company in the world, **Stora**). The truth, however, is that even if the name is the same, to become old in a successful way the interior organization of an old firm has "mutated" many times. Internal organizational change is what makes firms survive, and in the end all firms will probably die, or be acquired, since they were unable to reorganize. The distinction between mutations and routines, or rather new routines and routine management was Winter's (1964) story, and even though the changing of rules was a bit too simplistic behavioral reasoning, the principal idea was right. So here Penrose was wrong. Her (1959) story of the disequilibrium growth of a firm through constant exploitation of, and creation of new bottlenecks is, however, a fascinating, and empirically relevant biological story of the growth of a firm (also cf. Marris 1963). The nice thing is that if we combine the notions of the firm as an *experimental*, innovating *machine* driven by the *human competence* embodied in its organization towards *financially defined goals*, the story of the *experimentally organized market environment* can be derived. If sufficiently open, the EOE will give competence a fair chance to establish itself and to compete, which will be sufficient to prevent single individuals or firms from acquiring monopoly power. It is illustrating to note that kings, dynasties and dictators only occur in hierarchies.

Firm growth, monopolies, concentration and market competition

The firm of the old literature was looked at, by Adam Smith (1776), as a monopoly with bad efficiency characteristics that had to be checked by free competitive entry.

Besides the monopoly concerns, "big firms" did not exist in early literature, excepting the city states of Italy, possibly the Hanseatic league, the East India companies and the "warfare" enterprises of some kings. The first notion of big firms as production machines began to emerge with the railroad companies of the 19th century. Eventually, bigness became again a monopoly problem, giving rise to debate and eventually antitrust legislation.

The "monopolistic competition" studies since the 1930s are typical of this debate. The first analytical story was statistical. Firm dynamics was first introduced as a lottery, making Gibrat (1930, 1931) an early forerunner of efficient market theory. Gibrat asked the questions; is success a draw from a lottery? Is the rate of firm growth independent of the size of the firm? This possibility and the emergence of large business combines in the 20th century spurred a worried monopoly debate. Chamberlin (1933), Robinson (1933) and also Hotelling (1929) framed the problem analytically. The enormous literature that followed established anti-trust theory, legislation and thinking on a solid static foundation. Even

Schumpeter (1942) asked whether the big firm would be able to routinize innovative behavior, applying scientific methods to their R&D investments. A few firms -- a dismal Schumpeter (1942) concluded -- might eventually take over all markets and destroy not only the market economy but also its political image; democracy.

The organizational technology of big business caught the attention of economic historians like Alfred Chandler (1962, 1977, 1990), and people worried about the loss of political power to business. Robin Marris (1963, 1964, 1971a,b) was very early in arguing the need for a revised economic theory with the formation and growth of firms in core. How should we think about the market process in markets dominated by competition among a few giants? This analysis was, however, too early. Refined, neoclassical, macro theory was taking over the supply side of economic theory, rolling all phenomena that threatened its aggregation assumptions down into the mud. One or two decades later, however, the theory of the firm is coming back to life again, as the story has already been told above.

Marris and Mueller (1980, p. 50) are, however, still worried about monopoly profits. They find the private enterprise economy to be a *self-organizing process* that beats the market in earning a rent from coordination and leads to persistently increasing concentration at the national level and persistence of monopoly profits, resisting forces like international competition (rivalry). Smithian and early Schumpeterian dynamic competition are occupying a relatively small place in the Marris-Mueller text. They observe that neoclassical theory has to cope with economies of scale and that markets are inherently costly and imperfect, relative to the internal organization of the firm, and its potential to create synergies à la Coase (1937), Alchian and Demsetz (1972), Simon (1959) or Williamson (1975).

The monopoly and concentration stories culminate in Mueller's (1977, 1986a and b) attempts to demonstrate the persistence of corporate profits. These attempts rather demonstrate the need for a new theory of monopolistic competition outlining the circumstances under which such concentration should continue. This is one of the reasons for my attempts to formulate an alternative to the static, general equilibrium model that stimulates such reasoning as that of Mueller, namely the experimentally organized economy that endogenizes competition (see Sections II.5 and II.7). In the experimentally organized economy profits can be demonstrated never to persist for ever.

Most tasks ("dimensions") associated with the firm in business administration literature can be found also in the literature on the firm in economics. The difference is that business administration treatises focus on the running of the firm (control, strategies etc.) and discuss many features simultaneously. A profile of, or a strategy to run the firm is being presented. The typical economics text, on the other hand, usually an article, takes on one aspect in each article.

Of course, all aspects carry some importance. To study them all in one analytical context and to place them in a macroeconomic context as well is therefore impossible. A decision has to be made, deleting some and weighing the others together. This choice is empirical and depends on the problem chosen. In this sense the business administration literature is more "scientific" than the economic literature. The choice of problem and strategy to solve it has been made explicit.

The economists, on the other hand, provide all the components needed to make all kinds of cars -- but not all cars -- and leaves it to "us" to put together a car of our choice, often without instruction manual (theory).

MATHEMATICAL APPENDIX

Proof of the relationship between the rate of return and total factor productivity change

Proof of (III.15)

From (III.6) and (III.7)

$$PQ = wL + (r + \rho - \frac{\Delta p^K}{p^K})K + \varepsilon$$

Take differences, assuming (p, w, r, p^K) fixed;

$$P \cdot \Delta Q \equiv w\Delta L + [\quad]p^K \Delta \overline{K} + \Delta \varepsilon$$

Thus,

$$\frac{\Delta Q}{Q} = DQ \equiv \frac{wL}{pQ} DL + \frac{[\quad]\Delta p^{K}\overline{K}}{pQ} D\overline{K} + \frac{\Delta \varepsilon}{pQ}$$

$$DQ = s_1 DL + s_2 DK + \frac{\Delta \varepsilon}{pQ}$$

$$s_1 = \frac{wL}{pQ}$$

$$S_2 = \frac{[r + \rho - \frac{\Delta p^K}{p^K}]p^K\overline{K}}{pQ}$$

$$\frac{\Delta \varepsilon}{PQ}$$

is, by definition, DTFP.   QED.

NOTES

1. As did, in fact, also most books on strategic planning from the late 1960s and early 1970s.

2. even though some would say that this capital affects the demand, not the supply curve.

3. using Romer's (1986, p. 1015) formulation for an economy for a firm.

4. The Kim and Lau (1993) results are compatible with that interpretation. They show that increasing returns to physical capital and labor disappear when educational capital (measured by years of schooling) is added as an explanatory factor.

5. With this argument applied to physical capital all economic depreciation would be from physical wear and tear of the machines.

6. Which is the standard assumption in "human capital theory".

7. Note that K has been used in a different sense in Section III.3.

8. The balance sheet looks as follows:

K	DEBT
	E
K =	= Total liabilities

9. Making their equipment more valuable to them than to any possible outside buyer.

10. The mathematical derivation has been taken directly from Eliasson (1992b).

11. Rational expectations learning is normally not possible in non-linear models with explicit selection processes like entry and exit. See Lindh (1993).

12. For a critical view, see Penrose (1952).

13. LeRoy and Singell (1987) argue that *uncertainty* as distinct from *risks* is synonymous with an "insurance market failure". Therefore the firm arises -- my interpretation (1990b) -- as a competent team capable of ex ante transforming uncertainty into computable risks. The firm, hence, can also be seen as a "collective action" in Arrow's (1974) sense. The problem is what to mean with market failure, since the creating of these competent teams, capable of overcoming uncertainty, is exactly the opposite to market failure.

14. See the discussion on complexity and non-linear dynamics in Chapter II where no static equilibrium can exist and a natural distinction between uncertainty and risk arises.

15. This position is taken by, for instance, Solow (1990).

16.   The competent team so defined has all the characteristics of Alchian and Demsetz' (1972) jointness and the Marschak and Radner (1972) team. It is, however, not only the optimal design of incentives that matters, but the tacit competence of the top team to organize the firm so as to create an innovative organization capable of generating a monopoly rent.

PART II

PRACTICE

IV

THE FIRM -- ITS CONTROL SYSTEM IN PRACTICE

Until recently the firm in economic theory was presented as a factory established in a (given) price system, under complete internal control by its top management. The title of Thorstein Veblen's (1921) book; "The Engineer and the Price System" conveys the idea. This notion also carried the day in the policy world towards which economists directed their attention. It contributed -- I personally believe -- both to the unscientific and unprofessional debate on economic planning, socialization of industry and a host of ideological metaphors based on ignorance. It also caused the breakdown of communication between economic theory and empirical economic research, on the one hand, and business administration theory on the other. The previous chapter has illustrated this. Even though their purposes differ and the world is too complex to capture in one universal theory, both economic theory and the theory of business administration should have a minimum common foundation in the same relevant theory of the firm.

This chapter continues directly from the theoretical notion of the firm as a decision entity organized for *experimental* search in a largely unpredictable dynamic market environment, a decision body that is only partly controlled by its management. The purpose is to establish exactly how much top management knows about the interior life of its organization, and how much control it has. In passing I will give a well-rounded presentation of what really goes on within a business organization, hinged onto the theoretical structure presented in the previous chapters. The business organization as it appears also in practice is an organization endowed with human competence that uses physical capital to achieve financially defined goals. I will conclude this chapter by assessing the meaning and economic significance of the most critical competence manifestation of the industrial world: the competence to operate giant innovative and heterogeneously composed business firms; an attempt to give empirical meaning to the Coasian (1937) proposition.

IV.1   WHAT IS DONE WITHIN A FIRM?

Table III.2 itemizes the various tasks carried out within a large business organization. It has been structured on the "accounts" of the knowledge-based information economy in Table I.3. Even though it takes a few pages I will now go through the various activities listed in Table III.2 to convey a feeling for the amount of diversity top management has to cope with in order to run a large business organization.

There are four main categories; *Selection, creation of new knowledge (innovation), coordination* and *knowledge transfer* that I will go through in the order listed. Throughout this presentation I want the reader to keep in mind that the business organization functions simultaneously as a profit-oriented production, an "on-the-job learning" and a competence allocation career organization. No one makes out well at the top *selection* function without a broad-based experience from most of the other activities of the table, and few make it there without that experience.

The big firm that does not organize this in-house "business university" well usually does not continue for long as a big or independent firm.

Figure IV.1   Distribution of labor costs on functions
Large Swedish manufacturing firms, global operations, percent

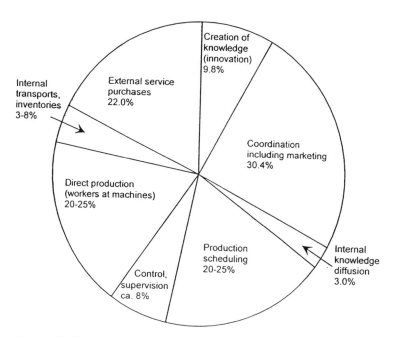

Total: 122%

Source: Eliasson (1990b).

There is a specific educational item in Table III.2 (item 14). This is the traditional, well structured form of "classroom" education that large firms increasingly carry on internally. The higher level "education" that leads to the top is informal. Performance is measured in terms of ability to understand, act and meet business objectives ("make profits"), not in terms of ability to articulate and document.

Finally, the table represents the various production activities of the manufacturing firm. The manufacturing firm is predominantly a service producer, and the private service firm is a specialized firm, in which the materials processing item 11 in Table III.2, is lacking.

Figure IV.1 illustrates the relative importance of the various tasks of Table III.2 in terms of resources allocated.

What is obvious from the earlier theoretical analysis and from the interviews is that *human or organization-embodied competence at all levels dominates the performance of the firm*. This means that competence capital somehow has to be made explicit in a theory of the firm, since the staffing of the firm with competent people is the dominant preoccupation of its top decision makers. This is not overly difficult. The hiring assignment and career (learning) problems of the business organization then become critical elements of a relevant theory of the firm. This is also clearly borne out by the organization of the firms' information system (see next chapter).

IV.2   SELECTION AND THE BREEDING OF A COMPETENT CORPORATE CULTURE

Already in Chapter III I introduced excess returns to measured capital over the interest rate as a return to the tacit competence to organize the firm as a hierarchy of competent teams (Eliasson 1990b). The selection of competent people at all levels, and in particular the selection of members of the top competent team that ultimately controls all other selections then becomes a critical "firm technology". The career system broadly defined determines the *mind of the corporation* (Eliasson 1990b, 1992b).

Decision making at all levels in a large measure consists of selection. At lower levels millions of small choices are made. It is impossible to determine the resources devoted to individual choices. Therefore activities are grouped in types of choices, represented by departments for which budgets can be separately composed. At higher levels choices often take on significant importance and can be identified. They, however, always interact which makes it next to impossible and almost always impractical to make up separate budgets even for major choice activities, since resource use cannot be meaningfully identified.

It is, however, always possible to describe the procedures leading up to choices or selections, and these procedures may tell as much as cost benefit analyses about the efficiency of the activity. Again, the selection mechanisms related to recruitment, especially higher level recruitment, is the most important.

The Varied Career

The career is a particular form of combined labor quality selection and on-the-job training. While the training for simple tradable labor skills can perhaps be separated from the job experience and a real job environment, higher management competence accumulation has to be integrated with the job, and the more so the more unique the competence capital of the business organization. The final qualities needed to run a firm are typically tacit and cannot be taught at school, even though some business schools pretend to have the competence to teach business leadership. The qualities needed of top managers are general and non-specialist. Their acquisition requires intense and risky work effort. To induce intense managerial effort and competence supply the contract has to be designed to allow the members of the top competent team to capture a significant part of the value contribution of their tacit organizational competence.

The "top competent team" makes the ultimate choices that decide the long-run survival of the firm. It is the final destination of a successful career. The top competent team determines the filter that selects people for the career. The whole organization of top level decisions and of career selection is very informal, as should be the case with unstructured decisions. Differences in procedures between firms are large. Such heterogeneity makes it less meaningful to characterize *what* is being done. One can observe and assess how. One can also characterize the qualities and the organization of the people that make the decisions.

The informal nature of selection and choice activities also makes it difficult to represent them in terms of resources used. The top competent team, as a rule, is also engaged all the time in lower level, routine management, which may absorb most of the time of its members. The outcome of selection and choices achieved makes all the difference for the firm: huge profits, no profits or losses. Recorded resource use for these activities at Central Head Quarters (CHQ) is a negligible factor in the context. *The large costs are foregone profits and recorded losses.*

Talent requirements are usually tough, educational requirements are not strict. Most people in an executive career today, however, appears to have attained an academic degree, usually early in life. A long academic career is often a negative signal, or as somebody remarked in an interview: "If you could stand that environment for so long, you wouldn't make it here". The filter procedure takes on a strong positivistic bias the higher up you go, reflecting probably the enormous scarcity of broadly experienced top level management.

Several large firms I have interviewed routinely weed out candidates without academic degrees from the group of career candidates they monitor. The reason is to keep the group reasonably small, but also notions like this: "If you could not pull yourself together to get an academic degree reasonably fast, most likely you will not be able to cope with the much more demanding tasks of a management career."

As for the rest of the career, candidates get plenty of opportunities, the filter being put to use not so much in order to avoid losing talent by accident, but rather to prevent lower quality human talent from progressing to high level positions.

An important criterion is willingness to take on responsibility and hard work, and also to move frequently internationally. This selection is often automatic. Candidates that do not like that life drop out.

From my interviews I have the impression that the competence to deal with mistakes is not well developed. Quite often a bad mistake, a subsidiary losing a lot of money, is the end of a successful career. My conjecture that should be investigated further is that a well-managed firm incorporates an experimental, curious culture, more willing to accept mistakes than alternative, more analytic and bureaucratic cultures. Analytic cultures are often based on the notion that careful prior thinking eliminates the risks of large mistakes, as in the case of central planning theory. The business culture recognizes that firm decisions normally have to be taken long before you are through with the careful thinking, that mistakes are, therefore, often unavoidable, but that the making of mistakes should be part of organizational learning at lower levels.

I was frequently assured that an individual that pulled himself together, after a seriously mistaken decision along the way, or an internal conflict, was never hindered in his new career because of this previous experience. But it was up to him to pull himself together. As somebody said: "This mentality is really what we want to promote".

I want to make two comments in this context. *First*, if real learning in management really consists of a broad-based career experience, and if the experimental character of business life is so important as indicated by Table III.1 (previous chapter), then learning to cope with, identify and correct mistakes is the core management experience needed. Anybody climbing through the hierarchy without a sequence of "managed mistakes" behind him or her, has either been very lucky or has avoided taking risks. Whatever the reason, his lack of experience or his attitude disqualifies him from top level positions, since being unable to identify and cope with mistakes at that level carries an extremely large, potential cost for the firm.

Second, and contrary to what I first said, the top level competent team take and represent the major decisions of the company and has to execute their realization with vigor, not rarely against lower level opposition, breathing complete confidence all the time. If a top level decision flops, the credibility of the team suffers. Team members cannot simply turn around and say let us rather march as vigorously in the opposite direction. This is so even though the top team really is a competent team, and even though everybody understands that the "flop" may not have been its fault or because of bad judgment. Hence, the top team normally has to leave after a major business mistake. It is therefore often rational to minimize the loss of talent by selecting a scapegoat and pay him off very well. Few can do what Napoleon did in Egypt 1798 when business opportunities suddenly appeared in Paris: simply leave the army and return to France.

The reason is -- again -- the complex, tacit nature of the business problem, the experimental nature of the decision process and the ignorance of lower level specialists of the large context in which the firm operates.

The explanation for IBM's success over many years probably should be looked for in its competence to manage talent; both in terms of filtering innovative competence upwards, and in preventing its internal bureaucracy from blocking organizational change.[1] This is a matter both of top level competence, of organization and of internal culture reinforcement (cf. Carlyle 1988). The technique appears to be to show disrespect for specialists and seniority, forcing steady job rotation and intellectual retooling, even at high level jobs, maintaining that those who cannot cope with that are not competent for high level positions.

The Specialist

A firm need both generalists for the career and specialists. One problem is that specialists sooner or later get obsolete. Another problem is that few people are intellectually flexible enough to begin as specialists and then reorient themselves for a general career. They tend to prefer to stay specialists.

The career possibilities for specialists have often been discussed. It has been observed that managers, section chiefs and people responsible for people usually are much better paid than even the very valuable specialists of so-called high tech firms. This problem sometimes becomes acute when a firm is about to lose a specialist who embodies a critical technology upon which the firm currently bases its earnings. In firms of "received economic theory" this specialist just then may be worth many times his or her salary to the firm, and much more than the top executives, which may be replaceable. So why not pay this specialist an enormous sum to keep him on the job.

There are many objections to this view. First of all the specialist may suddenly become obsolete and be worth much less. The task of managing other people, furthermore, is to make sure that the necessary lower level talent is around and to organize the firm such that it does not become dependent on one person only. This competence, in general, is worth much more in the long run than the unique competence of an individual just now. Part of this organizing competence, furthermore, would be to team up with specialists (of enormous value) such that they do not quit, and if they get obsolete such that the firm does not have to continue paying large salaries. If one person carries enormous specialist value in proportion to the firm, a participation contract, rather than an employment contract would perhaps be the proper arrangement. The growing importance of technical specialists in advanced firms therefore probably explains a parallel and very rapid expansion of technical consultants in the industrialized economies. This development has been made possible by technological development, a development that is radically changing the nature of production organization and firm management (Eliasson 1988b, 1990a,b). Thus specialist careers within firms -- academic style -- do not seem to be optimal arrangements, especially if specialist salaries come close to the compensation schemes for executive people.

The respect for specialists varies between firms. It is my impression that successful firms recognize that competence has to be developed continuously on the job and that its content varies over time, meaning that most competence capital embodied in people at high levels in a firm has been accumulated on the job. Hence, whatever specialist training the person in question originally carried with him means much less after a few years. It is interesting to observe that in one of the typical "engineering firm cultures" in a large Swedish multinational, two factory managers were economists by training.

The Internal Educational and Training System

Modern technology steadily increases demands on workers' skills and the quality of the nation's educational system. The failing educational systems of industrial countries, including the U.S., has been frequently discussed (Bishop 1988, 1989, Davis 1989) as the source of "the deteriorating manufacturing base". Firms are increasing their resources spent on internal education to develop specialized skills. They are, however, reluctant to invest in general education to compensate their employees for a deficient school experience. What the modern firm asks for is a good general educational platform that makes on-the-job training and retraining efficient and profitable. At recruitment firms are, therefore, increasing the attention paid to selecting quality. This is increasingly so even at the workers' level and the reason is to secure a high return on their growing internal educational investments (Eliasson 1992c, 1994e,f). Most often a lack of basic communications skills like mathematics, computer science and languages has been noted. It is remarked that students often take softer business degrees in order not to have to start at the low end of the career. Hence, a basic flaw in the career design has been not to make a down to earth technical and production experience mandatory in order to progress upwards in the career. This would have put a premium on having the right basic skills in the college and university diplomas.

Bishop (1988) also finds that a good basic training in active communications skills (language, mathematics etc.) matters for productivity even at relatively low level jobs in workshops. Such skills also appear to be decisive for the ability of the individual to learn on the job, and, hence, decisive for his or her ability to carry on a successful career (Eliasson 1991e, 1992c).

It is interesting to observe how a department store head of personnel argues "that we look for business degrees with a computer science minor", arguing that "we can teach technical skills ourselves" (Davis 1989, p. 68); i.e. just the opposite position.

A superior business idea is the first ingredient of success. Once a firm has established itself in a particular market with a particular product know-how and a particular process technology, its human competence endowment in that area increases in importance. If the business situation suddenly changes radically, the whole business may suddenly find itself in a crisis and quite often has to exit. All large firms try to ward off such situations through accumulating a portfolio of alternative competences, through diversification, through R&D investments, through mergers and acquisitions etc. Experience, however, shows that those firms that stretch their competence too far, soon find themselves in a costly, low-profit diversification ("insurance") situation, while those that stretched too little share the fate of the market through becoming better than their competitors, but unable to get out of a distressed profit situation that requires entirely different competences. Firms that have grown very large and old must have been very lucky (almost all of them remain in their original market and product niches) in picking this market environment. They have all weathered at least one, often several close-to-bankruptcy situations and they have steadily kept competitors at bay through product innovations and the organizational ability to accommodate new competitive designs. This observation raises two important problems. *First*, is there a learnable technique for firms to accommodate radical technological change internally.

Second, the position of standard finance theory (see Section III.17 on the theory of the firm) is that a firm should not attempt to manage the business risks, but focus efficiently on what it is best at producing. Hence, owners and specialists on assessing business risks should pull resources out of firms staffed with the wrong production competence, and invest the resources elsewhere. In this second case economic growth has to occur through entry and exit rather than through internal reorganization. There is, however, the question of how large the consequent bankruptcy and reorganization costs are compared to inefficient internal insurance, and the problem of who is better equipped to deal with the long-term decisions -- firm management, the owners or the market. This problem was addressed already in Section II.7. It is now coming back as an observed management problem. This takes us into the next section on the creation of new knowledge.

IV.3   CREATION OF NEW KNOWLEDGE

We now move into more well-structured, Schumpeterian terrain, where, contrary to the Schumpeterian notion, genuine unpredictability prevails. The bulk of (measured) resource use under this heading concerns R&D investment which takes on the average 10 percent of total labor costs in large Swedish firms (see Figure IV:1), the bulk of it for product development. This item is rapidly growing relative to traditional hardware investment, in the most sophisticated firms it is much larger than investments in machinery and buildings.

New products, especially radically new product designs, require reorganization of production, sometimes of the entire firm. A very radical such organizational change had to be implemented when IBM entered the PC market in 1981 and it appears to be needed again in the wake of the PC revolution (see *BW*, Aug. 24, 1981, p. 38).

Rapid productivity advance is often associated with new product design, the new product designs taking modern production technology into account. This illustrates how process and product design technology can be made to interact to the benefit of overall productivity performance.

It is also instructive to take note of another related experience that has often surfaced during my interviews. *Reorganization is either the source of, or the administrative vehicle for achieving, productivity advance.* The complexity and tacit nature of production, especially new types of production, normally makes it impossible to choose the best organization as a prior design. It has to be tried out through experimentation, and as environmental circumstances change, what is the best organizational solution also changes. It is, however, costly to keep experimenting with the organization of the firm, not the least because it reduces the reliability of the internal information system. Hence, most firms settle down with inferior solutions. For the same reason, an existing organizational solution can begin to deteriorate unnoticeably. Bureaucratic inertia builds, small autonomous kingdoms develop and new ideas are to an increasing extent efficiently resisted. Very slow *organizational degeneration* occurs in firms growing and operating for a long time in generous markets (see Ross Perot and GM in Chronicle under Computer Services, 9h). Such organizational decay is often the reason for the sudden death of a business organization when a new technology or a new competitive situation suddenly hits the market. To counter it, especially in time, drastic and seemingly arbitrary measures are needed, involving the replacement of top level people. The recent reorganization of IBM is one example (see further Section VI.4). Facit, the Swedish maker of electromechanical calculators, once controlled 20 percent of the world market. It understood early that electronic calculators would come, but was nevertheless caught unprepared and went out of business in 1973.[2] The Swedish shipyards commanded a 10 percent share of the world market in the late 1960s but they were all specialized on giant tankers. Most of them went out of business in the early 1970s, but took a decade to die because of enormous Government subsidies (see Carlsson 1983a,b). Many companies have in fact experienced productivity improvements from reorganization, even though they did it all wrong. The introduction of new computerized office routines is one example. The office computerization itself, using existing routines, did not improve productivity. The activity, however, revealed a number of redundant activities that were shut down, such that large improvements in productivity were achieved even though the office sometimes did not even become computerized. Failed attempts at factory automation offers the same experience. The reason; the reorganization has pulled down existing hierarchies and exposed internal inefficiencies, most frequently redundant activities. Often office workers, or whole departments, have found it difficult to explain what useful work they had been doing, and been laid off. The office has been reorganized or closed down.

A few sophisticated firms I have interviewed have turned this experience into systematic management practice. They invent a reason to reorganize regularly to prevent lower level hierarchical inertia from developing. Similarly, some large firms have rules preventing middle and high level managers from staying more than three to five years on their jobs. They are forced into a career life style whether they want to or not, and are induced to leave, if they don't like it. The official rationale is the need to accumulate a varied experience to be ready and flexible. Another reason is, as said, to prevent undesired local hierarchies. The interesting, related observation is the obvious disrespect for specialist education and training indirectly exhibited.

As a rule, operational and control people (in Figure III.1, previous chapter) resist such change, since coordination efficiency depends on a stable internal order (see Eliasson 1976a and Section III.2). Hence, organizational change is normally initiated at the top level in the decision pyramid. Part of the organizational competence of the firm is to organize itself such that (1) competence to reorganize exists there and (2) bottom up resistance is effectively overcome. This means that top level management maintains a certain degree of organizational isolation from lower level management. We can observe at this stage that all firms that have led a long life have experienced many internal and successful reorganizations.

IV.4   COORDINATION

The coordination functions include the management of well-structured, repetitive routine work, or what we normally call production.

Productivity advance through innovative *selection* comes from making the right *choices* on *reorganizations*, while *coordination* works on *production flow efficiency*, i.e. reducing slack at a given organization of production. The potential for productivity improvements through rationalization is rather small. On the other hand, the systems effects of coordination increase the more of the entire production flow that can be integrated. This is, however, largely a matter of organizational choice. The diversity of activities of a manufacturing firm is illustrated in Figure IV.1. The reader should note the large service or information processing element in regular goods production. Hence, the leverage on profits from "tiny" improvements in the organization that monitors and controls the entire business entity is very large. The large Swedish multinationals appear to have achieved large systems (or scale) economies in the 1980s from competently and efficiently integrating product development and international marketing and distribution with production.

Short-term ("static") flow efficiency through coordination requires stable internal information structures through which to communicate efficiently. Efficient information processing requires stable internal information structures. The extreme example is an automated factory that does not allow any ambiguities in information processing. This requirement conflicts with reorganization at higher levels, that, however, is the source of the really large improvements in productivity -- if successful. Hence, the coordination hierarchies of the firm always resist innovative organizational change, imposed from a higher level (see Eliasson 1976a). And long-term organizational improvement always comes at the cost of temporarily lower process flow efficiency.

This conflict of interest between the two levels of decision making is solved through organization, keeping the *strategic* and *control* levels in Figure III.1 organizationally apart, the *control* level being subordinated to the strategic level (see Eliasson 1976a, 1984b, Thorngren 1970).

Two administrative techniques take care of implementing strategic reorganizations into the control system. What Ledin (1988) calls *tactical* management has the purpose of imposing and integrating a new product, a new organizational solution into the flow structure of the firm at a minimum of disturbance. Ledin cites development of the AXE telephone switches and the "business information system" division as examples of strategic decisions in Ericsson that succeeded and failed, respectively, at their (tactical) implementation stage. IBM's successful move into personal computers is another example.

Another "tactical" device that links all coordination activities together systematically to meet top level profit targets is the *budgeting process*. Budgeting includes -- the way I define it (see Eliasson 1976a) -- both dynamic coordination through *investment* and production flow control through profit (margin) targets and more detailed cost control devices.

Through the CHQ controlled investment budget (allocation decision) the firm operates an *investment bank* function that competes with the capital market.

Risk management enters one step down in many firms. First of all the ability to convert uncertainty into subjective, computable business risks can be said to be the rationale for the existence of the firm (see Section III.17a). It enters at the top "idea" level. The big firms, however, also engage in more systematic risk management to control business cycle variations in profits (diversification), to control exchange risk exposure etc. and also enter the insurance market in direct competition with established insurance companies. There is finally one often unintended insurance activity in the sense that modern firms take on a significant responsibility for protecting labor from job and income losses and health problems, including also the provision for retirement schemes (see again on the theory of the firm in Section III.17). This internal insurance activity often runs counter to the interests of the firm in the sense that it is forced to equalize income differences to an extent that is detrimental to efficiency.

The monitoring of exchange position exposure of the firm is particularly interesting, since it requires an understanding of, a theory of, the interaction of prices in international markets, notably inflation, the interest rate and the exchange rate (Eliasson 1984c, pp. 49 ff). Apparently such risk management has been and still is very crude, exchange risks being controlled in isolation through adjusting foreign denominated assets and debt structures in the balance sheet continuously, and covering the rest in forward markets (Oxelheim 1988). A high interest rate, however, often tells something about expected inflation and expected exchange rate adjustments and relative international configurations in these three variables often have some predictive value that can be used for more efficient risk management.

Significant potential costs are associated with a firm's various types of risk management, that show up neither as implicit charges in profit and loss statements nor as implicit liabilities on the balance sheet. I have not seen any firms make such numbers explicit for internal use.

IV.5   ORGANIZATIONAL LEARNING

Organizational learning is a fashion term of recent origin that has been created to capture the fact that learning in firms is not only individual but also team oriented. Teams, the members of which understand each other and support each other, produce more than the sum of what each member does in isolation. The Coasian (1937) proposition is that when a combination of people and machines outcompetes the market in coordination costs a firm is formed. The firm breaks up when this is no longer the case. Organizational learning is the dynamic version of this organizational synergy, expressing the idea that such synergistic competence cannot simply be achieved through reorganizing the firm. Team competence has to be learned. It has certain characteristics explained in Aoki's (1986, 1988 etc.) comparison of Japanese and U.S. firms.

Organizational learning, hence, is something more than the training of individuals. It has similarities with the kind of team training that occurs in sports, and participation in college team sports is often an extra credit when being recruited for a corporate career program (Eliasson 1994e). Such organizational training is practiced more or less in most firms, and it is a typical part of the formation of the top competent team of a firm, that has to be composed of people that work well together.

Again, we have the problem (see Section III.17 on the theory of the firm) that organizational learning is not an intellectual activity, but a form of rote training, that breaks in the team as it copes efficiently with the repetitive management tasks of an ongoing business.

If the competitive situation changes radically the competent team may suddenly find itself incapable of dealing adaptively with the new situation. The situation of the team is then similar to that of a worker who has acquired his skills through rote learning. The team does not possess the explicit intellectual capacity of an educated individual to retool itself. As a rule a fast and brutal injection of external knowhow is then needed to get the firm back in trade, or save it. This requires that lower level resistance to change be brutally crushed through the removal of people who are in the way of change. This has been the situation of IBM during the last few years, attempting to change its mainframe mind. The role of executing such change is always reserved for the dominant owners represented on the Board. If such dominant and active owners do not exist the reorganizing capacity of the business usually does not function well.

But for all practical purposes *a firm* -- large or small -- *cannot be constantly organized for doing something else*, if need be. Hence, its current focus of internal competence accumulation has to be on its mainline business, technology, markets etc. The possible need for radical and brutal change has to be serviced through a separate stand-by organization to be called on only occasionally, most typically the Board. This task is supremely difficult. Hence, the typical fate of a firm subjected to sudden radical change in its competitive external circumstances, is failure. Attempts to save it are also often so costly, that the economically rational organization of markets for corporate control may be to facilitate shut-down and bankruptcy rather than management salvage operations, and to simplify the rapid reallocation of "saved" resources through the market.

IV.6   REPRESENTING THE FLOWS OF ACTIVITY THROUGH THE COST ACCOUNTS

The previous accounts of what goes on within a business organization serves the simple purpose of illustrating its complexity and the difficulties associated with making the firm transparent and controllable. The simplistic planning models of the 1960s and early 1970s are gone with the wind (Eliasson 1976a, 1984c). The notion of a plannable firm economy modelled on the organization of process operations, however, is still deeply ingrained in the profession which studies the firm from a normative point of view.

On this I want to reconfirm the results from my earlier (1976a) study, that the complexity just described and the unpredictable micro environment of the experimentally organized economy have thrown out most of the planning bureaucracy of large firms. Top management ambitions are to achieve reliable *remote performance* (profit and cost) control through proxy measurement, without getting involved in production details. To achieve that, easy and fast access to information on the format needed just then and there becomes critical. Major innovative decisions are still taken in an intuitive, ad hoc way at the top of the organization. To achieve efficient control of core variables without getting lost in the complexity and heterogeneity of a business firm, activities have to be reclassified and converted into a fairly stable measurement code, that is an approximate image of the organization of the firm. For the proxies to be reliable indicators of what goes on in the firm the links between the code and the control variables have to be stable. I will first describe this classification of the cost accounts, as they are usually found in large firms. Then I will discuss this (enormous) number system in terms of analysis, control, access and reach, and illustrate its shortcomings.

The final chapter brings in modern electronics-based information technology. What is happening in those dimensions? Is there a better, optimal solution that can be derived? What has come out of those billions of dollars that large electronics companies have spent on designing the ultimate business information product?

The functions and organizational hierarchies of many large corporations can be itemized in a stepwise fashion down to levels where quantifiable physical activities became visible, but in ways that still relate clearly to the corporate performance measures. The reader can see how the categories I use tie into Tables III.1 and 2.

Information Access vs. Control

The earlier text has documented two characteristics of the firm and its top management. *First*, the top competent team, through its tinted glasses, faces an enormous global opportunity set. Its particular appreciation of its local place in that global setting of opportunities defines its local competence (bounded rationality). Firms set up business *experiments*, test them in the market, learn and eventually find an organization, or a competent team structure that is capable of generating a satisfactory rent. The particular configuration of competent teams and individuals that achieves this rent embodies a total competence specification that is virtually impossible to encode. It remains "tacit" and is difficult to recreate elsewhere. For a considerable time the firm or its competent team enjoys a temporary monopoly.

Second, when turning around and looking inward, the top competent team faces an overwhelming complexity that is largely beyond analytical reach, even though some formalized control of the complex internal economy of the firm may be achieved (see Sections III.12-16). Inaccessibility of the opportunity set and the interior rationalization possibilities is partly a computational problem in the old Hayekian (1935, 1940, 1945) sense, partly a principal agent problem relating to limitations of language. The most important part of the internal communication and control system has to be solved through organizational technique, or an incentive system that links individual and corporate objectives, the visible hand of Chandler (1977).

Each successful business organization, hence, has found a balance between an analytical, formalized management system, and a dominant human-team-based competence input that controls the destiny of the organization. Literature on the organization and management of firms has documented the formalized system well, but also, unfortunately, proceeded to believe that the formalized system that can be observed and studied is what really matters. Some have gone so far as to believe that the system will gradually substitute for business judgment (Simon 1965). Some authors have been talking about "the" formalized planning and control system that would be invariant to its staff. Individuals could come and go. The competence would be embodied in the system. This is a strong version of classical growth theory; *capital* embodied technical change. This essay concludes that such simplistic notions of the firm are completely wrong and misleading. As a rule, new incoming management changes the organization, its control system, and quite frequently also its top people. In the next chapter we study how big "information companies" have gone broke to the tune of billions of dollars on the basis of the same misconception: the analytical syndrome of western civilization.

Third, very concrete conclusions on the nature of a relevant business information system follow. The recent reorientation of business internal information systems in this direction is obvious from my interviews. The improvement process is typically experimental. It was already in my (1984c) study compared to what little I could notice in the pre-oil-crisis interviews (1976a). The 1970s played a major rôle in forcing a reorientation.

Above all, the well managed business information system is "people" and "access to information"-oriented, reflecting the fact that *all* major decisions are taken outside the analytical "modes" of the organization, among groups of people that have to be coordinated spontaneously, needing access to information in a broad sense and of a kind not foreseen, on a new, unprepared format and fast. Human communication devices (!), easy access and flexible database designs are the keys. I will go through this in detail in the next chapter. In this chapter I will concentrate, finally, on one side of access, namely *interior reach*.

Table IV.1   The organizational hierarchy of a firm -- information access

(1) Level of aggregation	(2) Organization	(3) Activity	(4) Target (performance criterion)	(5) Database (measurement system)	(6) Market interface
(1)	Group ("concern")	Financial targeting	Rate of return on net worth	Balance & profit and loss statement	I,L,P,K
(2A)	Division	Financial and profit control	Rate of return on total capital	Profit and loss statement and partial balance sheet	I,L,P
(3)	Product group	Factory (production)	Profit margin	Profit and loss statement	I,L,P
(4)	Product	Process	Costs	Cost accounts	I,L
(5)	Component	Process element	Cost element	Cost accounts	I,L

I = Market for intermediate goods; L = Labor market
P = Product market; K = Credit market

Source: Eliasson (1984c, p. 75, 1987, p. 72).

Table IV:I maps several organizational dimensions into each other. The target column reflects the mathematical break down of the rate of return in equations (III:10-17), and maps into both the "organizational" or "responsibility" break down of column (2) and the corresponding detailed database or measurement system of column (5). Apparently both "responsibility", targeting criteria and measurement system to the extent possible tie one-to-one into the market classification of activities.

This reflects the observation of Williamson (1981) that divisionalization was one of the major organizational "innovations" of postwar industry, i.e. an information technology that made it possible to delegate process decisions and profit responsibilities without losing central control of costs and profits.

Divisionalization along well-defined market categories made it possible to operate a monolithic profit-related incentive and measurement system.

Table IV.1 also nicely illustrates the limit of central access to information about interior capacities, i.e. the limits of measurement: *First* of all, where external market (reference) prices are lacking, the quality of information depends on internal assessments, and the intentions that those who make these assessments want to convey. Such "pollution" of the quality of interior information dominates below the product group level. A *product group* is characterized by some joint production technology (being produced in the same workshop). Its different products are also sold in the same markets (e.g. different kinds and sizes of a product performing similar functions). This (*second*) means that the product group level (3) is the smallest unit to which profit responsibility can be delegated, i.e. where accounts "meet" free markets, that provide external reference data that cannot be manipulated by those responsible for compiling the data inside the firm. Table IV.2 gives an even more overwhelming picture of the complexity of the internal economy of a large firm to be managed from the top.

The product group level of a large firm, as a rule, is too small an accounting unit for central profit control. The large firms may have hundreds of product groups. Therefore, product groups are lumped together into divisions (level 2), each corresponding to a firm operating in one market. A division is defined such that it can have its own profit and loss statement and balance sheet. Thus CHQ can delegate operations control, still keeping effective cost and profit control on the basis of reliable (not polluted) internal cost data. CHQ normally then focuses on larger investment decisions at division level, but often (especially in U.S. firms) accesses cost information, and engages in profit targeting with division heads at the product group level (see Eliasson 1976a, Ch. II.3; 1984c, pp. 56-86).

The product group is the minimum organizational unit with well defined contacts with product, labor and capital markets. The big firm tends to centralize the capital market dimension and to delegate operations in product and labor markets to division heads. The firm of economic theory should be defined accordingly, in terms of its profit control and financial system, i.e. in terms of its own (statistical) information system (see Eliasson 1976a, Ch. XI; 1985a, Section II.2; 1992a, pp. 67 ff). A product group can be "physically" separated in a firm, even though it often engages in joint production with other product groups within the same hierarchy.

Depending on the nature of their business large firms have only a few product groups, or many. As a rule -- today also among European firms (cf Eliasson 1976a) -- CHQ accesses the full accounts of the product group directly through its central information system. Below that level database updating and definitional problems escalate rapidly, mostly because internal transactions at administrative (non-market) prices begin to dominate. The information content of databases -- at that level of disaggregation -- from the point of view of CHQ rapidly diminishes.

Table IV.2   Functions and hierarchies as viewed through the cost accounts of a firm

LEVEL 1 (STRATEGIC)
0.   Executive
1.   Finance/control
2.   Markets/Marketing
3.   Products/Production
4.   Distribution
5.   Administration

LEVEL II (COORDINATION AND
          CONTROL)
0.   **Executive**
0a)   Strategy, long term, ideas
0b)   Goals -- profit targeting
0c)   Organizational change
0d)   Acquisitions, divestment
0e)   Large investments
0f)   Delegation of operations
      responsibilities

1.   **Finance/control**
1a)   Long term; finance & investment
1b)   Short term; budgeting
1c)   Decision; investment
      (appropriation)
1d)   Control; reporting, profit control
1e)   Liquidity; cash flow

2.   **Markets/Marketing**
2a)   Market analysis, marketing
2b)   Sales
2c)   New product ideas

3.   **Products/Production**
3a)   Production idea, R&D
3b)   Design
3c)   Engineering design, Blue prints
3d)   Documentation
3e)   Production scheduling
3f)   Purchasing
3g)   Processing (plant operation)
3h)   Cost calculation
3i)   Quality control
3j)   Inventories

4.   **Distribution**
4a)   Delivery plans
4b)   Delivery administration
4c)   Shipping; organization
4d)   Shipping; execution

4e)   Transport organization
4f)   Inventory organization and
            maintenance
4g)   Insurance
4h)   Maintenance and repair
4i)   Reserve parts

5.   **Administration**
5a)   Central computing
5b)   Library, archives
5c)   Internal communication
5d)   Personnel
5e)   Wages and salaries
5f)   Education
5g)   Legal matters
5h)   Taxes
5i)   External communication
5j)   Insurance

LEVEL III   (OPERATIONAL)
1.   **Finance and control**
1a)   **Long-term**
      - Long term planning
      - Business model
      - Rate of return targets
      - Investment planning
      - R&D planning
      - Market investments
      - Investment calculation
      - Total finance and risk assessment
      - Credit market analysis
      - International risks
      - Internal resource allocation
        (divisions, profit center)
      - Portfolio management
      - Transfer prices
1b)   **Short-term**
      - Comprehensive budgeting
      - Budget model
      - Targeting
      - Cash-flow analysis
      - Tax analysis
      - Appropriations planning
      - Portfolio decision

1c)   **Decisions**
      - Pricing
      - Cost analysis
      - Reporting (against budget)
      - Ex post analysis

- Investment analysis
- Invoicing
- Customer credit risks
- Liquidity control (month, week, day)
- Sales monitoring
- Currency management
- Accounting

1e) **Liquidity**
- Receivables (payable)
- Invoicing
- Taxes
- Short-term financing (money markets)
- Internal banking
- Liquidity planning through daily money markets
- Exchange market planning

2. **Markets/Marketing**

2a) **Analysis/marketing**
- Research
- Forecasts
- Product R&D
- Product strategy
- New product (model) strategies
- Market and product design
- Competition monitoring
- Price and cost analysis
- Sales strategy and management
- New product launching

2b) **Sales**
- Inquiries
- Customer monitoring
- Customer manipulation
- Offering
- Order receipts
- Order management
- Order/inventory management

3. **Product/Processing**

3c) **Engineering design (construction)**
- Project management
- Technical information -- external
- Design and analysis
- Technical data bases -- internal

- Process costs
- Blue print design
- Graphical representation
- Model simulations
- Laboratory tests and analyses
- Prototypes

3e) **Process scheduling**
- Design and production data
- Inventory data bases
- Delivery forecasts per product specification
- Total production plan -- long term
- Investment and machine purchase plan -- long term
- Inventory strategies -- long term
- Short-term materials flow requirements
- Delivery stability analysis
- Order -- process analysis (optimization)
- Work scheduling
- Materials management -- control
- Inventory control (inputs, work in progress)

3f) **Purchasing**
- Purchase plan
- Selection of vendors
- Subcontractors other vendors
- Component purchases
- Goods reception
- Quality control

3g) **Goods processing**
- Process monitoring
- Factory design
- Machine configuration
- Machine design
- Machine programming
- Coding, communication
- Maintenance
- Machine support
- Machine control
- Materials flow -- transports
- Materials flow -- processing
- Quality control
- Inventory control (goods in process)

3h) **Cost analysis**
- Process budget
- Cost accounting
- Ex post analysis

Note: The classification of this table relates directly to that of Figure III.1.
Source: Eliasson (1984c, pp. 82 ff).

It now remains to explain how the accounts of Table IV.1 are built from the finest, systematic measurement grid of the company. Its cost accounts are divided up at finer levels of detail in Table IV.2. I will then systematically relate the items of the cost accounts to the control items of profit targets in equations (III:10) and (III:11) to prepare for the four examples of information systems biases in Section IV.7 that we know will affect real firm behavior; (A) *missing items,* (B) *inflationary* profit *distortions* and (C) *risk aversion,* accelerated charges of capital costs for precautionary reasons and (D) *wrong measures.*

The Cost Accounts

Table IV.2 is a standard breakdown of the cost and resource use structure of a firm. At level I, the first two sublevels normally represent the Corporate Headquarter (CHQ) unit. Underneath, the firm organization fans out in a number of divisions, each with a marketing, production and distribution activity, each reporting as a profit center to CHQ, where all major investment decisions are taken.

Levels 2 and below represent repetitive routine activities controlled by hierarchies that can be changed from the executive level. The normal cost account structure is very hardware oriented, keeping track of nuts and bolts at the process level 3 through deeper and deeper layers of costing, while softer activities before and after are normally dealt with in rough categories. Itemization on the hardware side is sufficient to build stock accounts on the cost flow accounts. This is not the case when it comes to other types of activities like marketing, product development and internal competence development, each of which have related invisible stocks that generate services that improve corporate performance.[3] For the purpose of control this means that the origin of profits cannot be properly identified from the cost accounts. Neither can the cost efficiency of various types of soft activities be properly assessed (see below under "missing items").

The cost and profit control hierarchy

The purpose of profit control is to relate properly defined cost accounts for easily identified profit units to targeted values of profits. The *additive targeting formulae* implicit in the break down of the rate of return in the fundamental control function (III.10) is used.

There are two sides to the targeting formula. One is based on the market assessment of the firm using the concept of an *effective rate of return* in Section III.9 (see equation III.4 and accompanying pages for explanation of symbols),

$$ER = \frac{\Delta MV}{MV} + \frac{DIV}{MV}$$

to control the costs of external finance, and the other, a rate of return on equity based on a further break down of (III.10) using (III.16) and accounting for more cost items than in (III.10);

$$R^{EN} = \alpha \sum_i M_i a_i - \sum_i (\rho_i - DP^{k_i}) b_i + \hat{\epsilon} \phi \qquad \text{(IV.1A)}$$

where for each profit center i;

$$M_i = 1 - \sum_j \frac{w_j}{p_i} \cdot \frac{1}{\overline{S_i}/L_j} - \sum_j \frac{P_j}{P_i} \cdot \frac{1}{\overline{S_i}/I_j} \qquad \text{(IV.1B)}$$

j being cost items of each profit center

and $a_i = p_i Q_i / p \cdot Q$
$b_i = K_i / K$

(IV.1A,B) are sources of information for top management's internal cost control and assessment of the origin of profits and losses (symbols are explained in Section III.11).

In a perfectly informed capital market measures ER and R^{EN} should coincide, barring a different time preference exhibited by the market agents and the top management of the firm. Observe here again the right hand side of the control function (III.10) namely that:[4]

$$R^{EN} = \frac{\Delta E}{E} + \frac{DIV}{E}$$

The main difference is to be found in the valuation of net worth, in the market (= MV) or in the internal accounts of the firm (=E) as discussed in Section III.12.

Top firm executives now have to take in a number of factors in managing the firm:
(a) the market may be more myopic than firm management, discounting the future heavily, thus lowering MV compared to E, thus increasing the costs of

external finance; either through the interest i in $\bar{\varepsilon}$ or through the value of capital in an equity issue.

(b) the market may have a different assessment of the future earnings capacity of the firm, usually more pessimistic than that of firm management, or simply be less well informed, thus also lowering MV compared to E.

A common representation of the latter is that the market projects a present value of future dividends while firm management knows more, and projects a present value in terms of future profits. Since the market knows that firm management has an interest in boosting the value of the firm, there is a credibility problem associated with all information on the "future earnings capacity" that firm management might want to tell the market (see Eliasson 1990b). Hence, the market will never be perfectly informed if it does not have *inside information*. Hence, top management may have to depart from what it considers an optimal strategy in terms of long-term earnings or value growth, adopting a more short-term strategy, thus foregoing long-term profits. If firm management is best informed, this would be a suboptimal strategy. Top management might, however, be less competent than some of the market agents, or entertain private and separate objectives, cheating on owners. Then, no assessment of the situation is possible, except that it should appear profitable for a non-cheating executive team to take over the firm. These are subtle theoretical issues, discussed in theoretical literature on asymmetric information problems that took on giant real proportions in the U.S. markets for control during the junk bond era of the 1980s. Also important is the fact that;

(c) top management may be badly informed about, or hold a biased view about, the internal earnings capacity of the firm.

This is very much a matter of concern for the internal information systems designers.

The first question to address (under c) for the information systems designer is to what extent *forecasts* on the various items of the profit accounts will be unbiased predictors of R^{EN} or the corresponding present value of all future rents.

The second question relates to *various biases in the measurement system*. These will be discussed in the next section.

The possibilities of making an unbiased forecast at all, putting firm management ahead of the market, is of principal importance. In the plannable economy of the equilibrium model, such unbiased forecasts are theoretically possible. In the experimentally organized economic environment of this exercise, they are not. Nevertheless, all firms make up such forecasts or assessments in their internal budgeting process. They may extend these computations to make explicit present value calculations, although the common convenient procedure (see Chapter III) is to assume an equilibrium setting and interpret the computed rates of return over some future years as a steady state projection.

Summing up

In this section we have demonstrated the mathematical relationships between top level corporate goal variables and shop floor performance measures. This analysis was based on the earlier target performance analysis of Chapter III. We have discussed the many measurement problems that appear when these, well-known relationships are generalized, as they are more or less in all firms. The most common approach is to take partial relationships from the mathematical accounts, that are believed to be stable over time and use them as proxies or rules of thumb. The next section will show how easy it is to commit serious business mistakes when using such relationships uncritically.

IV.7   FOUR COMMON INFORMATION SYSTEMS BIASES

The notion of a "boundedly rational firm" means that it interprets reality through an incomplete, unreliable, or biased information system. There are four typical biases; (A) *missing items*, notably assets, (B) *inflation* causing arbitrary distortions, (C) *risk aversion*, i.e. the discounting problem and corporate myopia, and (D) *wrong measures*. Let me go through the four examples of deceptive *measurement bias*, one at a time:

Rate of Return Requirements on Invisible Capital -- Missing Items

The most common bias of the internal measurement system of a firm originates in missing items, causing unexplained profits, or covering up losses on other accounts. A fairly extensive discussion of the associated measurement problem can be found in Eliasson (1990a, pp. 60 ff, 1990b, and in more detail in 1992a, pp. 9ff).

Capital stocks, representing capital service inputs, can be identified under practically all cost items in equation (III.6, Chapter III), even though the corresponding capital measures are not explicit. If capital is defined as any charges contributing to profits beyond a certain time limit, say one or three years, then any firm, and a large international firm in particular, carries a huge, invisible marketing investment forward in their accounts. Similarly, a huge stock of invisible product knowhow is embodied in past vintages of R&D charges to current account. In all firms, employers learn on-the-job, and frequently they spend time on-the-job learning new things or developing new ideas, that should not properly be charged as costs to current production. In principle, such measures can be made explicit in the balance sheet using the same principle of measurement as those applied to hardware capital. This is very uncommon in practice, barring some sophisticated firms with heavy expenditures on intangible investments that have tried, cautiously to activate such stocks. IBM occasionally has made software investment stocks explicit in its annual report. Astra has activated product development investments. These stocks of R&D investment included development investment for Losec, the new pharmaceutical bestseller that in recent years multiplied the MV value of Astra several times. How should such development capital be valued ahead of success? After success? How should failed development investments be recorded?

If soft investments are large, top management needs these numbers to properly identify the origin of profits and/or to exercise cost control on the same activities. Being unable to measure means accepting that such identification and control cannot be achieved, setting a limit to the ability of top management to understand and control what goes on within the firm.

On the other hand, each budget allocation of resources on items like production, marketing, product development and internal competence development reveals a decision based on an opinion about the marginal contributions to profitability of each of these capital items. Top management always has an idea about the profit-generating capacity of these assets, even though they have abstained from quantification. In fact, no quantification tradition exists among accountants, and the interesting question is how an external analyst should assess the economic value of a machine that has no alternative use, the profit generating capacity of which he knows very little about.

We have collected data on intangible capital stocks, using different sources and methods. They are shown in Table IV.3. The first column for 1985 was based on a careful reading and reclassification of the cost accounts of 10 large firms, separating out "investment categories" from current charges, more or less as it should be done if a new measurement system were designed. The problem is not that this is more difficult to do than for machines and buildings. The problems are in principle the same for all investment categories. As for machines we have established certain arbitrary accounting standards. Such standards do not exist for such capital items as marketing investment. We visited the firms and discussed their accounts with knowledgeable persons,[5] arriving at depreciation rate estimates that we agreed were reasonable. The other columns are based on direct estimates by responsible officers at the controller's office, most probably based on assumptions about the assets' earnings-generating capacity.

What do these accounts mean? First, the new, adjusted and the old balance sheets with book values differ significantly, at least half of total non-financial assets being unaccounted for in 1985.

Table IV.3 Balance sheets of the largest Swedish manufacturing corporations 1985 and 1988 including intangible capital
Current replacement values, SEK, percent

	9 largest manufacturing firms, global operations, end of		17 largest manufacturing firms, global operations, end of	Planning survey firms, end of 1988		
	1985	1988	1988	all sample	sample of subcontractors (ISIC 38)	sample of small firms (ISIC 38)
	(1)	(2)	(3)	(4)	(5)	(6)
1. Machinery and buildings	54	50	70	62	89	80
2. Software	n.a.	7	6	5	2	4
3. Technical know-how (R&D)	17	16	13	21	4	11
4. Marketing	20	19	6	10	3	3
5. Education	10	8	5	2	2	2
6. Total (percent)	100	100	100	100	100	100
7. Debt	65	66	77			
8. Market value (MV); end of year in percent of (6)	30	37	51			

Source: Eliasson (1992a, Chapter I, Table I.5A, p. 88).

Two things stand out. When the real rate of return from the 9 largest manufacturing firms 1985 has been adjusted for invisible capital items it is lowered from 11 percent to between 7 and 9.5 percent,[6] which is between one and three percentage points above the corresponding industrial loan rate. If one percent is regarded as a reasonable compensation for risks -- which I think is more than needed for a stock portfolio of these firms -- one could say that row (6) tells the value the firms should have had in 1985.

There is -- in addition -- the classical problem of how market values should be affected by taxes not yet imposed, that I disregard here. This would, however, be a small correction, compared to the huge differences between the market value of the firm, residually computed (assets minus debt = E) and the corresponding valuation in the stock market (= MV) as shown on row 8.

Bringing these soft assets into the open would tell the outsider market expert something about the resources invested in marketing, product development etc. Without complementary information about accounting principles (like depreciation rates, etc.) the external analysts would only be partially informed, but this would be true also about other capital items like machinery and buildings. The insider decision makers in the firm would, however, know a lot more, having access to complementary information and probably also having influenced the accounting assumptions made. For them the revised accounts should reveal a pattern of capital resource use that would be very different from the official one. Such accounts would at least make it possible for the insider executive to tell more exactly the value of the firm and the rate of return on its assets. Not having access to the same data might make him think that rate of returns are higher than they really are.

The very interesting complementary question to ask is whether -- in the absence of the revised accounts -- the official accounts give an interpretable or a deceptive picture of the state of the business.

The Illusory Profit Boom of 1974 -- Biased Measures

Rates of return are also affected by biased measures on the income side, notably biased measures of the capital gains part of profits, and notably again, capital gains on inventory. During inflationary times, nominal and real profits differ significantly, as can be seen from Figure IV.2 for 1974. Furthermore, different methods of correcting for inventory capital gains give very different profit measures. With all inflationary gains on inventories included -- the standard accounting practice -- a huge profit boom can be observed in 1974. The problem was that this year profits were extremely biased by nominal inflationary gains on inventories. The consequent problem was that significant decisions in 1974 where based on this biased measure. A political discussion arose around the question of income distribution and fairness. The really serious problem, however, was that firms, especially firms in basic industries with large inventories, erroneously regarded the peaking profit margins, including nominal inventory profits, as a permanent increase in the profit margin or the rate of return. Their assessments were supported by advisers, external observers, experts and academics of the time. Firms, therefore, initiated an enormous investment spending program at the wrong time and for the wrong market. When basic material prices collapsed in 1974/75, so did the profit boom, but then it was too late to correct investment spending plans. As can be seen from Figure IV.2 profit margins are significantly reduced if capital gains or inventories are properly deflated, and the profit boom in 1984 disappears altogether when capital gains in inventories are completely removed from the operating profit margin.

Figure IV.2   Gross profit margins 1950-1992 in Swedish manufacturing according to different definitions

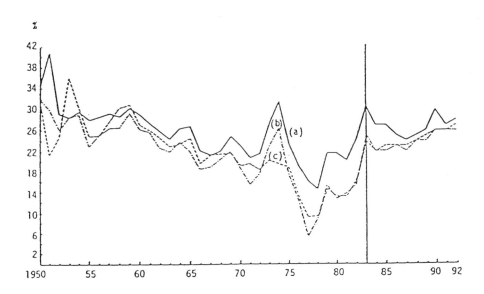

Note: a)   Gross operating margin in terms of value added, including nominal capital gains on inventories.
          b)   Ditto, including deflated inventory gains.
          c)   Ditto, excluding all inventory gains.

Source: Södersten (1985, p. 372) and updatings.

The issue at stake is really a matter of forecasting, even though it technically arises as a problem of using the correct deflator to remove temporary inflationary gains. Hence, the academic discussion around inflation-adjusted accounts supported such misconceptions by narrowing down the whole issue to an accounting problem, removed from the problem of interpreting data in a decision context.

Excessive Caution in Discounting

In considering bold investment ventures it is common to play it safe by applying high discount rates and/or fast depreciation rates to account for uncertainties. This is one possible manifestation of risk averse behavior. Hence, rates of return will be low, or negative during the first years of large projects, then excessively higher, possibly for a long time. Airlines often "suffer" from such problems, earning a high rate of profit on a fleet of airplanes overly depreciated in books, and "market experts" often take the numbers as presented.

Technical people in the laboratory or in the factory may not like this situation and push for modernization. The chief financial officer, on the other hand, being responsible for the external accounts of the company, likes the late phase of the project, since it is easy to present good profit figures. A firm ruled by the controller will be conservative, a firm ruled by the technical staff may be overly risk willing.

In a US-type financial market, specialists without operating knowledge of the firm, looking at its cash flow and visible capital will reinforce the controllers' view. The firm will be pushed towards conservatism, and -- which is the same in this case -- shortsightedness.

This situation of multiple misunderstanding is, of course, dangerous in a market environment, where firms compete with technological innovation. After a long show of high rates of return and no innovations, a new competitor all of a sudden can eliminate the economic value of the knowledge base of the entire corporation. The visible assets can only become "profitable" through the taking over and the replacement of existing knowledge (people) with new knowledge.

To prevent a situation like that the firm will have to be organized such that the controller is responsible for the operating or "static" efficiency of the firm, with an external risk-willing force, the top competent team (the top executives and some of the dominant owners on the Board), entering now and then to enact the necessary bold ventures.

However, if market experts exercise the controller's view in pricing the firms and if the firm is dependent on external funding, i.e. on its external market valuation, then the capital market will enforce myopia on firm management.

Wrong Measures

As a rule the measure one wants to have is not available and proxies have to be resorted to. Sometimes variables, such as capital cannot really be measured but they are measured anyhow, and used as information in decisions. But not infrequently the wrong measures are used and believed to convey information they don't contain.

Profit margins are often used and interpreted as rate of return measures even in the best academic circles. Firms frequently use the profit margin as an indicator of profitability. They may once have understood the risks of misinformation involved, but once a routine has been established they keep feeding the wrong signals into the decision process (Eliasson 1976a, p. 160 f).

The use of cash flow or pay back period analysis was presented in economic textbooks as similar cases of misrepresentation. But here I take a different view after having heard so many business people explain why they don't want rate of return calculations (Eliasson 1976a, Ch. VIII). In badly informed investment decision situations the pay-back criterion is an acceptable predictor of the rate of return.

A recent fad has been to aim for labor productivity targets and hours needed to manufacture a complete product, say a car. Those who use such measures had better check that they are reliable indicators of the profitability of the business. This is by no means obviously the case.

Productivity, as we have shown in Chapter III is a performance measure for the workshop in situations where proper rate of return measures cannot be computed. Too much focus on productivity measures in the workshops may, however, divert attention from the important decisions, for instance possible organizational changes, and the possibility of choosing something else to produce.

NOTES

1.   even though many observers think that IBM's "mainframe mind" has prevented it from moving rapidly in the right direction and caused its current distress. See Chronicle and Chapter VII.

2.   It was acquired by Electrolux which needed factories with skilled workers.

3.   See Chapter I in *MOSES Database*, IUI, 1992, Section 4.4. A separate IUI study that attempts to build such accounts is under way.

4.   in a taxfree world. For a proof see Eliasson (1976a, pp. 291 f).

5.   This was done by Fredrik Bergholm and Lars Jagrén and the results are partly reported in G. Eliasson, F. Bergholm, E.Ch. Horwitz and L. Jagrén (1985).

6.   depending on which depreciation assumption we use on invisible capital. Column (1) in Table IV.3 assumes significantly faster depreciation on invisible capital than on machinery and buildings (see Alt. II in Table I.7 in Eliasson 1990a, p. 80).

V

THE UNIVERSAL INFORMATION SYSTEM
-- A FANTASY OR A FEASIBLE NEW PRODUCT

> If at each stage the motion of a machine ... is *completely* determined by the configuration, we shall call the machine an "automatic machine".
>
> For some purposes we might use machines (choice machines....) whose motion is only partially determined by the configuration .... When such a machine reaches one of these ambiguous configurations, it cannot go on until some arbitrary choice has been made by an external operator. This would be the case if we were using machines to deal with axiomatic systems.
>
> A.M. Turing (1936, p. 232)

V.1   INTRODUCTION

The notion of a plannable economy that dominated economics and business administration well into the 1960s left significant traces in the design of economic planning, guidance and control systems of the *real* firms (Eliasson 1976a). The idea that firms should be organized as logical planning machines is still very strong and the notion that the "system", or the visible assets of the firm, embodies the technology, know-how or competence to run the business keeps recurring in literature. People can come and go. The system is what matters.

The experimentally organized economy, introduced in Chapter II, however, suggests (Chapters III and IV) an *experimental organization* of the firm and a completely different design of decision and control procedures than those of the planned firm. With tacit knowledge embodied in teams of people that make up the intellectual dimension of firm behavior, *management becomes the art of organizing people with competence rather than the logics of decision making*.

While this study shows that real firms increasingly have their information systems designed to focus on control, just as they should be in an experimentally organized business, we have also noticed that the ambition of computer and electronics firms to design "universal" and analytically based business information systems have been significantly influenced by the ideas of planning in the past and the engineering notion of automated production. We *also* established, however, through studies of the organization of actual business information systems (previous chapter), that they are, *in fact*, increasingly being organized to support organizational change, and identification and correction of mistakes rather than analytically oriented devices to support so-called strategic plans. This was obvious already from my earlier, pre-oil crisis interviews (see Eliasson 1976a), and increasingly so after the 1970s (see Eliasson 1984c).

This chapter takes a parallel look at the development, over the last decade or so, of an *integrated business information systems product*. The development story begins with analytically oriented information product designs on the analogy of the automated factory, development work typically being done by engineers, not acquainted with the nature of CHQ decision problems, and definitely not with the information and decision support needs of top-level management for whom the information product was originally intended. This product development, hence, has been typically "boundedly rational" and experimental and has left a series of bold ventures of the large electronics and computer firms along the road, together with billions of dollars worth of development money.

As expected, the outcome of the experimental product development process has been a fragmentation into different, specialized products, away from the *universal design* that was originally aimed at, and that still lingers on. Above all, the original hardware orientation of the information system, on which well-known firms like Xerox, IBM and Ericsson have lost billions of dollars, has recently given way to a recognition of what business information processing is all about; namely the art of making *teams of competent people work efficiently together*. The attribute "competent" is especially important. As observed in Chapter III, the art of running a business is the art of staffing the business with competent people. This means that devices to support selection of, and access to, people and information have been far more successful in the market game than devices for analytical problem solving. All surviving, large hardware firms, furthermore, like IBM, are now trying to orient themselves into end user "consulting" activities, competing head on with firms already established here. The game in a market previously populated by small businesses is, therefore, dramatically changing.

Before we look at the nature of this interesting product development I will outline the basic elements of a business information product and indicate the enormous and diverse technology demands that are required of those who attempt to develop the entire product, rather than specialized components, most of whom have so far failed.

The reader should also note here that long-term survival of a firm as an autonomous decision unit requires a prior history of frequent crisis experience, divestments and acquisitions, and numerous radical reorganizations. There is no economic theory of the firm to explain the operational side of such behavior. My theory (1987, 1990b, 1991a) of the *experimentally organized economy* only predicts that this has to be the case. The design of a universal information product, however, needs operational content, i.e. to improve the capacity of the firm as an experimental machine to cope with its experimentally organized environment. To do that well without theoretical guidance is impossible. There is a link, however, to some questions asked, but not answered in modern finance theory; what is the optimal size and composition of a firm? Should the firm internalize business risks through diversification, conglomeration, etc. (item 7 in Table III.2 in Chapter III), or should management opt for the optimum minimum scale for production and let investors carry the risks in their own portfolios. The principal answer to that question is trivial; the limits of the firm are set on the boundaries (the margins) where internal costs for coordination are lower than external market costs for coordination (Coase 1937). If synergies accrue from merging certain activities, lower internal coordination costs follow. Then, the size of the firm should grow through investment and acquisitions. This is no theory, however. It is only a statement of trivially true conditions. It does not explain *how* synergies to lower internal coordination costs are achieved. A formalized information system for top-level reorganizational decisions would support this task within the firm. But such an information system requires a theory, or at least a general understanding of how such synergies can be achieved. The embodiment of this understanding was one objective of the universal information system of the 1980s. Let us see what was achieved on this score.

V.2   THE NATURE OF THE UNIVERSAL INFORMATION PRODUCT

The Universal Information system of any organization consists of three elements: (1) a *description* (taxonomy, database, measurement system), (2) an *analytical method*, and (3) a *user-decision interface*. Figure V.1 illustrates.

In the model of the experimentally organized economy that we have adopted, bounded rationality prevails, meaning in this context that the representation of the business organization by its measurement system is *problem dependent* and unbiased only in the particular decision context for which it has been designed. I have indicated this in Figure V.1 by making the two top circles only partially overlapping.

The first problem of this chapter is to decide what bounded rationality really means in the context of an information decision system.

The nature of this problem can be illustrated from the area of manufacturing process automation. The automated machine station requires that the two top circles overlap exactly, barring a stochastic discrepancy, that describes the precision tolerance of production. The mapping of the two circles is one-to-one.

This automated machine station can sometimes include a prepared product mix and the economic problem of optimally mixing and sequencing the machinery, and the assembly of components can be represented at the analytical level. The feed-back loop, however, never changes the organization of the machine station, only the sequence of operations.

In terms of our decision theory of the firm in Chapter III a fixed process configuration that allows no choice takes us down to the operational level in Figure III.1 (in Chapter III). Performance improvements are achieved through a faster speed at individual workstations (rationalization). This may not even affect systems performance.

Figure V.1   The integrated information and control system of a firm

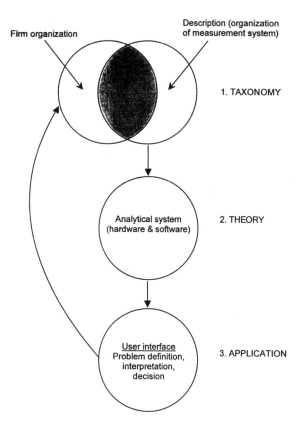

Source: Eliasson (1984c), p. 88.

If automated, profit or (flow) productivity-based mixing and sequencing are allowed. The machine station analogy is the automated budget process at the middle coordination level in Figure III.1. Programming models, aimed at maximizing profits over divisions or productivity in plants are crude examples of this (see Eliasson 1976a). One-to-one representation of the process in the database is necessary.

Once human discretion is allowed into the play (at the top of the pyramid in Figure III.1) the game becomes different. On the one hand, one can think of humans as "superior robots" that outperform the automated machine through their superior information processing capacity. The skilled worker at a complex machining sequence illustrates this. He will be "rationalized away" as soon as sufficiently improved technology becomes available. Middle management staffers, predominantly serving the function of intermediate, internal communicators (messengers) have been increasingly viewed in literature as candidates of elimination ("an endangered species", *Business Week*, Sept. 12, 1988), because of the rapid advance of electronically based business information systems that eliminate hierarchies make the business hierarchy thinner, the contacts between the top and the bottom more direct and the corporation "transparent", to use terms frequently appearing in business magazines. This development was amply supported by the evidence of the previous chapter.

On the other hand, one could look at both skilled workers and middle managers as problem solvers, able to take care of the steady flow of unexpected events in the midst of a production process, like break-downs of machinery; adding customer features to crude "idea-designs", or trying to get a new executive message transmitted through the organization on an unbiased form. For these two types of tasks and people, the designs of the optimal information system have very little in common. The first type is characterized by operational one-to-one, top-down and bottom-up representation, with "human automation links", the other by efficient access to data of choice specification and to competent people. Failure to recognize this distinction, pushing all information product designs into the first category, this is my conclusion, accounts for the many failures of bold ventures into the business information market.

The problem with the early development of the theory of business decision making and the design of a business information system was the attempt to merge all these levels into one comprehensive or universal information and decision system, notably on the idea of automated production scheduling. Suboptimization was a bad word. And the possibility that avoiding suboptimization was unprofitable because of immense transactions costs never occurred to most theorists of these days (see discussion in Eliasson 1976a, pp. 35 f and Chapter IV). This ambition was also supported by available background economic theory with built-in (by assumption) centralist planning conclusions (see Pelikan 1988a). The experimental approach to develop a universal information product, after a cascade of costly business mistakes has now fragmented into three types -- as the Chronicle and Chapter VII will show -- (1) *specialized* production control *products* at the operational level (transactions processing), (2) *accounting-based information systems* to support comprehensive budgeting work (middle level), and (3) *information support* at the top strategic level. Contrary to earlier ideas, the strategic information systems at the third level are not analytical or quantitative. They focus on *access to people and information*, and the earlier presentations of the theory of the firm and the theory of the experimentally organized economy explain why.

The three types of information processing are very different as to specification and required technologies. The range of technology needed to design them all in one package is enormous. I conclude that it is not efficient to merge the three types of systems. We will detail below the range of technologies needed to succeed in the full-scale business information systems markets. The next chapter tells what has, in fact, been going on during the last 15 to 20 years.

V.3   ARTIFICIAL INTELLIGENCE VERSUS ORGANIZATIONAL CONTROL -- THE PURPOSE OF INFORMATION DESIGNS

In his famous 1936 article Turing asked whether there was any question that he could ask that a computer would in principle be "unable" to answer intelligibly. He could think of none. The computer could in principle simulate the ability to think (see also Muggleton 1988).

The ambition to make human cognitive processes transparent, reproducible and computable runs through the history of documented Western European culture. The axiomatic design of language and mathematics originated in the Greek culture and with Euclid (ca. 300 B.C.) in particular. It is deeply embedded in scholastic literature and it surfaced again in the belief in the power of scientific inquiry and search for "the truth". The entire scientific establishment of western industrialized society is based on the belief that man will eventually understand it all, and consequently, that the computers will eventually be able to take care of it all (Johanneson 1968). The Heisenberg uncertainty principle, therefore, rocked the foundation of established wisdom. The associated notion of complete unpredictability or chaos occurring in a large class of non-linear mathematical systems, therefore, has been intellectually very disturbing, notably among the mainstream economists, who first rejected the idea. For the business man, it is not.

Western culture is, in fact, also characterized by a parallel experimental tradition, the origin of which is more difficult to trace, since it is not -- for obvious reasons -- accompanied by a parallel written documentation. This tradition is strongly manifest among people in the business community, operating in the experimentally organized, unpredictable competitive environment of world markets. Here the notion of tacit knowledge and restricted view (bounded rationality) prevails. Businessmen may ask the scientific community for comfort and advice but they often turn to many sources to tap the variation in opinions possible on the same subject matter, and they have to watch out, in order not to be pulled over by the unexpected. The two cultures clash at various places within the firms, creating a sometimes fruitful Hegelian dialectical process (Mason 1969, Mitroff 1971, Eliasson 1976a).

The old planning literature was footed in the belief that the future could be scientifically perceived and a successful life of the corporation systematically pursued (Eliasson 1976a, an idea entertained also by the old Schumpeter 1942). Artificial intelligence entertains similar ambitions. The same ambitions are clearly embedded in the idea of the universal information system of this chapter. Such ideas rest on the erroneous notion that fundamentals (facts, nature, technology) are independent of the ongoing economic selection process, i.e. of the decisions of all agents acting on a perception of what their competitors are up to.

We know, however, that each decision in a firm rests on some perception of itself in relation to its environment that is capable of resolving itself into a decision. This is the tacit memory of the firm, that essentially consists of a team of competent people conditioned by an organizational design (Eliasson 1990b). The task of this study may be said to have been to decode this tacit organizational memory *to the extent it is possible*.

The problem raised is again best illustrated with reference to Figure III.1 (in Chapter III) and the efficiency characteristics of the three types of control systems. The information system at the bottom (rationalization) level is synonymous with one-to-one production automation. At the middle (coordination) level information is transmitted through proxies, a higher level control language so to speak. The efficiency of this specialized language (Pelikan 1969, Eliasson 1976a) depends on how stable the relation between targets and proxies are. This efficiency of the specialized control language of the administrative system is identical with the efficiency of markets to communicate information on quantities through price signals. Erratic signals (prices or proxies) lower the efficiency of the market (or the system) in allocating quantities.

An efficient information system at the middle level, requires a stable grammar (a stable economy) so that identical signals tell identical stories all the time. The grammar (classification system of the databases) is a special language, a code of operation for the firm. *Any change in the organization of the firm, hence, changes the information content of the signals that come out of the information system*.

In order to handle the strategic organizational changes at the top level of the pyramid, the operating code (the memory), or the special language has to be universal enough ("the universal grammar" or "deep structure", Chomsky 1965) to include in itself a full description of the new, or any state, or organization of the firm.

This is all right *in principle* as long as all possible organizational states can be perceived and mapped into code. If this is possible, the problem of a universal information system boils down to the *practical* problem of designing, building and updating the appropriate databases. One could even argue that since there is an underlying, universal structure, the "system" has equilibrium properties in the sense, that in principle you could discover the globally best organizational solution, which you will stay with for ever. It should then be possible to design higher order (aggregate) information structures (special languages) that exhibit reasonable stability when intellectually dealing with strategic business decisions at the top of the pyramid in Figure III.1. Some such notions underlie ambitions in strategic planning and universal information systems design. The assumptions of the experimentally organized economy (see Chapter II), however, exclude the existence of such a state. Apparently successful business leaders have to be rational in a very different way than the rationality taught and practiced in the academic world. No wonder then that two, very different cultures have developed. I have called them the *plannable* and the *experimentally organized* worlds; and the difference lies in the implicitly perceived size of state space; very small and uniform or extremely large and heterogeneous.

If, for instance, a principal inability to perceive all possible outcomes exists, the universal grammar no longer exists and context-free code cannot be created. Unpredictability prevails. Ludwig Wittgenstein (1922, item 3.262) expressed this as follows: "What the signs conceal, their application declares". True tacit knowledge prevails, and can only be transmitted through an experiment or through action.[1] The new product cannot be evaluated until it has been tried. In this sense tacit, incommunicable knowledge exists in the experimentally organized economy of Chapter II. Since state space is unbounded and human understanding bounded and heterogeneous, no database that reveals the unknown can be created.

Hence, the question of how far up -- in the pyramid in Figure III.1 -- that grammar, or artificial intelligence can be brought, raised by Campbell 1982, is both principal and practical. It is, in fact, as comforting for science that the most abstract questions raised by philosophers long ago have the most down-to-earth practical applications in software development, as it is discomforting to know that this awareness removes several critical, supporting pillars of western culture and science. *Facts become dependent on the context in which they are observed*. It all depends, so to speak.

If you believe in equilibrium economics you have to face the practical problem of complexity only, as in Hayek 1935-36, etc. There is an equilibrium but you may not find it. If you buy the assumptions of the experimentally organized economy you have two problems. There may not exist any determinable equilibrium of the kind you are looking for, and if there happens to be one, occasionally, complexity will prevent you from determining its existence. This is a very practical problem for top-level management in a firm which has to arbitrarily change the course of the ship (see Table III.1 in Chapter III). The top-competent team solves this problem practically by keeping the top strategic decision makers and the middle coordinators organizationally separate, as is standard in most large firms (see again Chapter III). The firm survives on its ability (see Chapter III) to design viable business hypotheses (experiments), test them in the market, and on being very well organized to identify mistakes fast, and to pull out fast if found to be a mistake (see Table III.1).

All these complications notwithstanding, the fields of artificial intelligence and expert systems are progressing rapidly. The fields are so far not well defined but what is being done (see Chronicle) sometimes relates to the idea of a universal information system.

I look at *artificial intelligence* as a method of transferring *tacit knowledge to code without making the transfer explicit*. With that definition artificial intelligence is similar to organizational or team learning. It does not confer intellectual awareness and understanding. It is close to rote learning of skills. Hence artificial intelligence is a communication device. And many applications of *expert systems* (a subset of applications of artificial intelligence) have that quality.

The design of a universal information system (for cognitive support of strategic decisions), hence, at least in principle becomes an application of artificial intelligence. Let me elaborate.

Complexity in a technical sense and tacit, incommunicable knowledge requires that human problem solvers and decision makers interact with "the system". Complexity in a technical sense can be solved in principle. How to handle tacit knowledge is a different matter. The allowance for "tacit", not codable knowledge runs contrary to established, academic thinking, and the most common way of dealing with it is to assume it away, or assume that it can be coded at a (known) cost. This is the same as to assume that there is no principal limit to analytical decision making, only a practical, technical limit dependent on current information costs. Under this assumption the automated high level decision system can be viewed as an analogy to the automated factory. The limits are set by the present technologies of measurement, communication and computation.

The old notion of automated decision-making machines, once abandoned is currently returning under the rubric of decision support through artificial intelligence and the potential of developing *context free code* for enhanced communication. The limits of automation are drawn between *formulating* the problem and *solving* the problem. This borderline is becoming increasingly diffuse. The technique is to uncover, through artificial intelligence, the tacit knowledge base of individuals and make it transferable to all individuals and systems. Some of the new attempts within the artificial intelligence field are coming close to allowing the users of the system to develop more efficient specialized languages for speedy, within group communication, that will affect the ways problems are identified and formulated. The Xerox Palo Alto Research Center was experimenting with such a language at the time of my visit in 1986 (see Henderson 1986). However, the problem solving capacity of such systems is restricted to the problems the tacit code can handle. If the code evolves as a consequence of solving a particular class of problem, its applicability will be restricted to that particular experience domain.

Artificial intelligence furthermore can be seen as one way of *translating* "tacit" knowledge into machine code (see the Campbell soup case, *Business Week*, Oct. 7, 1985, p. 64 f) or into some visible code through which explicit communication is possible.

The automation of a machining sequence is a case of context free code, except for the context defined by the machine configuration. The automation of even a very simple machining sequence requires a very complex code. And the costs of transferring that code from the worker to the program were always grossly underestimated in the early days of automation. Above all, the necessary centralized knowledge of what was going on in the factory was almost always lacking (Eliasson 1980, p. 253 ff). The automation of more complex machining sequences, involving variation of dimensions and especially involving judgment have not yet been achieved. The more complex messages the more context required, like experience needed to interpret incomplete blueprints or instruction manuals and to pass judgment on to the user of the product etc. All this context has to be put on code as part of the work or decision sequence to be "automated". Most of this context has been acquired individually through experience or "on-the-job learning". It is tacit and difficult to centralize to one place (the computer) or to transfer to other humans or to "code". As a consequence *the development of appropriate context is an important part of artificial intelligence*, or rather, artificial intelligence is a language that through use can be modified such that tacit knowledge ("the context") can be communicated to others and to code. With this definition, artificial intelligence covers the systematic development of particular organizations (teams) of people, who communicate through specialized languages ("jargon", theory etc.) that are extremely efficient in their particular contexts. A top management group, whose members know each other well is such a team. Can their learning experience or intellectual breaking-in be systematized, not only through going to Harvard Business School, or hiring a management consulting firm, but through the application of computer software?

Yes, of course. Already the gradual learning to use a formalized information, budgeting and control system is such an example (see several cases in Eliasson 1976a). The new groupware "technology" (see Chronicle) with enhanced multimedia features will certainly contribute to such organizational learning where the team does not have to be physically close in the same room or building.

V.4 CONCLUSIONS ON THE UNIVERSAL BUSINESS INFORMATION SYSTEM (UBIS)

At first sight the logical results on information flows and on the notion of the economy as experimentally organized are frustrating for the analyst. This is so because of my mode of reasoning. Once you leave the linear world of standard economic theory you have to accept the possibility of chaos, phases of complete unpredictability and genuine uncertainty. There will be no information system capable of guiding a firm through such phases without an "arbitrary human leader", or "external operator" to use Turing's (1936) term, and there will be no insurance company, willing to insure for the uncalculable risks prevailing during such phases of unknown extension in time. One solution is to close your eyes to the fact that the world is non-linear, and act *as if* it is linear and predictable. The assumptions made in planning are such, and most decision makers do arbitrarily adopt such a prior equilibrium model of the world to "create" enough order to be capable of making the needed decisions (Eliasson 1992a, pp. 49 f.). The alternative approach is to disregard forecasts, and simply operate on the assumption that you know (the experiment) and correct the decision if it turns out wrong.

But also this is difficult. You need a good business hypothesis to set up a successful business experiment. However conceived, that experiment incorporates a prediction, which can be used as a benchmark for identifying business mistakes. This is exactly how the budgeting system of firms has always been used (Eliasson 1976a). The business information system is also used to support such comparisons of forecasts/plans/budgets and ex post performance. Sometimes the idea of predictability dominates, as was the case during the postwar period, which was seemingly stable and predictable up to the oil crises of the 1970s. Sometimes the uncertainty and skepticism of formal planning dominate, as has been the case since the 1970s.

The obvious conclusion is that all this has to be done and that the economic environment of the firm will be reasonably predictable for long periods. When "chaos" suddenly strikes, many players will fail, but those who are first at identifying and correcting mistakes, and pulling their resources out, stand a better chance than others of surviving. Those who have well designed information systems may be better and faster at identifying and correcting mistakes than other firms. This conclusion sets the limits of scientific information methods in the experimentally organized economy and in business life, but also gives such methods a rôle to play.

NOTES

1. Wittgenstein's statement implies that a language, to the extent possible, should have the properties of a stationary process.

The early students of communication theory were very clear on these limitations of language. See, for instance, Weaver's part in Shannon and Weaver (1949).

VI

THE EXPERIMENTAL EVOLUTION OF A NEW
INFORMATION PRODUCT

This chapter does two things. It (1) defines the business information systems product as it can be understood today and (2) demonstrates -- through examples -- the experimental nature of innovation and competition in technologically advanced markets for industrial products. It is my conviction that this case of the experimental organization of markets can be generalized to all advanced and growing market economies.

Modern industrial organization literature has a subfield of inquiry called R&D races. On the surface the story I am about to tell may appear to be an example of such an R&D race in which firms rush to be the first to discover *the* information product. But this would be a premature understanding of what is going on. The R&D race is an artificial game of finding the one solution. The winner takes all, and leaves all competitors dead. It is static equilibrium analysis.

In the experimentally organized economy there is no single winner, or a winner that can feel safe. There are many possible product solutions and which one of them is the best cannot be determined until they have all been tried. Even when you may believe that all have been tried, there will still, at each time, be many untried solutions that are even better. The new products being developed have not been foreseen. And the best solution coming up right now, might be the wrong solution a year or so later, that pulls its initiator with it, down and out. This is in effect the experience, since the late 1980s of more than half of the mini-computer makers.

In the beginning of the computer evolution it was all *computing*, number crunching in larger and larger volumes and at even faster rates. This was the manifestation of information processing in the early 1970s. Computer technology was presented under titles like: "Technology, Electronics, Research on new products" in *Business Week*. At that time *information processing* was not headlined as a separate technology as it is today. Also the concept of a computer begins to "fragment" late. *Home-computer* is a term used for the first time in *Business Week* July 5, 1976. In May 16, 1977 it is used synonymously with *personal computer*.

Rather than coming up with a winner the race in information systems business has continued and expanded into new markets (mainframes, micros minis, workstations, PC's, Laptops etc.) to converge again, to infringe on each others' market turfs, only to change character again (in the late 1980s) with the emergence of networking, open communications standards and corporate computing, etc. Since the mid-1980s software has taken over both as the driving force and the limiting factor in information industry. None of this was expected (before it happened) beyond the small circles of innovators and entrepreneurs that created the new orientation of industry.

This is the essence of the experimentally organized market. We may know today what was needed to get where we are, but we know practically nothing of what users will want in the future, and how producers will understand what they want and come up with the appropriate products. But there are hundreds of optimistic entrepreneurs who think they know, and some of them may be right. And if there are not hundreds of optimistic entrepreneurs the industry and the economy have a problem.

VI.1 THE PRACTICAL FEATURES OF THE INFORMATION PRODUCT

In this section I will summarize the various purposes for which information systems support is useful in a business firm and indicate in broad terms what that means for product design. I emphasize four features: a) *monitoring*, b) *control*, c) *access* and d) *organization of people*.

Monitoring and Overview

Transactions computing is still the main type of computing in business firms. The capacity of computers to monitor large and complex systems accounts for most applications. *First* of all, we have Corporate Headquarters' needs for central number crunching. The idea of a centrally controlled business system, shaped on the idea of automatic manufacturing process control that guides the realization of strategic plans drawn up at strategic planning departments is gone, something that was obvious already from actual practice prior to the crisis years of the 1970s (Eliasson 1976a, 1984c). The need to
-    *automate the maintenance of central accounts* is, however, still there, as is the need for
-    reliable *reporting against* agreed upon business *targets*
and special production tasks that can be transacted through computers are increasingly invented. To begin with inventory control, billing and accounts receivable, production scheduling etc. were computerized. Today the entire business is getting electronically wired, but the people are still there and the minds of the people still dominate the mind of the firm.

Reporting against targets is a method of identifying non-expected business problems early. Targets mean something as a joint reference for comparison for all participants in budget work. They have been worked out and negotiated in the budgeting process. As it appears in U.S. firms, known for detailed numerical control routines and tightly run operations, some of the extreme detail of reporting and targeting had been abandoned before the crisis years of the 1970s. Swedish firms, on the other hand, known for decentralized operating responsibilities were at the time moving in the opposite direction, for more detail and tighter central profit controls (cf. Eliasson 1976a, p. 227, 1984c). This development among large Swedish manufacturing firms, however, occurred parallel with the emergence of successful giant international Swedish firms in the 1980s, a contrary development to what happened among other industrialized nations in the 1980s (see Eliasson and Bergholm et al. 1985). The growing Swedish firms needed improved central profit control to rein in global operations. Since the large Swedish engineering firms were increasingly successful in the 1980s, while U.S. firms modified their central control methods as a consequence of bad performance, a careful and detailed comparison of Swedish and U.S. firms in this respect would be very informative. I have done a little of this, but only enough to formulate some hypotheses.

The technique in large Swedish firms (see Eliasson, Fries, Jagrén et al. 1984) has been to use more efficient measurement, information and communication systems, enhancing the transparency of the corporation, to allow operations decision to be decentralized, without losing central control. The technique has been to develop more reliable central profit controls.

Emphasis in modern control systems design -- as I noted in Chapter IV -- is on early *identification of profit problems* using agreed-upon targets in the budget as references, *rapid access* to more internal information on specification upon request. The engineering departments of firms in the information systems market that worked on the design of these general purpose information products were in general ignorant of how information was used at the corporate top, thinking rather in terms of the demands of manufacturing process automation, with exact one-to-one control of a repetitive production process.

In the beginning neither equipment nor software was available to support the flexibility now being demanded. *Easy access to information upon choice specification* puts a heavy demand on *database design*, coupled with *intelligent networks* and distributed processing capacity (the PC-revolution putting large computing power on everybody's desk), eventually evolving into a need for powerful local process capacity (work stations) and easily manipulable display facilities (graphics etc). Development is pushing in these directions.

Monitoring and Automation (transactions processing)

Second, a parallel need for specialized centralized *monitoring* and automated correction at local levels can be seen in global inventory control, maintenance monitoring of installed equipment etc. The productivity potential is enormous. This technology favors global scale and gives international firms a temporary lead in developing a competitive edge. A simple, early example is the central computerized reservation systems of airlines that were developed already in the late 1950s (*Sabre* of American Airlines). The competitive edge of centralized, individualized travel scheduling and reservations, however, was not fully understood before American Airlines commercialized its Sabre system globally in 1977 (see Chronicle). It efficiently automates some of the manual scheduling routines earlier done by travel agents, but it also effectively enters priorities, favoring the controller (the owner) of the system. The competing systems *Apollo* of United Airlines, ready in 1983, *Amadeus* of a group of European Airlines (including SAS), and *Galileo* (BA and Swissair), however, did not reduce the relative productivity gains in scheduling achieved by Sabre, only the economic value of the early, innovative product.

The airline scheduling and reservation systems, as well as automatic ordering and inventory systems, make use of the capacity of computerized systems to achieve instant overview of a geographically distributed and complex system. In that sense these systems technically resemble automated process control. They contribute to efficient production at the control and operations levels in Figure III.1 (in Chapter III).

The efficiency of these systems, however, depends on the establishment of *standards* and the consequent *economies of scale*. Such systems have frequently made it possible, at least temporarily, to achieve market dominance through scale. The Sabre reservation system of American Airlines has already been mentioned. Already in the mid-1970s American Hospital Supply provided hospitals with terminals to access its order system automatically (see Chronicle, specialized computer products). Many airlines are currently struggling to become dominant through global networks and reservation systems in a market that can only accommodate a few global players.

Another example of monitoring and transactions processing is centralized quality and maintenance monitoring, with automatic signaling of break downs (example: Otis elevators). It gives a competitive edge to an already dominant firm, that is difficult to break because of the large economies of scale involved.

We are now discussing monitoring systems of potential global reach that demand an initial systems investment (design, software and installations), that is so large that a very large market share is needed for the firm to recover costs. Economies of scale are what makes the difference.

The Access Feature

Data represent the business. People run the business. Hence, data are important to the extent they support the decision processes of people in the organization. Most important is the support of collective decision making in teams of people. Such support includes fast and efficient access to people (team members) and access to data of choice specification.

Access to people

While the human work environment is becoming increasingly abstract and removed from the rote production processes, higher level work is not becoming more man/machine-related, but rather *man/systems related*, the system being defined by its human participants. In principle one can even envision a work organization where all rote, codable tasks have been automated. Humans only enter -- to use the quote from Turing (1936) -- when "some arbitrary choice" has to be made. Such work is very competence demanding of people and it cannot be introduced faster than the needed receiver competence is being accumulated. It can, however, be observed in practice in many professional walks of life, top management being one instance. Here easy access to people, communication between people and the organization of varying combinations of people ("the calendar") is perhaps more limiting to performance than the other factors.

This is illustrated by the almost complete absence of "analytical information equipment" at the top of the business hierarchy, a rather frequent and increasing use -- often through assistants -- of access to data bases, but a dramatic spread of "human access" equipment in pace with availability. The mobile telephone and telefaxes are the best examples. Sophisticated local switchboards, for rapid tracing and connecting of people travelling is another example. Telecommunicated conferences and the spread of the "portable lap top computer" with "wireless communication" devices are also examples that many think will be very common in the future. The limits are no longer set by the advance of network and switching technology, but rather by the ingenuity and effort of software developers.

Access to data

Access is important also in other ways. The further up in the management hierarchy you go (top of triangle in Figure III.1 in Chapter III) the less structured are decisions problems. There are few formalized decision procedures, as in repetitive coordination of production. Before the problem has been defined the kind of data needed to support decisions are not known. And the information needed becomes known only after a series of questions have been asked and answered. At this level, rich databases with flexible designs and easy access are important. *Distributed databases, relational database technology, networking capacity* and *organizational computing* have become important features of the information system. It is obvious from the emerging technology (see below) that the access to information feature is demanded. Lotus' successful groupware product *Notes* is a good example.

The GM story of the 1980s illustrates the intelligence system through which the people and data in a complex organization can be wired together. GM was having problems, not only in understanding what to do with the new market situation in the late 1970s, but also -- once decisions had been taken -- with *how* to change its organization to be capable of coping with the new market situation. Ross Perot and EDS were brought in, not only to "rewire the incompatible computer configurations" of GM. The "computer wiring" of a modern business organization to a large extent reflects the wiring of "its brain". It links people together, and in affecting who meets whom, and who gets to know what, also shapes decisions. A major overhaul of the wiring of GM's mind was set into motion. GM acquired EDS and put Perot on its Board, only to find that what Perot wanted to see done was not what GM wanted. Perot was bought back out again (see *BW*, Sept. 26, 1988, pp. 32 f. and Chronicle).

Organizing People

Third, the full information economy is made unfeasible through shifting the description of the business environment from the classical model with asymmetric information and a potential state of perfect information to the model of the experimentally organized economy populated by competent teams (firms). In this world the attention of management will be changed *from* analysis and planning *to* innovation, experimentation, execution and control, i.e. *from the analytical information machine to the experimental machine*, populated by people who make "arbitrary" choices, and identify and correct mistakes. For this to be efficient, information has to be gathered in flexible ways and people have to be accessed easily. This means that the *efficient organization of people with* competence becomes the dominant feature of a business information system, tracking people down, scheduling meetings, organizing easy database access of choice specification at choice locations etc.

This again underlines the importance of the access feature (access to people and to information) and computer software that supports people working together both over distances and at one location (cf. Groupware in Chronicle under 9e).

VI.2   THE PRODUCTION OF INFORMATION SERVICES

The production of information services within a business can be organized in many ways. Above all, it is often impossible to distinguish the users from the producers.

a)   *Access vs. information*

The business information systems determine how far into state space -- or the opportunity set -- the firm can reach. The opportunity set of the firm has both an *internal* and an *external* dimension, i.e. understanding what goes on *within* the firm, and in the external market environment of the firm. In the experimentally organized economy, this does not constitute an analytical problem of collecting and studying coded information, but the art of organizing competent people making the experimental activities of the firm more relevant and more focused, and the people of the organization more alert and observant.

Most of the corporate planning literature of the 1970s and earlier was concerned with adjusting the firm to forecasts or its external environment, on the presumption that the internal capacities of the firm were known (Eliasson 1976a). Approaching business information systems from this end, however, is a complete misunderstanding. Some resources are devoted to forecasting what is going on in the environment of firms. And the attention of top management is largely oriented outwards. The bulk of coded information processing, however, is concerned with internal profit and cost controls to assess the internal capacity of the firm and to enforce a steady upgrading of performance. An important part of this business information task is to force deep internal information to be revealed to the CHQ teams. This is the purpose of MIP-targeting (Eliasson 1976a, pp. 236 ff). Top management pays attention to such internal matters, whenever the system signals problems, whenever the system has to be redesigned and -- most importantly -- whenever external matters demand a reorganization of the firm, a reorganization that invariably affects the effectiveness of the existing information system. These tasks require the presence of competent people, that can work in, coordinate and make sophisticated business decisions through a team in large and geographically dispersed organizations. This decision process requires easy access to people and to data. But business judgment is still exercised by the people of the team, not the system, even though the editing of the data, done through the system and the access features affect the decisions.

There are two, different sets of people to consider in this context; the *information specialists* and those who participate in forming the business decisions. It is often thought that these two groups interact or even coincide. This is not the case.

b)   *The information specialists – the CIO*

It is therefore interesting in this context to learn [see, for instance, Carlyle, 1988d, 1990 on the out-of-touch CIO, in *Datamation* (Aug. 15, pp. 31-34) and Chronicle, Section 9j] about the career positions of the Chief Information Officer (CIO). One would think that the CIO by the nature of his job would become the "spider" in the information network of the firm, a person that would naturally advance to the top on the basis of his or her superior information of the firm. Not so at all. Top level decision making is not a matter of using (coded) information efficiently. It is a matter of applying talent, experience and broad-based judgment to difficult business decision problems.

The CIO has not become a career person. The CIOs have rather learned that the critical information flows of the corporation and the knowledge put to work in top-level decision making are not communicated through their system. Hence, the CIOs have found themselves being systems experts with few career openings, not being involved in the top level use of the information communicated through their system. In fact, many CIO's who found that they were very useful in the beginning, when the system was installed, later found their specialist competence in less demand.

The rapid expansion of information equipment used in firms was accompanied by a parallel expansion of information staff with the "specialist" task of integrating business and technology. The first wave of computerization meant a centralization of certain information tasks to equipment and specialists, tasks that were earlier performed in conjunction with the job. In the 1980s a large hierarchy of (computer) information processing people had established itself in the large corporations. The information systems people, however, became specialists on the *language* or the *grammar* of the control system, not on its information *content*. They have rarely been involved in top level judgmental decisions, and not even in the judgmental aspect of control, i.e. identifying and correcting mistakes (see Table III:1 in Chapter III). They have remained typical specialists and narrow experts in a volatile technology field that has not yet even been hierarchically well established within the firms. The analogy would be a specialist on the grammar of the Swedish language. He or she does not necessarily write good Swedish, or even read or write very much. Worse still, the CIO appears to have stayed behind his desk, showing more loyalty to his profession than to the needs of his company. Thus the CIOs have become detached from an important management learning experience. As technology became communalized and removed from central computing, the platform of the CIO in the firm began to erode. Information systems people, who had not worked on it, therefore did not (as part of their job) get the opportunity to acquire the broad-based career experience needed for top level decision making and positions. They have largely remained specialists on the technical aspects of the corporate grammar. Being a CIO does not even appear to be a good intermediate station, on the upward career, but rather a dead alley (Carlyle 1989).

The information specialists still perform very advanced tasks. They are, however, separated and located in one of the machine rooms of the big firm. And the task of the information specialist is to support other people throughout the organization when they need rapid and reliable access to data and people.

Central computing suffers. Computer specialists are normally associated with centralized computer facilities. A casualty of the emerging decentralized networking technology has been the central computing facility, installed in the 1960s and the 1970s. With volume processing moved to the desktops or to the networks and a changing focus, away from "computing", the market for these facilities has diminished to specialized uses. This also hurt the mainframe computer market, beginning with the minicomputers in the mid-1980s. The advent of volume distributed processing, however, does not necessarily spell the end of the mainframe. Large centralized processing will always be in demand, and the distributed processing technology has not yet stabilized. While the network may be the computer of the 1990s, the large mainframe may still be a potent driver of the network. At least this was IBM's hope and strategy as it began to be formulated in the early 1990s.

VI.3   ELECTRONICALLY DISTRIBUTED SERVICES AND OUTSOURCING

A large and growing part of value added in general, and of manufacturing value added in particular, consists of knowledge-intensive service production. These services are becoming increasingly more specialized, technically demanding and also standardized. The bulk of these services have long been produced internally within the firms that use them. Whenever technically possible, however, trade in such services has occurred. Tradability of technical services normally means that these services are not part of the tacit, proprietary technical knowledge base of a firm. Electronically created, managed, marketed and distributed -- often very sophisticated -- services became a volume business in specialized areas already in the 1980s. And the number of not yet developed markets for such services appears large.

Better educated users and the new information technologies that we are discussing are increasingly making it possible to *distribute knowledge intensive services electronically*, rather than having people ("consultants") travel to the buyer. Complex tacit knowledge is increasingly being coded as information for artificial transfer. Industrial services are becoming increasingly complex and knowledge intensive, requiring that a team of specialists work together. The final product, however, may often be both simple and codable. As a consequence the actual creation of the service product is characterized by concentration of people to well defined locations, serving their customers electronically over long distances. We can observe how firms focus their own in-house production of services on the creation of proprietary know-how and on areas where they have particular competence and/or where economies of scale make internal service production especially profitable. Currently this means that marketing, distribution and designs to achieve market dominance in large international Swedish firms have been kept largely internal. The same was the case for the reservation systems of airlines, the quality and maintenance system of Otis Elevators, and the development of new sophisticated systems products in general. However, as competitors learn the design of such proprietary service production, the market rent of the original solution is competed away, as a host of services, including many auxiliary technical services, are being offered in the market. The trend is increasingly in this direction. New information technology has made outcontracting of service production and the distribution of final services easier and cheaper. The increasing heterogeneity of technical service inputs in modern manufacturing firms, however, makes it simply impossible to maintain and develop internally all specialties needed. Not even IBM was capable of acquiring the competence to supply digital PBX switching technology of its own fast enough to be a profitable long-run proposition (see case description below, Chronicle and *BW*, Dec. 26, 1988, pp. 33 ff). This has created a tendency towards concentrating the heterogeneous, knowledge demanding service production to particular locations where competent people can meet, and to organize the actual distribution of the services over electronically managed networks.

The services provided, like any other product, can be improved upon "technologically". Part of the product specialization is availability. Part of it has to do with technological features (process know-how, new materials). Another feature is global, includes reach, like market know-how, specialized financing facilities etc. Apparently the technology of electronic service production is rapidly becoming very complex but at the same time offering special, valuable features to the products service-oriented firms are offering (see *BW*, June 15, 1992, pp. 48-53). While a take-off has occurred in the 1990s, established firms find themselves being passed by, or failing, being unable to integrate the new technology with their established production. Hence, firms in the computer services field are becoming increasingly important not only to take over and run existing computer operations, but also to support the development of new service products.

While the upgrading of service know-how depends on human interaction, the distribution of services has forced the establishment of local agencies closer to customers. This pattern is obvious among large consulting agencies in marketing, advertising, management information and technical specialties.

The new information technology developing, hence, is generating three tendencies. *First*, knowledge-intensive service production can be integrated within the firm or be purchased in the markets. The new information technology makes it easier to reorganize this type of production externally and separately from the user. This means a tendency for manufacturing industry to fragment, creating a growing number of small scale, specialized and knowledge-intensive service producers, making manufacturing industry less and less distinguishable from the service sector.

Second, improved distribution capacity through an electronic medium should work for concentration of knowledge-intensive service production to particular geographical areas ("cities"), very much along the lines we can already observe, like financial services in London, manufacturing services in Stuttgart etc. People with competence have to meet in one place, but once the problem has been solved the result (information) can be distributed electronically. The benefit from that concentration is the tacit character of new technological development and the need for a university campuslike organization of their production that allows people to meet naturally.[1] A creative production environment can be organized in pace with the development of customer competence to receive electronically distributed services. This is not principally different from shipping a complex German machine to a U.S. manufacturing firm. If the firms do not have competent workers capable of using the machine, however, the transaction is not economically viable. In the service sector this means the creation of a knowledge-intensive communications system that makes it possible not only to decentralize certain service production geographically within the firm (like CAD access to component and inventory data) but also *to decentralize the firm hierarchy into the market through advanced subcontracting*. The increasing use of specialist engineering consultants is an instance of the latter phenomenon (see also p. 209f).

A *third* tendency, generated by modern information technology is being increasingly put to use to improve product designs of service producers (American Airlines' reservation system *Sabre* being an early, and perhaps the best example). This means that electronic service technology will become, during the 1990s, a driving force in the entire service production sector.

The *development of new products in financial markets* offers the best examples of electronically distributed services, and not in the least of their macroeconomic significance. The enormous superstructure of financial derivates like options, futures and swaps on top of the regular markets for credit transactions would not have been feasible without modern information technology. These new financial derivates make it possible to trade in risks and personalize the risk profile of your investment portfolio in such an efficient way that some argue that, when risks have been transformed to investors willing to take on risks, leaving riskfree contracts to risk averse investors, the total value of the stock market has increased considerably by becoming more informed and transparent to investors (see Eliasson 1994c).

The electronic medium has also removed the bulk of manual transactions related to contract handling and legal paperwork etc., thus eliminating the legal risks associated with "trust and voice agreements" over the phone, speeding up arbitrage further.

The creation of a host of substitutes to earlier straightforward financial transactions means that transactions that were earlier regulated or prohibited can now take place under new, non-regulated contract forms. Intermediary trading has increased heterogeneity in the market, reducing central policy overview and hence the possibilities of controlling financial flows. The consequence has been the effective integration of the world financial system, almost eliminating local (national) monetary control, increasing international financial pressure on national economies, hence enforcing the same rate of return requirements on the real production systems of all national economies.[2] *"Program trading"* is another interesting example of the automation of certain decisions based on rationality postulates of economic theory. Since the theory of finance "available" is typically static, it is interesting to observe that certain types of interactive mass behavior in the markets, not accounted for in theory, can be caused by such automated decisions. Even though markets may have become better informed, because of new information technology, it does not follow that they have become more stable.

VI.4   THE EXPERIMENTAL EMERGENCE OF A NEW, UNIVERSAL BUSINESS INFORMATION SYSTEMS (UBIS) PRODUCT

The development of a *universal information systems product* (UBIS) has been a huge *market experiment*, taking place in several parallel steps and resulting in many different types of product categories. The early engineering focus on the design of a centrally controlled, automated firm was a disastrous experience for many firms. What we can now see emerging as a useful product was virtually impossible to foresee 5 to 10 years ago. Any attempt to standardize, specify, plan and/or speed up its development by mobilizing more resources would have led the wrong way. In fact each firm in the game of establishing a "business information systems" division (the usual name) went wrong to begin with. The problem was not lack of resources, but lack of insight and experience among the designers of what kind of product the users wanted/needed and what could technically be done.

The experimental evolution of the new UBIS product is a gigantic, in-the-market-learning experience, that has many parallels on a smaller scale. There was the complexity and the rapid, unpredictable change of all the individual technologies that were needed. There was the almost overwhelming "technology" of merging all needed technologies into the one product that was not well understood to begin with. Most important, however, was the definition of the uses to which the product was supposed to be directed. Its evolution exhibits a slow reorientation away from an analytical, computational (planning) concepts towards support systems for people; flexible access to data and people, placing the competence of people in focus rather than the business system.

The business information problem turned out not to be a matter of "automation", or a substitute for human beings. The viable systems product concept rather was to enhance the capacity of competent human beings to work efficiently in teams. This is a positive realization. The technocrats of industry and academia, who dominated the early design process, have been corrected by market forces to the tune of billions of dollars.

There is an interesting lesson to learn from the Chronicle of events of the Supplement. While new technologies normally are developed as new products and new businesses in *new firms*, the universal business information product that was first conceived required resources on the order of magnitude of the very large firm to be realized. For the product that is currently conceived, however, hardware has increasingly become a commodity on which software producers can build. The new software firms are not intellectually locked into any particular hardware system, like a mainframe technology. While the bureaucracies of the large firms with large resources may be strangling the best ideas and forcing product development into known (to bureaucrats) obsolete solutions, new software houses may be on the right track with better concepts and needing only rather limited resources to do it (cf. Chronicle).

While "IBM" seems to have been alert and early in *understanding in principle* where technologies were heading, "it" has been late in, or incapable of, reorganizing to execute the introduction of the new technologies. One expression has been "that IBM can never change its mainframe mind". Similarly DEC got stuck with its "minicomputer mind", and *Xerox*, having an innovative scientific laboratory in Palo Alto, was rarely able to move these ideas onto industrial scale production. The PC idea was conceived in the Xerox Palo Alto Research Center (Parc) (around 1972/73) but realized by Apple and standardized to industrial scale production by IBM (1981). But the Chronicle also shows that most of the intellectual and hardware infrastructure was created, not in government and academic research laboratories but in the laboratories of large firms that tried to do the same thing, but failed. This is not at all a surprising observation. These firms were much more informed than anybody else about what technology could accomplish and what the market wanted. They failed to realize this understanding in turning their own organizations around and in the right direction.

The earlier presentation of the scope of the Universal Business Information Systems product (UBIS) demonstrates that only very few firms in the market will have the resources needed to come close to a full product range if the firm has the ambition to supply all the hardware itself. But this may be the wrong approach. The advanced and innovative U.S. markets for information and communications products have been capable of supplying most of what has been believed to be needed. It is no wonder then that optimistic entrants in the full-scale market have failed. The only firm that was for a while reasonably close to a full range product was IBM, but even IBM had severe difficulties in some hardware technologies, notably in office switches (PBXes), telecommunications and software, networking technologies that were and still are critical to engineer the flexible access features of a viable "higher level" information and decision support system.

While there was hardly any communication between computers in the 1970s, the 1980s have witnessed distributed data processing (DP) and local office automation. The 1990s appears to become the decade of networks, requiring that computing and telecommunications merge, and that appropriate communication languages be developed. But also another development is shaping up. Hardware development set the pace of information systems development through most of the 1980s. The availability of enormous computer power on the desk, fast networks with great capacities, and the "commodization" of hardware mean that software development and the provision of information systems knowledge are rapidly becoming the dominant drivers of the whole industry. Hence, the complementary major future technology will be *information* systems *integration*. The developing and managing of network services (MNS) will become one important product.

The whole range of components of a full UBIS is, however, produced in different combinations by a large number of firms. It is possible in principle for a well organized software-consulting-computer services company with a good idea and sufficient resources in the form of talented people to piece together a UBIS from "on the shelf" software and hardware components; very much as Sun Micro Systems did when building its first workstation. Most likely the high profit margins are to be gained at that end. While competition in the markets for standardized components will be intense, there should be a lucrative market for competent systems designers. The "maturing" of the entire computer industry is gradually forcing radical change on existing specialized producers (*BW*, March 6, 1989, pp. 40 ff).

The reasons for this modularization of the information systems market is *standardization* and *connectivity*; a development that has been hurting earlier vendors like IBM that have relied on proprietary software and hardware designs, making customers hostages to their "language". Small vendors have been trying to get out of the competitive strategy of proprietary designs for years -- notably minicomputer makers -- but been unable to come up with a full range of information products. This illustrates that success in the business information systems market very much is a question of talking the same language.

At the same time the increased complexity of the full range UBIS and, in particular, tailor-made demands of customers is boosting the downstream customer design part of the market. Competition has been stepped up fiercely in the increasingly broadened market for standardized components, especially on the hardware side. The enormous complexity of the business information systems market and the breath-taking speed of technological advance is best illustrated by examples. Let me therefore briefly tell how four companies (IBM, DEC, Ericsson and Xerox) with ambitions to become dominant players in the business information systems markets have gone about it. The IBM story also tells how new technology, allowing a steady reduction of the physical computing box in waves after waves lifted the capacity of centralized computing to suddenly explode in unpredictable directions with the microprocessor and distributed computing.

a)   The IBM Story -- Trying It All

IBM[3] was founded in New York already in 1896 under the name of *Tabulating Machine Company*. After a complicated early business life it merged in 1911 (see Sobel 1981, Chapter I) with *International Time Recording Company* and *Computing Scale Company* into *Computing, Tabulating Recording* (CTR, changed to *International Business Machines* in 1924) to produce mechanical and electromechanical office products. Thomas Watson Sr., who had been fired from NCR in 1914, then forty years old and a promising business leader, immediately took on a "would be" president position at CTR. Its history since then includes several successful changes of technology and reorganizations of a kind that normally wrecks a firm. IBM has dominated the computer market for decades. For decades it has had the ambition to be a full range supplier of information processing products for the corporate market. It has had enormous resources. As long as the computer market stayed within a reasonable range of products that could gradually be improved upon, IBM was either leading the development, or rapidly catching up. The range of computing products was reasonably limited as long as the mainframe and associated hard- and software constituted the core of computing. That hard core began to break up in the 1980s, partly as a result of IBM's own strategic move of entering the PC market in 1981 and supporting the introduction of a standardized operating system. A new information processing age began as PCs became powerful and prolific. As PCs were being connected through networks and as universal operating systems and software became the driving force behind development also the dominant technology of the information processing market changed. Then IBM's problems began. The full-scale product range was no longer a possible ambition within an organization integrated around a mainframe mind.

IBM has been through at least seven radical technological transformations; from a producer of mechanical (tabulators) to electromechanical products 1900-1990, via an electronic corporation in the 1950s and into the software consulting operation currently taking shape; each new technology coming faster than the earlier. A dominant transformation took place around 1965 when IBM established itself with the 360-system based on integrated circuit technology as the dominant player in the global mainframe market. About that time computing was almost synonymous with mainframe computing, even though a big mainframe at that time wasn't very much by today's desktop standards.

The microprocessor revolution (created by *Intel*) and the growing fragmentation of computing into smaller units was an emerging threat that IBM countered around 1981 by creating a standard and then a market for personal computing. It is illustrative to observe that the technology that made IBM the monolithic, dominant player in the information business market began to erode critically about the time the ambitions of the Federal Antitrust Authorities to break up IBM culminated (see below). Nobody understood at the time what was going on in the information industry, and least of all the antitrust authorities. The PC revolution, reinforced by the deregulation of the U.S. telecommunications industry, started the transformation of the entire information industry that all established players, including IBM, are currently trying to cope with, through a radical transformation of their product technology and their organization. The break-up of IBM that the Antitrust Authorities attempted has already taken place on the initiative of the market.

The early radical transformations; the punch card machine era 1900-1940

In the early 20th century the office information systems market, or the office machine market, consisted of accounting and bookkeeping machines, mechanical calculators, cash registers, and typewriters. CTR innovated the market by renting the machines rather than selling them and later focused its rental business on the punch, the sorter and the accounting machine. CTR started with electrically powered tabulators, a technique Watson brought with him from NCR. An innovation (over *Remington Rand*) was that the reading of punch cards (the sensing, Pugh 1995, pp. 49-50) was electric. Innovative electrification of office machines made CTR (IBM from 1924) the dominant office machine producer in the 1930s.

The computer revolution 1940-1955

A pioneering IBM machine was Mark I, a physically very large but programmable relay calculator that was ready in 1944; the largest electromechanical computer ever built. In 1940 IBM got the first patent on a vacuum tube computer. The first product was ready in 1942.

During the second world war the U.S. Federal Government needed even more accounting machines than before and IBM was satisfied through the 1940s with producing and renting such machines. It paid attention to, but took little part in the war-oriented attempts to build electronic computers, even though it was obvious that electronic computing might eventually be better in doing what electromechanical office machines were then doing. Because of federal regulations *Bell* was not allowed to enter the computing market, and had no intentions of entering the field of computing, except for internal use. RCA had been convinced by von Neuman (the mathematician at Princeton)[4] to start research in the area. By the end of the 1940s very little beyond *Eniac* (at the University of Pennsylvania and the Ballistics Research Laboratory) had happened even though *Burroughs*, NCR and GE had pilot projects in the field. But in 1945 the Eniac group at the University of Pennsylvania resigned and organized a firm, *Electronic Control Corporation* to design and make a computer for *Northrop*. After a series of problems and changes of name of the company the project called *Universal Automatic Computer* (*Univac*) was purchased by *Remington Rand* in 1950, despite reports that the total market would be no more than a dozen machines. The first Univac machine was a huge success and began to replace many Census Bureau machines, including IBM machines. William Norris founded *Engineering Research Associates* (ERA) in 1946 and from 1950 became a formidable competitor. Remington Rand acquired ERA in 1952 and became the undisputable leader (over IBM) in large-scale electronic computers.

IBM which had long been satisfied with the cash flow from its tabulating machines finally started a scientific computer in 1949. IBM's computers of these days were to move on, however, not as advanced as the Univac. IBM's superior resources, nevertheless, made it possible for the new Electronic Data Machine Division to move fast. By 1955 IBM was installing more machines than Univac, but losing money.

The transistor revolution and the second generation computers – becoming a global player 1955-1965

Around the turn of the century business machines consisted of *office* and *industrial machinery*. The former included tabulators, typewriters, filing cabinets etc. The dividing lines were sharp and well defined. As late as around 1950, the computer was regarded as a scientific or military machine. In business it was considered a specialized device, occupying a position similar to that of a tabulator 50 years earlier, useful only for a handful customers. The first private firm to acquire a computer was *General Electric* which bought a Univac in 1954. Also during the second half of the 1950s few computers were used in private industry. Watson Jr, who had taken over after his father in 1956 had a difficult time having devoted the cashflows of existing tabulator and punch card operations to building a computer company.

At the same time, in late 1952 the Federal Government brought antitrust actions against IBM for monopolizing the tabulator and the punch card markets. While the old Watson was worried about the consequences for the old products and patents, Thomas Watson Jr. believed that within a short period most of them would be irrelevant. Eventually the old Watson ceded to the young Watson's ideas and they moved positively to accept the Government's antitrust position , in order to be favorably looked upon in the later computer era (The 1956 *Consent Decree*).

By the end of the 1950s the first commercial transistors were being offered and IBM found itself behind. There were formidable technological competitors (GE, *Westinghouse, Sylvania, Philco*, RCA, *Honeywell, Bendix* and *North American Aviation*). AT&T would have been an even more formidable competitor but was barred from the market by the antitrust authorities. Most of these competitors were technologically ahead of IBM but had little experience of the office equipment markets. Each of these firms, hence, preferred to remain at the scientific periphery of the computer industry.

In that sense, the old office equipment manufacturers were more dangerous competitors. They were interested in computers but their efforts were all half-hearted, except for *Remington Rand* (which merged with *Sperry* into *Sperry-Rand* in 1955), which was ahead of IBM in transistors. Sperry-Rand moved energetically in the late 1950s. *Business Week* wondered whether IBM would be able to maintain its lead (Sobel 1981, p. 150). The Univac division had good products but the two merged companies could not make the two parts work together and they lacked the office market know-how of IBM.

For IBM the contract to deliver a high-speed computer for the Atomic Energy Commission's Los Alamos Laboratory offered an opportunity to shift from vacuum tubes to transistors into the second generation of computers. The *Stretch* computer, on which work began in 1955 (Fisher, McKie and Mancke 1983, pp. 47 ff) never returned development costs. But the indirect benefits were large. It set the standard for IBM's transistorized 7000-series of commercial computers, announced in 1958 and also contributed to the 360-family announced in 1964. Despite heavy competition (from among others *Control Data Corporation*, founded by William Norris in 1957) CDC claimed to have developed the first solid state transistorized computer in 1958) IBM weathered the transition on the basis of its financial muscle, marketing knowledge and good back-up service.

In 1955 IBM introduced the *magnetic disk memory* and in 1956 the first *Fortran* version. In 1956 IBM, furthermore, began work on the second generation, transistor-based computers. The first 7070-machine was announced 1958. There were, however, several technologically advanced competitors. GE developed the *time-sharing* technology and the *Datanet* communications processors which allowed computers to talk.

Potentially more dangerous for IBM, however, was RCA's massive assault on the computer market in the late 1950s. Its giant 501 computer of 1959 was good and favorably received. It became, however, a business disappointment. And even though RCA continued to spend hundreds of millions from its television business on computers, it never made it in computers. IBM, however, realized that it was not ahead technologically, despite making many attempts, and had to do something about it.

Even so, on the basis of its total strength in products, marketing and production efficiency, IBM continued to dominate computing, country by country in the industrial world, through its *World Trade Corporation*.

Dominating the mainframe business – integrated circuits and the third generation computers 1965-1975

In 1955 Bell Laboratories had solved the technical diffusion problem of placing several transistor functions on a single silicon chip. By 1965 integrated circuits were being used in the Apollo guidance system and the Minuteman missile program. Only a few firms, notably *Texas Instruments (TI)* and *Fairchild Camera*, developed and produced integrated circuits which became the foundation of the third generation computers in the mid-1960s.

By the mid-1960s it looked as if the computing industry had achieved a measure of stability. The market appeared to be dominated by hardware producers, and parallels were drawn to the automobile industry. Several contenders would vanish, and a few would soon dominate. Such was the verdict by those who understood.

Then it began.

With IBM barely and late into second-generation computers, IBM's market position was being challenged in the early 1960s by new machines, notably from *Honeywell*. At the same time the market was shifting in favor of larger machines in the *Control Data* niche. Then IBM decided to go for the new third generation technology, designing a very large machine that could also be redesigned to compete with smaller machines. IBM's salesmen began to inform customers that a new IBM machine would soon be out, using new technology. Internally within IBM, however, the new machine was resisted since it was expected to kill the "new" second generation transistor machines immediately. Internal mess seemingly prevailed within IBM. Watson, however, supported by Learson's leadership, Amdahl's technology, and William's financial acumen (Sobel 1981, p. 222) moved. The first 360-machine was installed in 1965 and the computer market soon thereafter changed.

The market soon realized that small or medium-sized companies could not use a whole powerful 360-machine. Besides, possible new applications were difficult. Electronic service firms were established, for instance EDS by the former IBM salesperson Ross Perot. With the possibility to connect all kinds of accessories to the 360 system a whole new market for plug compatible equipment was created. Time-sharing arrangements around central *computer centers* were established and the entire market changed during the late 1960s and early 1970s. The computer services and software industry began to acquire significance.

In the wake of this change, all of a sudden a demand for smaller machines made itself felt. New firms were established or old firms reorganized (*Digital Equipment*, HP, *Varian Associates, Data General* etc.). While IBM had suddenly moved up into *Control Data* territory, it missed the significance of the emerging minicomputer market. It was also worried about what *Xerox* might do and about the significance of the "office of the future" revolution. In that vein IBM began to develop its own copying technology. (In the early postwar period it had missed the opportunity to acquire the Haloid-Xerox corporation). In 1970 and later, IBM released its first copying machines.

Just about the time the huge and fairly long success story of the 360-system established IBM as the dominant leader in mainframe computing and its mainframe mind, and a new era in computing was being borne (in 1969), the Justice Department filed a new antitrust suit against IBM, based on its dominance in the then known mainframe hardware market.

The desktop revolution, the micro processor and fourth generation computing, 1975-1985

The minicomputer market was spawned by the opportunities created by the centralization of computing around the 360-system. Very soon, however, the *Intel* microprocessor of 1971 (and the PLM operating system of 1973) made the PC and the desktop revolution possible.

The desktop computer was the exact counterpart to the centralized computing organization around the 360-system. Again, "IBM understood" what was about to happen. It waited, and did not move until 1981. As earlier, operational departments were expected to resist the change, so IBM's PC introduction was organized separately from the rest of the company, and the necessary standardization of the operating system was contracted out to *Microsoft*. In 1981, almost overnight, with the enormous resources of IBM, the computer market changed again.

With centralized computing on a mainframe, the leader can control its position in the market for a long time, or so, the Justice Department thought. Decentralized technology, however, also decentralized technology development to chip manufacturers and software developers. The entire industry became customized in the sense that an enormous range of high-technology computer products could be created around a set of easily available components.

Deregulation of the telecommunications market and the networking revolution, 1980-1990

The new situation in the computer market was, however, not to last long. *General Electric* had introduced time-sharing technology in the late 1950s. Linking computers in the office or locally was a technology envisioned by many in the 1960s, and the Xerox Palo Alto Research Center (Parc) began developing a local area network already in the early 1970s (the *Ethernet*). Simple distributed processing technology was being introduced in the mid-1970s. Significant technological change in the intersection between computers and telecommunications had, however, been held back by the antitrust authorities, forcing IBM to stay with computers and AT&T to stay with telecommunications.

The deregulation of the telecommunications market in the early 1980s released a new explosion in technological competition. It was not only the big players against each other. Potential technology had not been effectively exploited by the large firms. Hundreds of new players entered the field, attempting to wire computers in offices and firms together, and threatening the dominant roles of IBM and AT&T. The "network is the computer", even though still only partly realized, was already on its way. IBM, even though it had tried, had so far failed in acquiring the necessary networking technology. It went in and out of satellite communications in the 1980s. It failed to develop competitive digital office switching technology internally, it failed doing it together with Canadian *Mitel Corporation* and lost enormous amounts of money on its *Rolm* venture (see Chronicle). Rolm was sold to *Siemens* in stages 1989 and 1992. IBM's mainframe-based dominant position was rapidly beginning to erode and its PC and workstation businesses, although successful, were not as profitable as IBM had been used to, and were constantly threatened by newcomers.

With computing power beginning to be distributed over offices and firms the creation of a common language to communicate became central to success in the market. With central computing IBM did not have to worry about compatibility. With distributed computing and networking technology the development of a standard software design became critical. With the computer on the desk, the computer was no longer a machine only for the specialists. It became easy to use. Database access, presentational convenience etc. opened up a sea of new opportunities for innovative firms, especially in the software industry. As it became challenged from all angles, IBM was suffering from internal competition between its mainframe central computing division and the new PC-based division.

Towards the mid-1980s IBM, however, began to open up. To convey a feeling for the enormous technological task confronting the once dominant computer maker a glimpse of the complexity is in place. In the first phase of change IBM (Carlyle and Moad 1988a) was to slowly open up its whole downstream range of software products through adjusting to an *open systems network* (OSN), through its planned to be compatible *Systems Application Architecture* (SAA), withholding, however, its source *objective code* as a proprietary design [the IBM *object code only* (OCO) policy]. For the majority of customers this meant nothing. They did not want to become computing specialists. They did not want to customize their own information systems through manipulating the object code, although some did (Carlyle and Moad 1988, p. 40f). The catch was that if a firm customized its information systems design through changing the object code, portability of the system to new hardware was negatively affected. IBM was then working on a new 48-bit operating system, code named "Planet" that would have an enormous addressing range, being able to host SAA and IBM's *Systems Network Architecture* (SNA), being IBM's system to make IBM internally an open system. At the same time the extended version of IBM's OS/2 operating system was being designed to include a communications manager, a database manager and a user interface. This was the other strategy IBM was pursuing in the late 1980s, using its dominance in the market *to create standards around its own software* -- rather than proprietary designs -- the first example being MS/DOS for PCs.

The new software product range centered around the network management product *Net View*, the PS/2-OS/2 operating language and the relational database product (see more below). Included in this product offering was again the programming, user and communications interface Systems Applications Architecture, SAA, designed to insulate both users and program developers from the architectural and compatibility problems within the IBM product range[5] (see further Moad 1988a.). As it appears IBM also pursued a parallel strategy in making its mainframes the servers (through the SAA) of huge distributed processing networks, connecting computers of all sizes (see *BW*, Sep. 10, 1990, p. 30).

At the time IBM had also recognized that workstations would be the wave of the future that would cut into its mainframe business. IBM's PS/2-OS/2 workstation products were being designed to that end. IBM was even aiming at becoming the No. 1 Unix-based workstation producer (Leibowitz 1990). IBM's minicomputer activity (the ABS division) had also, unexpectedly, turned a success (Moad 1991). While the market for traditional minicomputer applications was shrinking, the AS/400 minicomputer was increasingly being used as a server for local area networks. IBM hoped that mainframes would be the drivers of future networks that tie workstations together. Competitors were, however, working on other network designs. But this "new" networking phase did not give the market a chance to stabilize. As computing and communication technologies continued to merge the software market exploded, again fundamentally rocking the established vendors. The technology to develop all kinds of user friendly access products was in place (see Chronicle).

The final test – entering computer and management consulting

While IBM controlled enormous resources and wielded an impressive technology arsenal by the end of the 1980s, its mind was still centrally wired. One could not say, however, that IBM was unaware of the directions the market was moving. Already in 1979 (*BW*, Sep. 17, 1979, p. 42) it took steps to enter the then not even existing multimedia market. The final organizational challenge of IBM entering the 1990s illustrates the enormous technological product complexity facing a full range business information systems provider. I will present IBM's attempts to come to grips with the third market transformation since the mid-1970s in terms of its strategy to remain a full-range information systems provider.

Since the late 1980s IBM had been attempting to reshape and slim its once 400-thousand-plus-member organization. Having outsourced essential intellectual elements of its technology to *Microsoft* and other vendors its strategy no longer appeared to be to keep control of the language of its system, but to adjust to the languages of the individual customer ("translation"), leaving the intermediate range of hardware and software products open to competition. The expectation was that future profit margins might very well be in the customized information systems design ("consulting"). This left the whole intermediate range of software and language design down to hardware technology open to competition. This was an unusual situation for IBM attempting to enter a new market with its bottom line hardware technology being subjected to fierce competition from new technical solutions, itself having its mind wired on an old centralized mainframe format, that top management was struggling to change. The complexity of this task was mind-boggling.

The new market situation is illustrated by IBM's "break" with its earlier partner, Microsoft, over Microsoft's new, and apparently successful *Windows* operating system, which directly challenged IBM's OS/2 system. Microsoft's further attempts to break in on special Apple territory (higher quality graphics computing etc) further aggravated IBM's market position. With OS/2 not yet ready (the 32-bit version, McMullen 1991), and the partner responsible for developing the central intelligence (the operating system) for the new market about to break loose, IBM was not in an enviable situation. Microsoft was in fact moving right into the territory into which IBM had been attempting to organize itself for several years, trying to achieve dominance in the entire software field (see Software, general in Chronicle and *BW*, Feb. 24, 1992, pp. 32-39). To counter the threat IBM announced (in 1991) an agreement with *Apple* to cooperate in a number of development projects, notably multimedia, an object-oriented operating systems standard and a new powerful Risc chip (*Power* PC) together with *Motorola* (*BW*, Oct. 7, 1991, pp. 28-30). In this context, this could only be interpreted as an open acceptance as a fact that IBM had been incapable of developing, through its own organization, all the technology needed to become a full-range information systems provider.

But IBM top management appeared to have understood in principle where the market winds were blowing and had extensive development work in progress since the 1980s to open up its systems technologies. The main idea with IBM's SAA had been to become popular with software houses. SAA is IBM's OSN system, a set of strictly defined rules for connections between programs and computers to make it possible for customers to "connect" to networks and hardware of all kinds. To make SAA popular IBM needed a lot of software written for it, fast. Since a large business bureaucracy is not the right place for creative software production and also keeps programmers isolated from the market, IBM needed outside help fast. Thus, a radical reorganization of the company and its philosophy was needed (also see Carlyle 1988b), in addition to outside partnerships.

The open end of IBM's change from a hardware-based equipment manufacturer to a vendor of software-based customer solutions involves an enormous investment in internal education and retraining and in new software development (Moad 1988a), which in turn required enormous investments in retooling the sales force (McWilliams 1988a).

Reshaping IBM to suit this strategy required a parallel reorganization and retraining program. Even though reorganization and continued training belonged to IBM's tradition to combat internal bureaucracy (Carlyle 1988b), IBM's past history was one of gradual technological change, or IBM pushing the change. Since the late 1970s change had been extremely fast even by the standards of the IT market and IBM had been gradually losing control of development. Some critiques also warned that reorganization and retraining was too much focused on marketing, leaving an inflexible engineering and manufacturing organization prone to turn out lackluster hardware.

As computers had become commodity products, IBM had found it necessary to create new proprietary designs through software applications and even through entering into direct consulting. IBM supported its fast (*BW*, Aug. 7, 1989, pp. 51-52) refocusing on software to keep its margins from slipping, by taking equity positions in a range of software companies. To achieve results IBM also made big changes in its bureaucracy, reorganized responsibilities, e.g. through moving responsibilities for the new partnerships into the important Market Operating Group and through creating new job positions.

As users increasingly turned to large peer-to-peer networks based on workstations and distributed systems they needed a technology to manage and distribute software to scattered resources. IBM's *Net View* was supposed to do that, but was still being developed. It was also designed to make it difficult for users to leave IBM's SNA (Systems Network Architecture) for OSI and products of IBM's competitors. To succeed with such particular product designs, IBM had to be successful with its entire product range for the corporate market.

IBM's *relational database* (DB2) including the *Structured Query Language* (SQL) and supporting advanced data dictionaries and facilities to handle new objects besides data was another element in the IBM software structure to drive corporate computing.

IBM's move to become a universal business information systems supplier (Dunn 1988) including associated downstream consulting in the new market environment of the 1990s had been indicated early in partially revealed strategic signals. Realizing that program, without offering "connectivity" was, however, pushing off users that desired certain features from specialist vendors. IBM was, hence, attempting to encompass simultaneously both its own SNA network architecture and links to international standards, such as OSN (see figure, p. 80 in Dunn 1988).

Realizing that the demarcation line between *voice, text and data systems* would disappear, and that all traffic would become digital, IBM had started early to develop its *Integrated Services Digital Network* (ISDN) and various *multimedia* approaches (see Chronicle). To move fast in this area and to enter the full-scale business information systems market, advanced switching and networking technology was needed. This IBM realized already in the early 1980s. This technology, however, is and was alien to mainframe computing. And even though IBM management had understood what was needed it has so far failed to realize that understanding through the development of products for the new markets. To acquire the networking technology critical to connectivity and the full-scale business information system, IBM had been (Dunn 1988) cooperating with *Ericsson, Siemens, Nynex, Bell Atlantic* and others. Switching (including central office switching and more recently broadbased ATM switches for volume data communication) and telecommunications had been the particularly difficult areas. Despite internal R&D, partnerships, among others with Canadian *Mitel*, and the enormously costly adventure with *Rolm* -- the once-state-of-the art office PBX producer (see Chronicle) -- IBM has so far not succeeded.

IBM's past covers the history of traditional computing and its ability through part of the 1980s to lead or catch up with new technologies at increasing rates of turnover (electromechanical devices, the vacuum tube, the transistor and the integrated circuit) is well documented. Until the mid-1970s technological competition was, however, still a matter of coping with straightforward, central computing technology. Coupled with IBM's massive corporate marketing experience IBM easily stayed on top of the market.

With the PC, networking and the deregulation of the telecommunications market *technology became increasingly organizational and complex* and the turnover rate began to speed up. IBM's centralist hardware mind suddenly became obsolete, and a hindrance to adaptation rather than support, and even though top management appears to have understood in principle where to head, it could not realize that ambition in practice. It is also interesting to observe that in the mid-

1980s IBM targeted DEC, another computer maker with a centralist mind and proprietary systems as its most dangerous competitor, at the time when DEC was beginning to experience problems similar to those of IBM. IBM's increased software/consulting service attention to customers meant entering a new field that had to be opened up in competition with a large number of both new and established firms. Competition was ferocious as the Chronicle shows. In entering the PC market IBM did not have the capacity to develop its own operating systems standard and thereby relinquished control of a critical intermediate technology to *Microsoft*. Success also did not come and the early 1990s has been a period of frustration, internal turmoil and (for IBM) unusual shedding of people, including top management. Employment world wide has been halved and with Gerstner as CEO, for the first time an outsider took charge to reorient the once giant organization.

The central grip on IBM exercised from CHQ in Armonk and White Plains has not been altogether positive for the ability of the giant company to orient itself downstream, away from hardware to decentralized management applications, software and consulting. The top executive hierarchy had understood that and made several moves to loosen the grip, something that was not easy, considering the tangle of interdependent technologies that IBM had developed around its mainframe technology. The organization, once exceptionally competent in coordinating diverse technologies into unique products, had grown into a state of Babylonian language confusion. In creating a federation of relatively autonomous divisions in 1992, internal bureaucracy was, however, significantly reduced. In 1992 a new IBM was born (*Datamation*, Dec. 15, 1992, pp. 39-43). It consisted of the following subsidiary companies:

(1)   Programming systems (software)
(2)   Technology products (chips)
(3)   Applications solutions (package solutions)
(4)   Pennant systems (printers)
(5)   Personal Computer Co.
(6)   Adstar (storage products)
(7)   Applications Business Systems (ABS, minicomputers)
(8)   Enterprise Systems (ES, mainframes)
(9)   Network Systems (communications)

Most of these separate companies were the largest in their market in the world. Thus, for instance, (Moad 1991) IBM's ABS minicomputer division earned more revenue than Digital in 1990.

It soon turned out, however, that the new organization was not well conceived. While its practical implementation had gone wrong, the original business idea of maintaining an organizational competence to merge diverse technologies into unique products was becoming even more important than before. IBM had been early in understanding that communication and computing would soon merge and that multimedia technologies would eventually dominate the products IBM was developing for business and other applications. IBM, in fact, "tasted" multimedia already in 1979 when forming a joint venture with MCA and a Californian entertainment group (see *BW*, Sept. 17, 1979, p. 42). Even though IBM had no plans to enter the telecommunications and switching markets, *networked computing* would have to be part and parcel of its main technology, and customers were increasingly demanding complete solutions to their business problems and complex tailormade systems products. That required (of IBM) a viable competence to merge the technologies now being developed in separate IBM companies. Thus, in May 1994 IBM decided to turn back, and brought all separate companies except the *PC company* together again, restructuring its business organization into new divisions, for instance bringing the mainframe (ES), the minicomputer (ABS) and the Unix workstation activities together in one division. In the new matrix organization generic product technologies like computer hardware, software etc. are translated into 12 specific applications "products" like health care, government, travel etc., each requiring the specific competences to understand problems of the customer and the information technology simultaneously. While the downstream software and consulting oriented solution to entire business problems is now emphasized, IBM has also begun (contrary to earlier times) to market standard products and components directly from its technological divisions. The main market for IBM is, however, systems products for the "networked corporation" in which geographically dispersed people can work together on complex tasks. The acquisition of *Lotus* and its successful groupware technology in June 1965 is part of this ambition to build a presence in networked computing.

On the surface it may look as if IBM is now back to where it started in the 1980s. At a deeper level it is all different. IBM has done with the entire company, and with a giant company, what has often been done on a smaller scale; by restructuring the organization and then reversing the restructuring, enormous redundancies have surfaced and been removed. With redundancies removed merging the diverse technologies critical for success in networked computing is considered possible. While the original business idea was right IBM had failed in its execution, and reorganizing is the instrument by which execution can be improved.

Summarizing IBM's attempts to develop an UBIS product

The complexity of the general business information systems product is illustrated by IBM's attempts to counter competition from all directions. Above all, the thousands of different customer specializations needed, and the several dozens of different technologies required to put such a product together cannot easily be administered within one centralized organization, especially at the rate of technical change typical of the IT market and the rapid diversification of the software market. The new customer-oriented organization of IBM illustrates the impossibility of a universal business information system (UBIS), that was demonstrated theoretically already in Chapter V. Adaptation was made even more difficult by the fact, that the core of the central IBM organization in the early 1990s was the mainframe, third generation computer design initiated with the 360-system in the mid-1960s. The potential to coordinate an UBIS-like product development program, on the other hand, might be found in the software development market, and a software firm freed from the intellectual constraints of mainframe computing. Even though this problem had long been understood within IBM, it took a crisis to enforce the necessary change underway since the beginning of the 1990s. Thus, market competition has done a much better job than antitrust policy in preventing monopoly formation in the computer market. The main impetus to this effective market control has been the removal of antitrust regulation in the telecommunications market. This took until 1982 for the Federal Antitrust Authorities to understand, when they terminated the wrongly conceived antitrust suit against IBM.

Summarizing the IBM story so far two interesting observations surface. *First*, the top level IBM executive bureaucracy may have been intellectually aware of the strategic problems IBM was facing each time. This time, however, it has not (so far, June 1995) been able to execute the organizational design needed to turn the company around to become the leading contender on the right track into the future. Is the reason internal resistance or lack of necessary inhouse competence?

Second, the reasons for IBM's early recognition of the initial strategic problems appear to have been its enormous marketing know-how. Could it be the fact that this time completely new (non-mainframe) technology was needed (like telecommunications technology and decentralized computing) and/or a sheer complexity that went beyond the "intellectual" capacity of a centralized organization like IBM? Our earlier theoretical analysis would suggest that complexity has played a central role.

Just in passing, the desktop, the networking and the software revolutions that have completely reshaped computing business since the early 1980s have also effectively forced a reorganization of U.S. computer industry, and pushed Japanese competition back into the hardware field, where they are excelling. A new U.S. computer industry has emerged, notably through the establishment of new firms, the exiting of failing firms and the dramatic reorganization of earlier dominant giants. It will be interesting to see whether the Japanese and, for that reason, Europe will ever come back with dominant players in this market and also whether IBM will experience a comeback as the, or (only) a dominant IT company.

Table VI.1   **The office machine market**
Percent of selling (market shares)

	1928	1939	1945
Burroughs	18	18	9
IBM	11	22	35
NCR	27	21	17
Remington Rand	32	25	32
Underwood Elliot Fisher	11	14	7
Total	100	100	100

Note: Bell, RCA and General Electric were also in the market, but mostly as suppliers of hardware component technology.

Source: Sobel (1981, pp. 75, 87, 105).

Table VI.2   **Market shares 1965 in U.S. computer market**

1.	IBM	65.3
2.	Sperry Rand	12.1
3.	Control Data	5.4
4.	Honeywell	3.8
5.	Burroughs	3.5
6.	GE	3.4
7.	RCA	2.9
8.	NCR	2.9
9.	Philco	0.7
Total		100.0

Source: Honeywell v. Sperry Rand, p. 157. From Sobel (1981. p. 169).

Table VI.3   From vacuum tubes to semiconductors
-- the ten largest producers

	1955 (Vacuum tubes)	1955 (Transistor)	1960 (Semi-conductor)	1965 (Semi-conductor)	1970 (Semi-conductor)	1975 (IC)	1980 (LSI)	1982 (VLSI)
1	RCA	TI	TI	TI	TI	TI	TI	Motorola
2	Sylvania	Transitron	Transitron	Fairchild	Motorola	Fairchild	Motorola	TI
3	GE	Philco	Philco	Motorola	Fairchild	National	National	NEC
4	Raytheon	Sylvania	GE	GI	RCA	Intel	Intel	Hitachi
5	Westinghouse	TI	RCA	GE	GE	Motorola	NEC	National
6	Amperex	GE	Motorola	RCA	National	Rockwell	Fairchild	Toshiba
7	National Video	RCA	Clevite	Sprague	GI	GI	Hitachi	Intel
8	Rawland	Westinghouse	Fairchild	Philco/Ford	Corning	RCA	Signetics	Philips
9	Eimac	Motorola	Hughes	Transitron	Westinghouse	Philips	Mostec	Fujitsu
10	Lansdale Tube	Clevite	Sylvania	Raytheon	American Micro	American Micro	Toshiba	Fairchild

Source: Foster (1986), p. 133.
Note: Among the two European semiconductor companies in this league, *Philips* and *Siemens*, only Philips made it into the table. Philips has been slipping in the 1980s and Siemens may have been gaining ground compared to the companies in the table, but not compared to the Japanese and more recently the Koreans. See further *Chronicle*.

b)   The XEROX Story -- Beginning too Early

Xerox is the innovative copying machine producer which built a global firm on the basis of the patent[6] IBM refused to consider. In 1959 it launched the first commercial plain paper copier. Xerox management realized early that copying and computing technologies would eventually merge and that copying alone would not be a viable business. In 1968 Xerox targeted *computers, education* and *medicine* to move beyond xerography into a global communications company (Smith and Alexander 1988, p. 2). It entered the field, however, much too early when it acquired *Scientific Data System* (SDS) for $900 million in 1969. After many costly mistakes, Xerox left the mainframe computer market in 1975, and unloaded SDS.[7]

In the 1960s Xerox enjoyed a virtual monopoly in copying and could afford a large number of experiments. In the early 1970s IBM entered copying and soon Japanese competition also began to make itself known in the volume end of the copying market. Xerox eventually responded in the late 1970s, having learned the quality discipline of its Japanese affiliate *Fuji-Xerox* and began a tough restructuring program. It is interesting to observe that Xerox' management headed by Kearns was able to orchestrate a successful comeback in the copying field through focusing on the high quality copying end.[8] During the 1980s, not least because of continued competition in the volume end of its copying market, Xerox realized that a systems approach was necessary to survive. Xerox now approached the *office of the future market* from a new and different end. Xerox saw itself no longer in the general office automation field but in the *document, electronic image processing, and electronic printing market*, emphasizing storage, filing and access of information through documents. Xerox expected this to be a huge market and also that paper would continue to be an important information medium (*High Technology*, Dec. 1987, pp. 46-49. Also see Chronicle). William C. Lowe, who engineered IBM's original PC success, was hired. His ambition was to integrate the work of the groups within Xerox that make workstations and those that make copiers and printers. Scanning technology and color copying have been added to the product range.[9] Xerox was arguing that most businesses are now, contrary to the early 1980s, ready for these advanced office systems (*International Herald Tribune*, July 15-16, 1989, pp. 9 and 11).

Xerox is interesting for its inability as a production organization to commercialize the output of an extremely innovative research laboratory. In its heyday the Xerox Palo Alto Research Center (*Parc*) had developed a multitude of new ideas which Xerox itself, apparently, was unable to develop into profitable industrial production. The concept of a "user friendly" computer was created already in 1972 in the form of the *Dynabook* computer (later called *Alto*) with *windows*-type graphics and short, simple commands (1981). Already in the mid-1970s Parc began looking into *electronic publishing* and some early applications were used. Xerox Parc also invented the *laser printer*. The most spectacular case, however, was the *Alto PC* that Steve Jobs saw and went on to create the Macintosh on.[10] The *network as a computer* was also a Xerox Palo Alto Research Center idea (*BW*, Nov. 26, 1990, p. 76), and Xerox was instrumental in developing the *Ethernet*, as well as the *workstation*, the *mouse* and a *windows* program for PCs (*BW*, Feb. 13, 1989, pp. 48-51). Xerox' early ambition to create a complete business information systems architecture was, indeed, ambitious (see *BW*, Jan. 9, 1989, pp. 6 f). But the Xerox bureaucracy was unable to make good business of any of it. Despite its copying document orientation and early experimental attempts at word processing, electronic editing, and publishing, Xerox missed the desk top printing market. *Apple* picked up the idea, and HP became very successful in the laser printer business.

It is interesting and sad to observe that while so many of the technologies that Xerox invented and initiated are now core technologies in the networked computing era of the 1990s, Xerox itself appears not to be an active frontier player in the field (see e.g. survey article on information technology and the networked corporation in *BW*, June 26, 1995, pp. 46 ff).

c)   The DEC Story -- Good but not Good Enough

DEC was founded in 1957 by Kenneth H. Olsen, an MIT engineer who saw a market niche for small, scientific computers and laboratory equipment in the shadow of IBM's and *Control Data's* large computers. DEC and most other minicomputer makers began directly with third-generation integrated circuit technology. The minicomputer market took off with the introduction of IBM's huge 360-computers. The 360-system left a niche for smaller systems based on the new technology.

For many years, until the beginning of the 1990s, DEC or *Digital* was the second largest computer maker in the world. It first specialized in scientific computing with its innovative minicomputers introduced in the early 1960s but later on entered corporate transactions computing. The DEC 10, DEC 11 and VAX families of minicomputers introduced in the 1970s opened the door to the corporate market. Also DEC had long entertained ambitions to be a full range supplier for the business market, basing its product range around a minicomputer. The DEC world began to become unsteady as minicomputers were squeezed between the mainframe and the powerful workstation in the 1980s, almost killing the market, or at least a large number of its inhabitants.

Both *Apple's* and DEC's ambitions to enter the "corporate" or "commercial systems computing" market dominated by IBM have been strewn with set backs. Being the second largest computer manufacturer in the world DEC for a long time probably was the strongest threat to IBM in the business information systems market. As late as the mid-1980s IBM in fact targeted DEC as its most dangerous competitor (*BW*, Nov. 17, 1986, pp. 86-91). However, DEC encountered the same enormous complexity of the business information systems market as IBM. While its "mind" may not have been as shaped on central mainframe computing as that of IBM, it did not have the same resources. And it was observed as late as in the late 1980s (see McWilliams 1988b, p. 56) that "unless DEC could come up with answers" to a handful of key IBM "products and technologies" for the corporate market it would face a very serious problem. These problems also arrived in the 1990s. The handful of general software products needed between end user applications catering for the various functions in Tables IV.4 and 5 (in Chapter IV) and the underlying hardware and hardware-oriented software were slow in coming. DEC's ambitious *Enterprise Management Architecture* never became a viable competitor to IBM's Net View, PS/2-OS/2 workstation products and DB2 (Moad 1988b), even though these IBM products never became successes. IBM itself, in fact, did not judge itself capable of doing it all and, hence, formed (in 1991) a joint venture with Apple to mutually exploit each other's competitive advantages and to develop new products, notably on the software side.

Kenneth H. Olsen had long realized that the computer business is much more than building machines (*BW*, April 21, 1986, pp. 98 f) and was very early in making all DEC computers communicate. While IBM's key product lines could not communicate, all DEC machines shared the same (albeit proprietary) operating system (*BW*, March 10, 1986, p. 69) and could communicate through *Ethernet*. DEC was early in entering the Risc and Unix (somewhat modified) workstation market.

In the early 1980s DEC suffered its first slump in earnings, being squeezed between mainframes and the growing PC market (*Tempus*, No. 36, 1983, 8-14 Sept. Also see Interview). Kenneth H. Olsen returned out of semiretirement to reorient the organization. A number of measures were introduced to strengthen DEC's position in traditional technical markets and networking technology (where DEC was an innovator) to penetrate IBM's largest commercial accounts. A whole range of successful, new products related to networking technology was turned out (*BW*, July 20, 1987, p. 78). Olsen also carefully guarded DEC's position in scientific and technical computing (*BW*, Nov. 25, 1985, p. 82). However, even its core market position in factory automation was at peril when (in early 1985) DEC managed to introduce its Micro VAX II workstation and a stream of new products. Then things turned for the better and DEC was for a while looked at as the computer phenomenon of the late 1980s. The star of Route 128 again became Wall Street's star (*BW*, July 20, 1987, p. 78 f). But bad times struck again (*BW*, May 16, 1988, pp. 50-55; *BW*, Nov. 21, 1988, p. 86), and DEC's proprietary operating system was declared out of fashion. Its PC operation was too small, and PCs and workstations were taking a large part of VAX's traditional jobs. Olsen tried again to reorganize the company to move into fast growing markets (*BW*,

Aug. 13, 1990, pp. 32-33). In 1986 DEC had claimed that it was ahead of IBM in connecting computers (*BW*, April 21 1986, p. 98). IBM had responded with Net View and a mainframe-based network. DEC had no mainframe and suddenly found itself again on the defensive, attempting to market its *Enterprise Management Architecture* (*BW*, Oct. 8, 1990, pp. 66-72).

In 1990 DEC, pushing hard into software, had developed a layered software, called the "middle one" on top of its proprietary operating system, including graphical user interfaces, database tools and network connection software. DEC hoped this kind of software, called Network Applications Support would help firms integrate multivendor systems and also help DEC become a leading supplier of open systems (Bunker 1991). The strategy did not work. Since Olsen could not bring himself together to restructure and fire 25 000 employees he was forced out of the company (*BW*, Aug. 3, 1992, pp. 46-47). DEC is now banking on its new 64-bit Risc processor *Alpha* and VAX machines that can be upgraded to Alpha machines (*BW*, May 4, 1992, p. 27). This strategy gives cause for optimism the *Economist* (April 17, 1993, pp. 67-68) observed. The dramatic collapse of IBM's turnaround plan also shifted attention away from DEC's problems, which, in fact, are very similar; the difficulties of turning a huge organization with a hidebound management around fast enough (BW, Jan. 18 1993).

The new CEO (Palmer, taking over in 1992) began to cut costs and reorganize DEC around nine business units. In 1994 this restructuring was abandoned and key executives left (*BW*, May 9, 1994). There were rumors that Digital, once the No. 2 computer company, might not survive (*BW*, June 19, 1995, p. 77). But Palmer stayed on and enacted an even sharper focus on high performance computing and networking, arguing that with its new Alpha server Digital is both retaking the lead in networking and becoming capable of offering mainframe applications and a huge memory at about one tenth the price of a mainframe (*Datamation*, May 1, 1995, pp. 61 ff). Even its *HiNote* lap top gets excellent reviews. But critics still wonder about the substance of these arguments. Is this really a permanent turnaround for a firm still not really freed of its past technologies, and generating low revenue per employee compared to competing firms (*BW*, June 19, 1995).

d)   The ERICSSON Story -- the High Ambitions, the Early Rise and the Final Collapse of the Swedish Computer Industry

The potential of electronic computing was understood in principle long before the micro chip revolution. This was so in many advanced industrialized countries. With one of the world's leading electromechanical calculator producers *Facit*, *Ericsson* in telecommunications, *Saab* in aircraft, and an advanced technological university community, *Sweden was early* into electronics and computers, but failed miserably in computers.

An early start

The first Swedish vacuum tube computer (*Besk*) was ready in 1954.[11] Its design was successful and the Besk computer was directly copied in several places.[12]

In 1956 *Facit* opened an electronic data processing department and hired most of the Besk development team. A copy of Besk was ready in 1957 as Facit EDB, but the vacuum-tube machine was then already technically too old and Facit for some reason abandoned its ambitions to go on in electronic computing and to develop a new computer.[13]

Axel Wennergren, the founder of Electrolux corporation started a computer company *Alwac* (Axel Wennergren Automatic Computers) in California. They developed reliable computers with very few vacuum tubes. Alwac 3 was ready in 1954 and sold well (more than 200 computers). This design was acquired by Wennergren's Swedish operation and integrated in Sweden under the Alwac name. About 40 computers were produced and sold. At that time (around 1960), however, the vacuum tube technology was already obsolete. A transistorized version of Alwac 3 (called Vegamatic) was developed but was abandoned around 1962/63 at the time of Wennergren's death. The development team went on to build a transistorized version of the Besk computer, mainly to exploit all the software written for Besk. Two transistorized Besk computers were used for a long time, but development work was abandoned.

Saab founded a computer division *Datasaab* to develop computer competence for its jet fighter program Lansen. It built the first transistorized mainframe in the early 1960s, called Saab D2, the fastest machine in Europe. It also installed (in 1960) the first computer for industrial use in Sweden. (See *En bok om Saab-Scania*, Stockholm 1987, p. 65).

Around that time Sweden had an impressive electromechanical calculator industry. *Facit* was the leading company with a 20 percent world market share. *Åtvidaberg* (changed to Åtvidaberg-Facit in 1950) had acquired the well known calculator company *Original Odhner* in 1942. In the early 1960s Facit began to build electronic calculators. To expand its presence in world markets it acquired *Addo*, another well known calculator company in the late 1960s. Facit's electronic calculators were, however, not successful. It suddenly (in the mid-1960s) found itself lagging technologically in the calculator business, and established a relation with *Sharp* of Japan; Sharp produced the electronic calculator hardware, and Facit put its label on it and sold the product through its global marketing system. Facit's mistake then was to attempt to build its "strength" on its international marketing organization and put its own label on somebody else's product. This only worked temporarily. Very soon Sharp was ready to go alone, and Facit had no satisfactory electronic calculator of its own developed. The whole firm failed in 1972. It was acquired by Electrolux, which used some of the existing factories with a staff of skilled labor to produce its own products. Electrolux, however, continued on a cautious scale with Facit products, only to sell the whole activity in 1983 to Ericsson.[14]

A Swedish PC, called ABC 90, developed by *Diab, Scandia Metric,* and *Luxor,* was ready for the market in 1978. This cooperation continued until 1985, but failed, partly because of the large resources needed and partly because a proprietary operating system was used. K.J. Börjeson, who had developed the ABC later started *Jet Data,* which failed but again designed an Intel 486-based DOS computer 1993 in PC *Leo Jet,* which also failed commercially.

Diab went on to develop a Unix-based computer in 1983. It did not help that Diab was owned by Ahlsell, and was taken over by the Swedish Telecommunications office (now Telia) in 1986. In 1991 Telia sold 75 percent of its Diab holding to *Bull.*

In 1984 *Datatronic,* a Swedish PC maker, acquired ailing *Victor* and managed to rebuild the company into the second largest PC vendor in Europe, only to sell out to Proventus in 1988, which sold it on to *Tandy* (now *Tandy Grid*) in 1990, which had ambitions to enter Europe. Tandy Grid attempted to market Victor PCs under the Tandy label, but failed, and in 1993 AST acquired Tandy Grid to become the fourth largest PC maker in the world. AST later ran into problems and was partly acquired (1995) by *Samsung* of Korea. Mats Gabrielson (the creator of Datatronic) tells[15] that the choice in 1988 was between risking everything that he had created so far, or sell.

The Ericsson attempt at the business information systems market

In 1982 *Ericsson Information Systems* was formed with the ambition to become a full range information supplier for the corporate world, organizing its product range around a PBX, its telecommunications know-how and the enormous cash flow from its successful AXE telecommunications technology.[16]

Again, however, the enormous width and diversity of the technology base needed soon began to make itself felt in the form of lacking human competence, stepped-up internal demand for investment financing, increased competing demands for the parallel development of the Ericsson AXE specialty and, above all, from increasing international technological competition in the business information systems market. Ericsson gave up and sold its PC and Alphascope activities to Nokia in 1988, and its Facit operation to the Norwegian Entranator group. Nokia, in turn, sold its computer division to ICL in 1991. Not even ICL was, however, capable of weathering the technological competition in the computer market and was acquired by mainframe-based Fujitsu, intent on learning the PC market. It is ironic that Fujitsu bought a basically Swedish-developed competence that can be traced via Ericsson, all the way back to Saab's early development of military computers in the 1950s. This was the end of the hardware part of the Swedish computer industry. What remained was a very successful telecommunications company (Ericsson), which is based on a specialized dedicated computer system and the specialized process computers that i.a. ABB produces.

It is interesting to speculate what caused the demise of the Swedish computer industry. One plausible reason is that it found itself alone in the midst of an extremely dominant and successful mechanical engineering industry which absorbed the high-quality attention and talent. Firms attempting to enter the computer market all did it as a side activity, placing priority on its main activity. Side activities are never attractive for recruitment of internal firm talent. The Swedish mechanical engineering industry, however, was very early and quite successful in integrating electronics in its mechanical products. Since hardware technology defined the limits of the capacity of information systems it is easy to understand that entrants into the business information systems market were mostly hardware-based, failing to notice early, that success required first of all a broad range of software competences. Another reason for the failure probably was Ericsson's all absorbing attempt to enter the business information market, enrolling most of what was going on in Sweden in electronics, computers and software in its endeavor. When Ericsson failed, it took the lot with it,[17] and Sweden entered the 1990s with practically no producer of hardware in its computer industry.

In the mid-1980s nine software firms[18] were registered on the Stockholm (OTC) stock exchange, the largest being the software houses *Programator* and *Enator*, the nine employing together less than 2000 people. Programator was partly a computer services firm, partly a firm specialized in programming support of other firms. In the early 1980s Ericsson engaged in a joint venture with Programator, lacking software competence for its attempts at the business information systems market, but soon pulled out. Programator was acquired by *Cap Gemini* in 1992 under the name of *Cap Programator*.

Enator was partly acquired by IBM, and later (1994), together with *Dialog* (earlier Kommundata) by Celsius. In 1991 *Celsius* had acquired *Telub* which in turn acquired *Dotcom* from Ericsson, specializing in internal firm networks. Together Celsius now manages a broad-based competence in information technology covering both computing and telecommunications, with sales in information technology of almost $1 Billion and more than $1 Billion in defense technology. It has recently (1995) announced a concerted drive into the information technology market. The logics looks perfect,[19] but skeptics draw parallels with Ericsson Information Systems which was based on the same argument, and also point out that the Board of Celsius has none with IT competence and is dominated by politicians and people from the earlier State Holding Company. This is natural for a company that is to 67 percent (votes) controlled by the state, but no good signal for the market and the future. Celsius, however, is the only genuine Swedish operation of any size that is left of all attempts over the last 40 years or so to build a computer industry in Sweden.

Datema, a firm in the Johnson group was one of the largest computer services firms in Europe in the 1970s. After a series of economic problems originating in mismanagement it was acquired by the Finnish software house *Tietothedas*. Probably very little of original Datema software activities still exists.

The Swedish development of a business information industry is interesting also in another way. Two suppliers of office information systems (Ericsson and Esselte) were operating in seemingly similar markets, applying very different technologies and entirely contrary business strategies.

Comparison of Ericsson and Esselte

Esselte and *Ericsson Information Systems* for some time operated in a common market segment. They were both supplying equipment for a similar set of office information functions, but were pursuing entirely different technological and commercial strategies. None of the product concepts, however, had a potential for serving top management, even though ambitions to that extent were voiced, especially in Ericsson's advertisements.

Esselte was earning good profits on staying with an old binder/labels type document technology, staying clearly away from the manufacturing of hardware and rather operating as agent for other firms' products in the office information area, keeping a steady watch -- as they said -- on the advance of alternative, electronics-based document technologies.With many years of experience Esselte was very clear about which segment of the huge office market to focus on, namely local office filing systems (binders and hanging folders). It had no ambitions to enter the database markets, managing large data systems, where computers were successfully entering, and only had a peripheral interest in management tools and information systems. Esselte supplied systems developed by other firms. It did not design its own systems and it stayed away from downstream consulting. Here the Esselte strategy was clearly different from that of Ericsson, even though Esselte, towards the end of the 1980s had entered segments of the market for distributing "database content", like financial information.[20] *Esselte*, or rather *Dataindustrier* (later *Diab*, that was acquired by *Bull*), as mentioned above, developed a computer of its own. Ericsson, coming from the electronics side, on the other hand, opted for the electronics-based office document and information systems, entering too early, misconceiving the product the market wanted and lost billions of SEK, only to sell out most of its information division to Nokia in 1988. Esselte, on the other hand, stayed successful for the time being.

Both "extreme" strategies were, however, dangerous. Esselte argued that it was ready to go electronic, whenever the right software-hardware configurations and the users were ready. They had also been supplying electronics-based equipment (made by external suppliers) for years, and argued that they were technologically prepared. While Ericsson could not develop the office information product demanded within a "profitable" time and cost limit, the Esselte strategy, on the other hand, could misfire, if a competitor suddenly entered the market on a large, industrial scale, with a product that rapidly would make the Esselte products obsolete. Both Xerox and Kodak have had the strategy to make paperless document handling a reality. If so, the "Facit case" could be repeated. The difference is that Esselte was supplying a system that requires considerable learning before use, while Facit was producing a well-defined piece of hardware (the electromechanical calculator) that did not require much prior learning.

This was the story until the late 1980s. While Ericsson's business information systems activities are gone, Esselte is still in the market. It has suffered ownership problems, and undergone several reorganizations. The company was split into an information systems part in 1992 called *Scribona* and the rest, called Esselte supplying standard office hardware from the shelf, like binders, Dymo- and Pendeflex products etc.

VI.5   THE NEW INFORMATION PRODUCT -- SUMMING UP

The integrated business information system builds on the merging of *computing, telecommunications* and *office equipment* technology (see Figure VI.1). The functions of this information system can be divided up into at least the eight categories of Table VI.4. Each places different competence demands on the developers of information systems. To begin with hardware producers (electronic components and computers), carried the initiative in developing new applications. Until the 1980s the software people, working closer with the users, were too few or too locked into the proprietary culture of a financially strong hardware producer to be able to initiate change. In the 1980s hardware became standardized and the PC-revolution began. Many large, resourceful and very competitive software companies emerged as driving forces on the U.S. scene. In the 1990s software producers commanded the initiative.

Data processing and *analysis* (items 1 and 2) are the traditional tasks associated with the computer. These functions are still important.

The *production* (item 3) task means asking the system to do what was earlier done manually.

Coordination (item 4), or scheduling of people means using the system as an organizer, a memory or a calendar book.

Monitoring (item 5) involves, inter alia, supervising the enactment of scheduled tasks or events, reminding the system or people of upcoming events, checking that things have been done, or that performance is up to targets etc.

Presentation (item 6) is a form of production that deserves its own itemization, since the new information systems being developed will allow *such powerful presentation technology that the character of group decision making may be significantly influenced*. One example of this would be the potential for live simulation of unexpected events, and synthetic rehearsals of decisions to cope with the unexpected.

Access (item 7) is fundamental and a relatively new potential, not paid attention to until the 1980s and the telecommunications revolution in computing. This is where top management eventually may find its business information system of direct practical use, enhancing access to both data and people, making database and networking technology, on the one hand, and combined data, voice and picture communication, on the other, a critical technology combination.

Cognitive support (item 8) is when the "intellect" of the computer is put to use to support the "mind of the group". Ambitions are high, speculation on this matter has a long history, but headway has been very, very slow. Intelligent software capable of transferring the "tacit" skills of craftsmen onto code is gradually developing (see Chronicle under Artificial Intelligence). Important developments are occurring in the field of team communication of complex messages (groupware like Lotus' *Notes*) and new "tacit" and devoted grammar can be developed through systems use, a form of "on-the-job learning" [Trillium of Xerox; see Henderson (1986) and Chronicle]. The next step will come when software is developed to help structuring new problems, i.e., making complex tacit knowledge explicit.

Software development in "presentation" is expanding into both cognitive support for "executive teams" (most important for our analysis) but also into technical and engineering applications, like "software to develop new software". An important "group cognitive" development is the "groupware" experiments, designed to keep teams, working at geographically dispersed locations intellectually together.

The information systems developed so far are usually specialized to perform well on one of these functions. Manufacturing automation is principally different and separate from other activities, although both parts and finished goods inventories, marketing and product development and CAD functions in some applications have been integrated with the production process. Computer integrated manufacturing (CIM) aims at such general integration (see Eliasson 1995b).

Printing and graphics functions are usually kept separate. Not until recently has a workable integration between word processing, graphics and printing become available. *Apple* seems to have been the innovative firm. Lack of standardization of filing and communication systems have made this technology, so far, overly difficult. Monitoring, access and cognitive support systems live their separate and specialized applications lives at different places in an organization.

Production and engineering databases are almost always principally different from the economic databases used at Corporate Headquarters and, hence, not integrated.

The information system envisioned, however, means that a combination of all the "items" of Table VI.4 be achieved. Suppose that a complex message is to be communicated to a decision group somewhere (Table VI.5). The problem has to be defined, and its presentational form and mode of communication ("session") determined. Thereafter follows the actual "transporting" of the message by first announcing its destination. Then the transport route (the network), including the choice of "vehicle" or "protocol" follows. Finally the message is communicated physically. This may look unnecessarily cumbersome to the outsider, but the inability of the systems product designers to get a realistic grasp of all the complexities involved, is what has caused all the disappointments and mistakes in this field over the last couple of decades. We are concerned here with tasks much more complex than automating the entire domestic railroad and local (rail-based) passenger and goods transport systems of a country. The fact that messages can be treated more brusquely than people, that safety regulations are not as demanding and that transactions are taking place at lightning speeds, however, makes automation possible.

The complexity is, nevertheless, so overwhelming that integrated systems are almost always developed for special applications by each user. Some of these systems are impressive indeed; like the early Sandvik global inventory control system development more than two decades ago, Philip's internal cost control and pricing system[21] etc. But the cases illustrate that a good system is not enough. The users also have to understand how to use it (see item 9, Table VI.6).

To integrate all these functions into one information system a very large number of technologies have to be mastered within the same organization; at the R&D labs, at the design departments and in production. Table VI.6 gives an overview of the basic technologies that will have to go into the product. Each of them are represented by one or more departments at a Technological University. They can be clustered under the four different functionally oriented headings of Table VI.6. Table VII.1 that organizes the Chronicle presents a further break down with overwhelming complexity. While the principal design of technology demands in Table VI.6 are tough but possible to overcome, the Chronicle explains why almost all entrants failed.

Figure VI.1   The integrated business information system

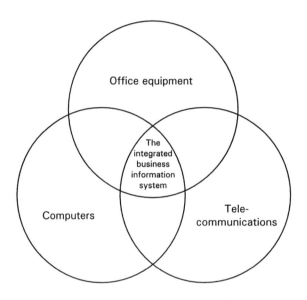

Table VI.4   Functional orientation of hardware and software development

	Functions	Examples
1.	Data processing	
2.	Analysis (computer capacity)	
3.	"Production", rationalization	– automated manufacturing
		– invoicing
		– correspondence
		– updating of files
		– library
4.	Coordination (of people)	
5.	Monitoring	
6.	Presentation	– printing
		– graphics
7.	Access	– distributed databases
		– distributed processing
		– communication
		– compatibility
8.	Cognitive support	– artificial intelligence
		– expert system

Table VI.5   Layers of communication

1.	Application	- define problem and data
2.	Presentation	- define presentational format and tell
3.	Session	- manage connection between programs
4.	Transport	- deliver
5.	Network	- format of data packets
6.	Data link	- change vehicle (protocol)
7.	Physical	- medium of transmission, do it

Source: Musgrave (1988) and Cerf (1991), p. 45.

Table VI.6   The technology elements of the new information systems product

Representation
1. Process knowledge (operations)
2. Taxonomy (concept)
3. Data base

Analysis/Data processing
4. Languages
5. Computers

Communication
6. Networking
7. Switching and telecommunications

User contacts
8. Software
9. Man-machine interaction (user competence)

Table VI.7   The critical design technologies

Access	- Networking
	- Open systems design standard/portability
- Access people	- Telecommunications
	- Mobile telephones, faxes
- Access data	- Database
	- Distributed processing
	- Portables
Representation	*- Graphics, visualization*
	- Multimedia
	- Electronic printing
	- PBXs

VI.6   THE MANY TECHNOLOGIES THAT HAVE TO BE MERGED IN THE UNIVERSAL BUSINESS INFORMATION PRODUCT

A common experience with new technology or new product development is that the complexity of the task is underestimated. Often, this kills the project. Wise managers, however, usually factor in significant negative surprises in their budgets. A typical method to exert effort from the development departments in firms is to let them come up with their own optimistic budget, and when the development people fail to achieve agreed upon targets, a new compromise is negotiated requiring crisis management and harder problem solving and night work by the researchers and developers, *if* they want to continue. In fact, as I have argued elsewhere (Eliasson 1976a) most progress would cease if budgets would be accepted only for safe projects.

The Product Idea -- the Experimental Evolution of a New Technology Combination

All new development is experimental. The universal business information systems product, on the one hand, exceeds most earlier experience in complexity, misunderstanding and failure. On the other hand, it probably had to evolve like this. There was a tremendous technological push to exploit the new information technology. There was a tremendous and curious potential demand on the part of users with resources to spend on new ideas. There were hundreds, perhaps thousands of daring firms, rich in ideas that wanted to try, and each entered the market from a different end. Without this multiple approach and the many failures, development would probably be decades behind where it is now, because the new product requires the simultaneous presence of a critical mass of technology with a sufficiently varied composition. Without the messy experimental composition of this entire, disorganized venture, it might not even have happened. When the evolution of business information systems began no one was capable of envisioning where we are now -- which is quite unusual -- and even if someone had, no simple institution, not even IBM would have been capable of executing what it envisioned within a centralized organization. This was not a Manhattan project.

Tables III.6 (in Chapter III) and VI.6 give a rough idea of the multitude of technologies involved, and the break down of the same table in Chapter VII (Table VII.1) and in the Chronicle tells the same story in a much more detailed way. Each item in Table VI.6 corresponds to *at least* one discipline at a Technological University, pursued, as is typical at academic institutions, in isolation. The new information product required that they all be integrated. This integration is still taking place experimentally in the market.

The Chronicle tells the story of how new hardware development creates a platform for software development that in turn is now beginning to create the multiple technological platforms for customer solutions that will drive the development in the future.

Each new technology is challenging the commercial conditions of existing technologies. The *transistor* opened a new second generation technology of computing in the mid-1950s, to be followed in the mid-1960s by the *integrated circuit* and the third generation of computers, to be followed again by the micro processor and the forth generation of computing in the 1970s. In the late 1960s the minicomputer (DEC, *Data General, Prime* etc.) moved into an empty niche in the market that mainframe producers had not paid attention to. This niche continued to grow well into the 1980s between the mainframes and the low-capacity PCs. The increasingly powerful PCs, however, and after 1980 so-called "powerful workstations" (*Apollo, Sun* etc.) began pushing the minicomputers out of the market in the late 1980s. The force of this squeeze between workstations and mainframes was increased by the fact that minis -- like mainframes -- were locked into proprietary operating systems designs, making them unable to communicate efficiently with other computers via networks. Workstations as a rule use the Unix operating system which has good networking features. This made the workstations ideal computers for the emerging networking technology and for graphic-intensive applications, like CAD, and minicomputer makers were forced to reconsider their product strategies, putting small producers with small resources at a disadvantage (see *BW*, Nov. 21, 1988, pp. 84-86). With the microprocessor experiencing wave after wave of upgraded capacity, and networking technology distributing computing over the firm, software was becoming the dominant restriction on computing, spawning thousands of new specialized applications, and firms.

The Management Task -- Integrating at Least Nine Fundamentally Different Technologies

The product development task now becomes overwhelming. Nobody has yet defined the entire business information product ahead of its experimental development. All development has been extremely piecemeal and tailormade, and not focused on a viable concept of a future integrated product. The experimental mode has dominated. The integrated product I am attempting to sketch may not be the best concept, even though it realistically takes in both the user side and technological limitations.

Table VI.6 summarizes the various technologies involved in putting the whole product package together under four different functionally oriented headings. Organizing this effort is a formidable, almost impossible task.

First, we have the *representation* function, i.e., the task of orienting the system towards its use; knowledge about the production process, the necessary classification system for measurement (taxonomy) and databases. This whole area was hardly observed by the information industry for decades. The task was supposed to be handled by the users. Finally, towards the end of the 1970s, increasing attention was being paid to database technology (see Chronicle).

The *second* main category is the *analysis/data processing* function. Here, of course, the computer industry was born and almost all activity until well into the postwar period was in hardware. The first version of the *Fortran* programming language (for IBM computers) was introduced in 1956. In the 1970s standards began to be introduced in the operating systems and computer language areas.

Communication and computing ushered in an entirely new era in information systems in the 1980s. The enormous potential associated with gaining flexible access to people and data began to bring results. *Access technology* is currently dominating the development of industry.

User contacts finally was a long forgotten task, left to the user. The development of high-level languages and artificial intelligence, special applications programs etc., mostly associated with the PC have revolutionized the computer industry since the 1980s. Each of the (at least) nine subtechnologies involved, however, is entirely different from the others. Merging them into a complete systems technology has posed major difficulties. Paradoxically, this has been especially difficult for the established giant firms with enormous financial resources, that have had their organizational minds shaped in hardware and centralized computing. No one has so far been successful in this cross-disciplinary development work. No firm so far, not even IBM, has the complete repertoire of needed competence established in-house. While IBM has been unable to acquire the needed telecommunications technology, AT&T has so far been unable to learn computing such that it can compete successfully in the field. Learning in this context means achieving competitive price/performance. Similarly Xerox never learned computing, while IBM really did not learn to master the mechanical engineering knowhow to manufacture copiers profitably and so on (see below).

With the PC revolution created by IBM, however, hardware has become a commodity and a large part of the software industry has fragmented into standardized systems (database management, operating systems etc.). The merging of them all appears to take place in new companies in the software industry that are not intellectually constrained by a history of past hardware solutions. To get a feeling for the extent of the task (see the Chronicle to follow) we will include a sketch of the experimental product development history so far. What remains in this chapter is to put the "integrated product package" together from the bits and pieces known to be available in the market.

VI.7   THE EMERGENCE OF THE ELEMENTS OF THE NEW INFORMATION PRODUCT

The break through of modern computing occurred in the beginning of the 1960s, when commercial applications based on volume *transactions processing* forced mechanical punch card machines out of business. *Integration* of computing and data storage on magnetic tape allowed efficient *control of inventories*. *Production scheduling* became another frequent application.

Early technology development

Disk memories replaced magnetic tape during the seventies and a large development step towards *database* management prepared the way for *data comununications*. *Terminal* and *time-sharing* systems increased in numbers and on-line stations replaced "batch-stations", only to be replaced gradually during the 1980s by PCs and *distributed* processing. CAD applications increased with the local processing power of PCs and workstations and their capacity to handle graphical information (see e.g. Hedenklint 1991).

The rationalization motive dominated early conceptualizations of the business information system. The new fantastic machines could carry out the numerical calculations earlier done by hand calculators at lightning speeds. Focus was on computer hardware capacity to replace rote human labor. This period lasted through the 1960s and well into the 1970s. Unintelligent terminals tied into a time-sharing arrangement with a mainframe, first introduced by General Electric, began to show up in the late 1960s. The languages of the computers were machine language or crudely compiled codes. Work on *Fortran* began in IBM in 1954. Fortran was introduced commercially in 1957/58 (the first version in 1956), and rapidly became the standard programming language of the 1960s. Already in the 1970s, however, higher level languages like APL were being introduced. Use of computers was very knowledge demanding on the part of the user. A whole new profession of programming experts appeared in the market.

Visions of the computer age and even the information age were conjured up in literature, but they were imprecise, revealing in retrospect the almost complete lack of understanding of the "experts" of the potential of the new digital machine, as well as of the organization of the production which the new machines were supposed to monitor, control and run, and above all make possible.

The early attempts to design a business information system

The first visualizations of the *business information system* began to appear already in the 1950s. Xerox realized early that in the long run copying and computing belonged together. It acquired *Scientific Data Corporation* (SDC) in 1969 to learn computing, an unsuccessful idea, as was the whole project of a system of "architecture of information" that was initiated and carried on at the Xerox Palo Alto Research Center in the early 1970s (see Alexander and Smith 1988). IBM entered copying in 1970. The business was carried on separately from computing and was initially successful. IBM left copying in 1987. The merging of computing, text editing, data storage, graphics and printing on a digital basis is still to be seen even though the "multimedia revolution" is currently moving very fast. The first workable desk top publishing "systems" to be introduced commercially were pioneered by *Apple* (see *BW*, June 27, 1986), even though a development project had been initiated long before in the *Xerox* Palo Alto Research Center.

The early focus of information systems was on rationalization. They copied existing work processes onto computer code. This ambition was pursued parallel to a new development in the 1970s; flexible manufacturing and the automated factory. It is interesting to observe that the complete reorganization of the actual business to optimally exploit the new information technology, which the Japanese have successfully pioneered appears to have been such an overwhelming task in practice that it has been given a separate name, *re-engineering* (see Chronicle).

Office *rationalization* was a popular idea of the 1970s, and examples of failed attempts abound. The story often was that computerization of existing office routines yielded no productivity effects. However, going back to manual routines again often created a large positive systems effect, since the two-way procedure had revealed to management a multitude of redundant office routines that could be removed.

The *office of the future* theme first surfaced out of copying quarters. Xerox' ambition in the late 1960s to merge copying and computing had failed. The next attempt originated among several telecommunications firms that wanted to build an office communications architecture around their digital PBXs. Here we have Ericsson, AT&T, Northern Telecom and many others. They did not succeed. One mistake was purely technical. Product developers did not understand the limited capacity of the PBXs to transmit digitally stored information compared to the needs of a viable business information system, and local area networking and data switching technology was not generally available. The interesting thing is that ambitions presented by the firms in the market (see Chronicle) included both "office automation", "the office of the future" and "the business information system".

A parallel attempt was launched by *Wang* in the early 1980s to build an office information system around its early wordprocessing, networking and computing technology. Again the portable word processing systems built around the PC and standardized operating systems killed all early proprietary systems in the early 1980s. New and potentially more successful attempts have been underway in the intersection between the PC and the network (distributed processing, the computer as a network) and may eventually perhaps realize the "architecture of information" dream of *Xerox* from the early 1970s. IBM's acquisition of *Lotus* and its successful *groupware* technology indicates the trend towards the *networked corporation*. Office information technology, therefore, appears to experience a "new" take-off in the early 1990s, offering a wide range of new functions and *access* products for users, rather than possibilities to increase their internal office productivity through rationalization.

The *automated factory* illustrates a parallel development. It represents the ultimate engineering idea of a computer application; the one-to-one representation on code of a real production process. It has so far only been realized in practice in partial applications, like local machine stations, inventory control, accounts receivable, quarterly consolidation of accounts etc. What we currently see developing is not so much successful rationalization efforts with large productivity effects, but *new decentralized ways of organizing product development and production simultaneously* and the capacity to achieve low cost, small batch product quality variation in large-scale industrial production. So called *integrated production* (see Eliasson 1994d) involves the systems competence to coordinate specialized engineering consultants and subcontractors through the market. This systems competence makes it possible to develop and produce very complex products like large aeroplanes requiring a broad and very diverse spectrum of specialties, with great reliability, bypassing costly testing and avoiding mistakes and bad product designs. Business information systems development first mistakenly followed the engineering-based rationalization idea. The business information systems product now being developed is not shaped on the idea of factory automation but designed to support, through easy access to people and data, complex team work at all levels in firms.

In the beginning, technological advance in hardware equipment generated product development. Hardware is still setting the outer limits on business information processing, but other limits make themselves felt before. Since the mid-1980s, with large-scale and growing computer power on the desk and fast computer networks with high capacity in place, *software development* is setting the pace, driving business information systems development in a direction where its potential can be effectively used; its *access* features.

The *unintelligent terminal* of the late 1960s was the first step in the direction of *networks*. Its first use was to punch in locally distributed data for central computing and then to retrieve the result. Central processing units grew up around the world being the highlights of the computer system by the mid-1970s. They began to be linked up (communications). Terminals gradually acquired some intelligence and central storage (disks, tape) and databases began to be organized. Table VI.6 (or the more detailed Chronicle) illustrates the gradual spread of hardware applications away from the *central processing unit*. Specialized applications programs (software) for central processing accessed through terminals dominated the scene as late as the early 1980s.

Two "technological" innovations made for a decisive change in the direction of an *information system*; the emergence in 1977 of the first commercially distributed *personal computer* of Apple and the development of *computer networks*. These technological advances were conceptual/organizational rather than "technological", although a number of technical innovations paved the way for their introduction, notably the *microprocessor* of Intel, first introduced in 1971.

The engineering approach to computerized problem solving was, however, still in focus well into the 1980s. *Distributed processing* was originally used to rationalize database consolidation to exploit the (still limited) central computing capacity. Small applications were concentrated to the local data bases and local computer capacity, while heavy computer applications were moved to the central processing unit.

Distributed processing and the PC, however, opened up database network facilities and the local computer intelligence needed for a revolutionary redesign of the organization of economic information (organizational) processing in the entire firm and the advent of a new business information technology. Powerful workstations have moved processing away from the central mainframe to the desk. High capacity and fast networks make it possible to retrieve and focus the data to the local station where they are needed. The central mainframe may, however, experience a comeback. IBM has long argued that it will be used as a server and organizer of the entire network. Standardization of operating systems and networking protocols allowing for open systems networking (OSN) that can accommodate many different computers have been slow in coming but are gradually emerging. Even IBM joined the "Unix revolution" during the 1980s.

The potential of the merging of computers, networks and sophisticated software was, however, not released until (1) a fair amount of *standardization* had been achieved to ensure compatibility of networks and computers, and portable software designs, and (2) the telecommunications market in the U.S. had been deregulated in the early 1980s. The ability to impose a *standard* offers the benefits of economies of scale. The IBM PC operating system (MS DOS) offered large economies of scale to IBM production units. Software producers gained economies of scale from writing programs in the IBM standard which in turn benefited IBM volume. However, IBM clones also benefited from the automatic compatibility with all IBM components and software, which eventually meant increased competition for IBM. Many argued that IBM prepared for its own "collapse" in the 1990s by introducing a PC standard (see Chronicle). The dominance of GM in the U.S. engineering subcontracting market and GM's ability to impose the MAPS standard (see Chronicle) on component manufacturers offered the same economies of scale to GM and large parts of U.S. engineering industry. We can talk of a privately created infrastructure, a collective good induced by the profit motive. In fact IBM for some time during the 1980s appeared to make the creation of "standards" part of its business strategy.

At first sight, this dominance in, or rather control of market information processing achieved through the creation of a standard, could be seen as an instance of Schumpeter's 1942 prediction of ever increasing market concentration. The standard would be the platform from which one company took forever control of the market. Neither Schumpeter nor anybody after him, however, studied the phenomenon of scale and concentration in the context of the experimentally organized market environment. Their analytical setting was the narrow state space of the classical model. In the classical model, as we all know, a superior technology, will create the Schumpeter (1942) concentration effect. The winner of the R&D innovation race will achieve monopoly status. The scale, or competence or monopoly rents observed so far, however, have all been temporary, as would be expected in the experimentally organized economy. Information technology in particular offers almost unlimited alternative solutions which soon, through competition, reduce the value of the first, innovative solution. Not even the dominant PC operating system standard of IBM-Microsoft (MS/DOS) was "safe" for more than a few years. New solutions exhibit new and superior capacity capable of handling new, high-performing hardware, and alternative solutions [like the Unix system and perhaps the competing OS/2 (IBM) and Windows 95 (Microsoft) systems in the mid-1990s].

The largest boost to innovative activity was, however, released by the *deregulation of the U.S. telecommunications industry*, allowing computing and telecommunication companies to confront each other in the same market. The enormous potential released from this combined merging and standardization of technologies has in turn released an enormous entrepreneurial activity in the U.S. information industry. Small innovative firms have put the giants under competitive pressure, forcing a break-up of IBM, and creating a number of large firms in a short period of time. The Japanese entry in the information market through hardware technology has been stalled. The PC revolution created by IBM's standardization of the market and the deregulation of the U.S. tele-communications industry started it all.

Networking technology, standardization of computer languages and software technology are setting the pace. The core hardware technology moving this "software" technology has been the PC.

Integrating the computer and the network

Currently the thrust of development is towards corporate processing or the *integration of the computer and the network*, a development that will blur the whole taxonomy of information business. It will put increased pressure on the established firms to acquire the technologies they lack, as witnessed by IBM and AT&T, entering the market from their respective technological ends. *Compaq* and *Sun* are entering through *open systems networking* by way of their workstations. *Tandem* is entering the mainframe and network market through its fault tolerant dual system and so on. But the technology is extremely difficult. IBM has not succeeded in acquiring the needed switching and networking technology. And even if technology and designs are moving its way AT&T has not found itself capable of doing it alone in the technology area where it appears on the surface to be the expert firm. It acquired NCR through an almost hostile takeover in 1990 to move fast into the integrated computing and networking technology.

This road, however, has been strewn with $ Billion failures, as the giant electronics companies of the world have unloaded their ambitions in the field, beginning with all major electronics companies in Europe and in the U.S. in the 1980s. Currently only a handful U.S. firms remains in the race, many of them new start-ups from the 1980s, while Japanese potentials wait along the roadside to watch the development of a product that is still not conceptually ready.

The reason for failure has been the *lack of understanding* of the information requirements at all levels in the large corporation (i.e. the user contacts in Table VI.6), the *underestimation of the effort* needed to understand and centralize all detailed process knowledge (item 1 in Table VI.6) and the *enormous investments* in new technology needed to bring the many elements of the new product together into a whole.

The staffing of design and product development departments with engineers is probably a major reason for the early failures. Product developers had no or little experience of the economic management of a firm. The two groups of people normally do not communicate within firms. The engineering know-how of a firm, in addition, is usually based in a technology of the past. It is sometimes argued that IBM's mind is shaped in mainframe thinking, which will make it difficult, perhaps impossible for the giant firm to adapt to the new distributed, computing technology (*The Economist*, 1991, Dec. 14-20, pp. 67 f).

There are three different clusters of technology to consider:

(a) How to design the information product to meet the demands of management in the experimentally organizational economy.
(b) How to merge the large number of very *different technologies* needed to design that product.
(c) How to cope with lacking *receiver competence* among users.

I will go through these aspects in turn.

How Should a Business Information System Designed for the Experimentally Organized Economy Look?

The purpose of a business information systems product designed for the experimentally organized economy is not to substitute for top management in the formulation of business strategies and decisions, using sharp analytical methods but to
a) help *people work* more efficiently *together* and *access information* (data) more efficiently, and

b) to effectively *identify* and *support the correction of business mistakes* (see Chapter III, Table III.1) and to facilitate the coordination of activities within the firm.

To make the firm statistically transparent in terms of its business objectives (targets) is one desired property. The second desired property is efficient support in coordinating people. These two tasks are principally different but can be integrated within the same information system to the extent that the information system can handle *access to data* as well as *access to people*. It is interesting to observe that the early business information systems approaches, emphasizing *access* to people features were designed as communication devices around a PBX.

The early focus of business information systems, however, was on analytical uses and the mechanical processing of quantitative information, or on items 1 through 3 in Table VI.4. This more or less meant doing the same thing as before. The integrated information system, on the other hand, allows production not only to be organized differently but also makes the true business information and control functions of the experimentally organized economy more efficient, namely (see items 4 through 8 in Tables VI.4 and III.1) to support business intuition, and to identify and correct mistakes. This is not a matter of analysis, but of organizing people with different competence characteristics into efficient teams (Eliasson 1990b). Access to people and information then become the critical capacities of the business information system, not analysis. The new developments, hence, originated in two different technological cultures; computing and telecommunications. Since a decade and a half these technologies have been gradually merging, and this technological merge, which would not have been possible in the regulated U.S. telecommunications environment of the late 1970s has opened up a new technological agenda. Had deregulation not occurred in the early 1980s, U.S. information industry, therefore, probably would have looked very different today; very obsolete by today's standards and dominated by Japanese firms. Deregulation of U.S. telecommunications industry, therefore, probably saved U.S. information industry from Japanese competition by simply taking off the bureaucratic shackles. It is interesting to speculate about what will happen to European IT industry, notably French IT industry, which is still pinned down by regulation and government "support".

I will first discuss the access features of the information product. I will then, based on Table VI.6, discuss the product design problems associated with merging a large number of totally different technologies in one product design. Finally, I will address the problem of user or receiver competence. One side of this fascinating story is the early misspecification of the product because designers did not understand what the potential users were doing. Another, equally intriguing business problem is the intellectual capacity of users to learn how to use a new product, designed to support their problem solving (receiver competence).

The Access Feature

In the experimentally organized economy, the focus is on problem solving in a decentralized organization through teams and people with diverse competences, not through analytical problem solving. Hence, the access features; access to people and access to communicable information become critical desired features of viable information systems. Networking and portability (open systems and standardization) are key technologies.

Access to and scheduling of people

The demand for access and scheduling features of business information systems is illustrated by the enormous success of fax technology and mobile telephones.

The fax machine made early, rapid inroads on the telex market (Siemens' original territory) due to easy use. The spread of its use boosted economies of scale of the system. In a larger context, however, the fax machine gradually disrupted a whole set of related communications services;

- meetings
- messenger boys
- mail
- telegrams
- telephone
- teleconferences
- telex
- electronic mail
- data communication.

There is a substitution effect due to lower costs and easy handling, but the fax machine also opened up new communication possibilities that were before difficult and costly.

This development, of course, was guided by the type of communication demanded. With a few exceptions the fax executes the telex, telegram, messenger boy and (also) mail services faster, more reliably and more cheaply. Fax messages are often in preparation of later, faster, telephone communication or meetings. Hence, the fax technology will easily be integrated with voice, graphics and data networks that are being installed, serving complementary support functions. And it adds, and will continue to add, new features such as automatic electronic storage and copying capacity, and also (through improved scanning and word interpretation capacity) editing capacity, moving the received messages on to the word processing and electronic mail configurations. The scanner and text interpretation has already created an interface between the fax and word processing. But new competing technologies are already in use. Electronic mail, based on enhanced data communication network capacity, albeit somewhat more demanding to use, offers new intriguing features, that are more naturally integrated with local, multimedia-based IT installations.

We could go through a similar survey for mobile telephones, that have been spreading as rapidly as the fax machine. Again, also the advantage of the mobile telephone is access, this time notably to people, but networked, wireless computing is already being introduced for sophisticated users, and the current orientation of telecommunications is towards merging data, voice and video communications with an increasing share of the total message volume being carried over wireless networks. The technological potential of this particular market is large enough to make it virtually impossible to predict in a meaningful way how it will look only a decade from now. Development will proceed through a large number of experiments that will be sorted out through competition in the market.

Access to information – database and networking technology

Besides networking and portability, database technology is the critical feature in developing the access dimension. Access to information (data) is part of the "office of the future" idea. The problem, however, was that office rationalization and the development of new, sophisticated internal service products mixed up from the beginning.

Mobile telephones facilitate access to people. The fax does the same, but it also makes it possible to transport reasonable volumes of data fairly conveniently. The fax requires, however, a sender. The ultimate data access feature is when you can tap into your own files from any place, without support. This is already possible through computer networks that have been organized to make this possible. It is also possible to access public files through terminals. The French *Minitel* is an example. Field representatives of large firms can already enter inventory files far away, and service engineers can look into production systems from a distance to locate errors, and so on.

This is possible because the systems have been set up to make this possible, but the possibilities are so far specialized. Technology offers considerably more potential when the necessary communications compatibility has been established. The problem is that such facilities are more demanding on the user than the fax and the mobile telephone.

Receiver Competence

What has been said so far emphasizes the importance in business of human *receiver competence*. Receiver competence ultimately determines the ability of the user to successfully introduce new (information) technology. The importance of receiver competence has habitually been underestimated, and slowed the introduction of new information technology compared to optimistic engineering forecasts. This was, and is so in factory automation, office automation, distributed processing, distributed database management and so on. Even though literature and expert reports breathe a vague awareness of the importance of receiver competence, this issue has rarely been subject to special inquiry, nor has the concept of receiver competence been addressed directly (see Chronicle). It is difficult.

The information system of a firm has the characteristics of a language; in our case the problem is the learning of a new language and to use it in the particular organizational context of a firm. This learning has to take place, the right organizational mode has to be found and the properties of the entire system have to be understood for the business problems to be solved. The learning is particularly troublesome because it has to be achieved in two dimensions. *First*, hundreds of new techniques have to be expertly understood and operated at different places by experts. *Second*, also a universal understanding of the integrated technology has to be achieved, at least in some places, for the entire system to work. This is no minor task, and it poses problems in two ways.

First; "installations" of new, normally very incomplete systems have failed. *Second*; feedbacks to the developer and producer of the information systems have not worked.

Making Users of the Business Information System Hostages of the Systems Developer's Knowledge

Access to the know-how to use the information system is normally solved through embodying as much of the know-how as possible in the equipment and the software, reducing the competence demands on the user. As a consequence "access to the PC" for a long time was limited to specialists, or those with the time to learn, and with the time to maintain their know-how. Furthermore, the *easy access* features of the system (to people/to data) that I have emphasized repeatedly took a long time to develop. Thus the PC has not yet really made it to the CEO's office and the Boardroom, except by way of assistants (cf. Pinella's (1991) discussion of a particular LAN-based executive information system). As software of the right kind and familiarity from school is increasing through the new generations, the situation is, however, rapidly changing. The fax machine, on the other hand, spread immediately, because it needed almost no prior learning to use.

This little summary pinpoints the intersection between the appropriately designed general information system of a business organization and the kind of "product" on which the advanced industries of the West can make sustainable profits. It is not through selling ready-to-use products in large numbers off the shelf. It will be done through downstream *integration of hardware and software developments*, moving the product specification into the user's production system.

The product I see coming, however, is going to be extremely demanding on *receiver competence*. It has to be, since it is going to involve the entire corporate production system, and *embody, in relevant form* a lot of information of that system. It is going to be tailor designed to suit the user around a standard language. Hence, the introduction of that information product is going to involve -- reluctantly on the part of the user -- the transfer of significant tacit "team knowledge" of the user to the producer, and also a very large "amount of systems know-how" from the producer to the user. The latter is obvious, or at least becoming obvious. The producer of a business information system that wants to succeed has to shift his focus from hardware to downstream software production and on to consulting and knowledge transfer. This is at least where the profits will be generated and where customers can be integrated with the particular knowledge base of the systems designer. You teach them your language, which is no small thing if you have a good product, and they become hostages of your system. In one sense this "hostage" arrangement goes much deeper than the earlier dependency on supplier hardware. It involves the intellectual dimensions of the firm. Several firms *in this market* have long understood this possibility and been pushing in this direction. IBM has a long tradition from the hardware side of this kind of customer relations. Since the 1980s IBM has been attempting to reorganize its position in the business information systems market in the downstream software and information services direction. To what extent it will succeed remains to be seen.

Revealing Proprietary User Knowledge to the Information Systems Supplier

The *user knowledge* that has to be "embodied" in the information system is partly proprietary. It is largely tacit, meaning that firm management itself will have to be involved in the transfer to a new *corporate language*. Management will not happily share its knowledge with the producer's systems people. Hence, the solution of successful systems, so far has been that the user itself has acquired the systems competence and both designed, built and "installed" it. This is all right for the very large firms, that I have interviewed, and especially, of course, for the large electronics and computer firms that are themselves in this market. This very fact, coupled with the initial absence of inhouse systems knowledge and the reluctance of top level management both to learn the new system and to allow proprietary knowledge to be diffused through the system, has slowed the introduction process.

For the large firm, this is part of the general problem of remaining productive and competitive. If competitors in general raise their performance through the introduction of new information systems, they also have to learn the new technique. Small and medium-sized firms, on the other hand, cannot support the required inhouse knowledge themselves. They have to buy a "turn-key" product, which is, as I have argued, not the right approach, since we are dealing with a *generic, intellectual support system of the entire firm*, not with a separate production activity. For the medium-sized firm that wants to grow big, this system is also exactly what it needs. The management of small firms generally do not have the organizational knowledge of big business needed to coordinate all its disparate activities. The business information system, on the other hand -- if appropriately designed -- should come with some of that organizational competence embodied.

VI.8   SUMMARY CONCLUSIONS ABOUT THE NEW INFORMATION PRODUCT

Scheduling of people and information access, not analysis, define the properties of the integrated business information system. This means that we are not looking for an engineering design, but for a software organization design that captures the needs of executive people and teams of people having to be in contact from different locations and needing access to information of choice specification at any moment in time.

This is what I expect will happen. A number of engineering and software design features have to be ready before this integrated product can be put together. I don't think the same company will develop all elements of this system and also launch the integrated information product. The technologies are so disparate, referring, on the one hand, to business representation and database design and user interfacing, on the other. When the right hardware and software configurations are ready, possibly at different locations, I can see a complete outsider, a consulting or software firm, putting the bits and pieces together into a successful whole, probably a system customized for each firm.

In the first round (a few years back) many companies in the field thought -- very logically but too simplistically -- that advanced networking and switching know-how would be the entrance technology to the new product. Networking know-how at the time came out of two sources; (1) telecommunications firms like AT&T, ITT, Ericsson, Northern Telecom etc., and (2) computer manufactures that individually or in teams had developed computer networks [Ethernet (Xerox, DEC etc) or Token Ring (IBM)].

As I have already demonstrated this "analogy" was far too simplistic. The advanced computer networking technology now emerging is something very different from the old (even) digitally based telecommunications technology. The trend towards digitally based joint voice, word and data communication networks wiring workplaces together and demanding heavy minimum data carrying capacity means that telecommunications firms to survive in their fields have to acquire computer know-how, not the other way around. Digital data communication and switching is a different communications technology that the telecommunications firms are currently rushing to learn. The parallel product development called multimedia, including interactive TV that in the first round caters for the consumer market, is emphasizing this trend, and will soon appear in business applications. The experience so far has been that telecommunications firms have failed in acquiring the needed computer technology and computer firms have failed in acquiring the needed telecommunications technology.

The push towards organizational processing in which the network becomes the computer is blurring the two technology fields. Both technologies have to merge (the Chronicle contains an account of what the players are currently doing). The interesting question to ask is whether big players like IBM and AT&T, with large resources will do it, or whether it will be an innovative outsider with the right idea.

NOTES

1.   It is interesting to speculate whether developments in access products, like groupware, will make it possible to disperse also knowledge-intensive and creative service production.

2.   A first causality was the Bretton Woods system of fixed parities in the early 1970s. The possibilities of enforcing exchange controls have been gradually eliminated in almost all countries, in fact reducing the capacity of the nation to carry out autonomous economic policies, thus changing the nature of the world economy.

The refusal to remove, for a long time, exchange controls in Sweden appears to have imposed a significant cost on the nation in the form of a higher interest rate, but with no more monetary autonomy in return (Oxelheim 1988).

3.   On the early history of IBM, see Sobel (1984) and Fisher, McKie and Mancke (1983).

4.   who is also the father of the still dominant internal sequential architecture of computers.

5.   These incompatibility problems and product line fragmentation are mostly to be blamed on IBM's historical mainframe, hardware orientation (Moad 1988a, p. 67). IBM still has difficulties reaching out of its mainframe culture.

6.   *Haloid*, founded in 1906, buys Chester Carlson's xerographic patents in 1947, launches the first commercial plain paper copier in 1959, and changes its name to *Xerox* in 1961.

7.   Note that IBM entered copying on the same idea in 1970 and produced copying machines for more than 15 years before selling the unit to Kodak in 1987, citing production cost reasons.

8.   See *BW*, June 30, 1986, p. 7 and *BW*, June 22, 1987, pp. 62-64. Also see Jacobson and Hillkirk (1986).

9.   Note that *Kodak* is refocusing in the same direction under George Fisher, the new CEO hired from *Motorola* (*BW*, Feb. 13, 1995, pp. 40-45).

10.   See Smith and Alexander (1988).

11.   Before that a *relay* calculator called BARK had been built.

12.   Saab needed a computer and bought the design and built a copy in 1955 called SARA (Saab Automatisk Räkne Apparat). The University of Lund built a copy in 1956 called SMIL (Siffer Maskiner i Lund). The Academy of Engineering Sciences in Denmark built another copy in 1958 called DASK (Danish Arithmetic Sequence Calculator). BESK stands for Binary Electronic Sequence Calculator.

13.   About 1960 Facit got a defence order for computers to the Swedish battle management system and the Besk design was used. But these computers were never commercialized.

14.   Ericsson, after having failed in the business information systems market (see below) passed Facit on to the Norwegian *Entranor* group in 1988. After years of losses Swedish *Nordbanken* took over and placed it in the *Securum Industry Holding* of crisis companies, from which Mats Gabrielson of (earlier) *Datatronic* and *Victor* picked it up in 1994 (see *Affärsvärlden*, Feb. 2, No. 5/94, p. 18) mainly to use the Facit trademark to sell peripherals and office equipment.

15.   See *Computer Sweden*, Jan. 8, 1993.

16.   See for instance Vedin (1992).

17.   A repeat, so to speak, of the *Facit* failure, which brought down *Original Odhner* as well as *Addo* and the whole Swedish calculator industry.

18.   Programator, Data Logic, Enator, Finansrutiner, IDK-Data, Mods, Modul, Turn-key, Kontorsutveckling - see *Svenska Dagbladet*, Sep. 9, 1984 (Näringsliv) and *Affärsvärlden*, No. 38, Sept. 20, 1989, No. 38, Sep. 22, 1993 and No. 38, Sep. 21, 1994. See also *MikroDatorn*, No. 15, 1993, which includes an overview of the Swedish computer industry.

19.   See *Affärsvärlden*, Feb. 8, 1995 (No. 6), pp. 32 ff. Also see *Affärsvärlden*, March 22 (No. 12) 1995, pp. 120 f).

20.   A profitable business that was sold to Dun & Bradstreet during the ownership crisis of the early 1990s.

21.   Even though this did not prevent Philip's top management from experiencing a gigantic loss-surprise in 1990 (see Chronicle). For references to the system, see Cattela (1981) and Weezenberg (1981).

PART III

A CHRONICLE OF EVENTS THAT MARK THE EXPERIMENTAL EVOLUTION OF A NEW INFORMATION PRODUCT

VII

SYSTEMS COMPONENTS AND THE NEW INFORMATION PRODUCT DEFINED

Introduction

The Chronicle to follow on diskette, but to be presented and discussed briefly in this chapter, demonstrates the experimental nature of innovative product markets, and most notably the development of the new product that I have called the *Universal* or total *Business Information System* (UBIS). Even though I have frequently called this a new information product, it neither exists, nor has its design been presented. What the market has witnessed over the past decade or so is a steady flow of ambitious and optimistic attempts to offer bits and pieces of a whole that may eventually materialize as a definable entity. In this book I have tried to define the characteristics of such a product from an analysis of the *informational requirements* of a firm operating in an experimentally organized market environment (Chapters I through III), a study of business practice (Chapter IV) and an assessment of what information technology offers and will offer (Chapter V). The final, concluding part (in Chapters VI and VII and this Chronicle) is to compare this "synthetic product design" with actual offerings in the market over a couple of decades. Is the UBIS a possible real thing or an intellectual illusion?

The Chronicle is based on a fairly complete listing of "clippings" from business and information industry journals, from 1975 up to the present. It was closed around mid-1995. The prime selection criterion has been to track the origin of all technologies that eventually have gone into this product as defined today. As it happened -- and not entirely expected from the outset -- the Chronicle appears as a brief history of the development of the modern information (IT) and telecommunications industries and the merge of the two technologies from the mid-1980s and on. This is so, even though I have not expanded on other product lines than those that eventually have gone into general business information applications.

The selection criterion has been to choose those events that led up to today's situation and trends in business information systems development. There are five problems associated with this selection. *First*, what we see today may not reveal the trends of the future. Development of product technology may currently be heading the wrong way, to be corrected later; a sequence of events that is, in fact, typical of the *experimentally organized economy*, discussed in Chapter II. If development again radically changes direction, the particular "path" this Chronicle has followed will become outdated and uninteresting. This has happened before, as my Chronicle shows. This time, the risk of misunderstanding the direction of development is, however, small. I venture to say that business information systems development is finally taking shape after a large number of mistaken starts. And the main reason for such a strong statement is that the product developers in the IT and communications industries are finally beginning to learn what business management demands of a viable information product. This Chronicle, nevertheless, shows the impossibility of analytically deriving the future from information registered in the past. Development has been truly experimental and the road littered with failed business attempts. This will be even more clearly demonstrated if my assertion that "now we know" turns out to be wrong. The picture presented in the Chronicle is probably correct as a whole, but it also exhibits and illustrates some of the large number of false starts and unforeseen details. The Chronicle ends very dramatically, and typically of the experimentally organized economy with the distress, and complete reorganization of IBM.

Second, the early simplistic target of some firms in the market to develop a complete, unified product or system has fragmented into a spectrum of specialized and sometimes very successful products and markets. To cover all of these in this Chronicle has been impossible, and any choice will be somewhat arbitrary. It is, however, important to recognize that the coverage of new features, technologies or products has to keep increasing, since new producers of systems later tend to integrate these parts as standard features.

Third, the original ambition to get into the *mind of the firm* -- my interest -- is still very much alive, even though the product developers are finally understanding that *the brain of the business firm is its people, not its information system*. This reorientation of understanding has been made visible in the Chronicle, as it shifts attention from hardware equipment for analysis to software intensive communications equipment designed to provide *access to people and information*, and to help coordinate people, and to serve them in flexible ways.

Fourth, and perhaps most important, what I have had problems with -- in this brief summary Chronicle -- is to illustrate the large number of *failed attempts; the real costs for innovation in the experimentally organized economy*. The Chronicle simply gets too large if they are all to be documented.

Fifth, and somewhat technical, *the taxonomy of the Chronicle (in Table VII.1) has been designed to tell the story of the evolution of the UBIS product, not its current definition*. Some technologies that were long kept separate through regulation, notably computer networks and telecommunications, have merged during the course of the Chronicle. This is an important part of my story which, however, makes the taxonomy less efficient for somebody who only wants a quick overview of the UBIS product as it looks today. Since the current state of development is still in a flux, I think, however, that to understand the current situation you have to be quite familiar with the technological history of the last two decades. Besides that, the taxonomy that looks obvious and efficient today was in nobody's mind when I began to work with the Chronicle. Whatever, since the Chronicle is presented on a diskette, anybody can reorganize the clippings to suit his or her mind.

In selecting items for the Chronicle the ambition has been not only to trace the development path but also to illustrate the enormous range of technologies and knowhow needed to make it in the business information systems market. There is a particularly tricky selection problem here. *Corporate computing* involves much more than the technologies needed for the business information system. But it touches on most categories in the table below, before it settles as described in earlier chapters. Therefore, a selection of related events from the whole range of computers and information technologies has been entered. From that range the business information system emerges out of the PC communications and software revolutions. However, a whole range of related items in corporate computing also falls into the specialties and applications listed at the end. Office automation and factory automation, or rather Computer Integrated Manufacturing (CIM), small business information products and financial products. Unfortunately, sheer volume in combination with late awareness has made it impossible to come even close to listing all critical events under these headings, with the exception of *office automation* and *office information* systems, which for some time was considered almost synonymous with the *business information* system.

The Chronicle, finally, has a strong American bias. This is fair. Practically all technology supporting the postwar information and communications revolution was invented, developed and brought to industrial volume production in the U.S. Japanese firms have imitated and learnt and improved upon U.S. information technology, being successful in their specialties; large-volume hardware manufacturing. European firms are not only laggards and imitators, there are few surviving successes to report on the computer side, despite heavy subsidies in some countries. On the telecommunications side the picture looks a bit brighter in some European countries, but the current merging of computer and communications technologies is forcing European telecommunications firms to rapidly learn computing and digital data communication, so the survival capacity of many of the old European telecommunications firms can be questioned, at least when confronted with the best players in the world in open markets. I have taken the liberty to overrepresent Sweden somewhat in the Chronicle. Sweden is an interesting case. It was technologically and industrially early in both fields, failed completely in computing but currently sports one of the most successful telecommunications companies in the world, but in a market challenged by an accelerated turnover of technologies.

Sources of the Chronicle

In addition to interviews my main sources of systematic information gathering and in organizing this presentation of the "information product" has been *Datamation* and *Business Week* (referred to as *BW*). *Datamation* captures the information problems early, as they are understood by users of information products in firms and by vendors of products. Normally, only products already in the market, or about to be launched are presented and discussed from a technical user point of view. *Business Week* captures the corresponding problem as the products are reaching a commercial (market) awareness among business journalists. As a rule this is late, only after new products have been in their development stage for years. I have also used the Swedish *Teldok publications* systematically to get an overview of what has been happening in some specialized fields. This documentation has been complemented with interviews of both producers and users of business information systems. Interviewed firms are listed at the end of the book.

The real market awareness of the problem, however, is rarely reported, except when a crisis has hit a firm or a product, or when an executive becomes philosophical about the future. The task I have taken on has been to put together a puzzle from a set of very incomplete pieces.

This Chronicle of events tells the story of the experimental evolution of the new information product, with many attempts, most of them failed ones, and an eventual evolution of a useful concept. There is also the partial story of the enormous synergistic potential associated with a generic technology like "electronics" or "information technology".

A typical comment has been that only a few big companies, perhaps only Governments can make it in the future information market, and that only big companies can mount a real challenge to IBM. Such assessments, voiced frequently, for instance, in *Business Week* were based on interviews with "the experts". As Japanese manufacturers learned to compete in the semiconductor markets, concerns voiced by these experts shifted from assertions that the U.S. producers would be able stay ahead through increased R&D spending to concerns about the Japanese challenge. Then all of a sudden *Intel* surged ahead, and deregulation of the telecommunications market changed the core technology of both computing and communications and successful innovative initiatives were taken by new and small firms that rapidly grew to become big challengers. What "killed IBM" was not the Japanese but innovative and very competitive entry in U.S. markets.

Classification of Technologies

I have organized the presentation around a taxonomy of elements (see Table VII.1) that together constitute both the universal business information system, as it has been conceived by some, and the actual UBIS as it is still evolving. The various elements have been grouped under five broad headings (*Representation of the Business, Analysis* (computing), *Communication, User Contacts and Applications*), five groups of information activities that will all be more or less represented in such an information product. From this evolutionary story one can observe the early obsession with *hardware* (under B, Analysis, Data Processing) that gave way to a *software* awareness (Section 8 in the Chronicle) by the end of the 1970s. The computer architectures of these days were based on centralized data storage and processing with proprietary operating systems and terminal/mainframe interfaces. These systems architectures are now "aging" and impede adaptation at the user end, or among old producers of new solutions and features. Large, previously successful firms appear to be hindered by their existing technology (read staff of experts) in adapting to entirely new technologies. This is so even though these now large firms often understood what should be done, but were unable to execute their objectives. Internal administrative resistance or simply lack of *receiver competence* are frequently quoted reasons. Technological *locking-in* effects are therefore typical of technological development. With some notable exceptions, which may be accidental (see below), this means that the *new products* and *technologies* appear to be *developed in, and implemented by, new firms*. Several very small startup firms have grown rapidly to become very large firms in a few years. Small size and financing appear not to have prevented them from becoming major, industrial scale producers in a decade or so. It is interesting to note, however, that *new technologies introduced* are often *based on previous research in the laboratories of large companies, not so much (!!) in Government sponsored or university-related laboratories* (Eliasson 1994d). This means that *large*, established firms have often served as private *infrastructure providers*, through their R&D, a service that they were unable themselves to exploit fully and commercially, or through training people who later left to set up their own innovative businesses.

**Table VII.1   The Content of the Business Information System
                -- a Classification of Technologies**

A   REPRESENTATION OF THE BUSINESS

    1.   Process knowledge
    2.   Taxonomy
        - The Organization of information and of the business
    3.   Database

B   ANALYSIS, DATA PROCESSING

    4.   Language, standards
    4a   General
    4b   Operating systems
    4c   Higher level languages
    4d   Standardization
    5.   Computers and hardware
    5a   Computers, general
    5b   Supercomputers
    5c   Mainframes
    5d   Mini/Micro computers
    5e   Powerful workstations
    5f   The Personal computer (PC)
    5g   Portable and Lap Top PCs
    5h   Notebook or pocket computers
    5i   PBXes
    5j   Sophisticated components incl. terminals and storage technology
    5k   Accessories and peripherals

C   COMMUNICATIONS

    6.   Networking
    6a   Networking, communication, general
    6b   Compatibility, standards
    6c   Systems integration
    6d   Intelligent networks/The network as a computer/organizational
        computing/distributed computing
    6e   Local Area Networks (LAN)
    6f   OLTP (On-Line Transaction Power)
    6g   OSN (Open Systems Network)
    6h   Electronic Data Interchange (EDI)

6i   Integrated Services Digital Network - ISDN
6j   Cooperative processing
7.   Switching & Telecommunications
7a   Switching
7b   Telecommunications

D   USER CONTACTS

8.   Software
8a   Software in general
8b   Technology of developing new software (Case)
8c   Integration of hardware and software (computer firms integrate downstream into software)
9.   Man Machine Interaction
9a   General
9b   Receiver competence
9c   Presentation/graphics/electronic publishing/imaging/virtual reality/visualization etc.
9d   Access incl. executive informations systems
9e   Software that organizes people (Groupware)
9f   Artificial intelligence
9g   The portable executive
9h   Computer services (Users contract out their computer systems)
9i   Education
9j   Information and computer management
9k   Systems integration with customer uses
9ℓ   Multimedia

E   APPLICATIONS

10.   Process Knowledge
10a   General
10b   Office automation and office information systems
10c   Factory automation (CAE, FMS, CIM etc. incl. CAD)
10d   Financial products
10e   Specialized corporate products (not functions)
10f   Small businesses

From Hardware, via Software to Netware and the Lap Top

The deregulation of the U.S. telecommunications market appears to have been an extreme stimulus to innovative activity in the IT markets, that has unleashed a wave of new technological innovations and new startups. This probably saved the U.S. information industry from the Japanese onslaught in the 1980's. The Chronicle shows the potential for new product technology development in the intersection between computing and telecommunications to have been enormous.

A typical development, however, appears to have been that a new, innovative product has been launched by a U.S. firm, only soon thereafter to be copied in a Japanese firm and sometimes moved very successfully there to large-scale volume production. In Europe, on the other hand, Government policies have played a much larger role, locking firms into the technological mode that Government bureaucrats happened to be familiar with. By the end of the 1970s and for a decade or so this happened to be a centralized mainframe and hardware mode, while, at the same time, U.S. information industry shifted downstream into software, and decentralized networked computing at PCs and workstations. This is why the Chronicle, when mentioning European progress, mostly reports on problems and industry voices calling for Government help.

The early limitations to hardware technology is reflected in the orientation of product development. Roughly speaking (Tesler 1991), *batch* technology dominated the 1960s, and *time sharing* the 1970s. The 1980s witnessed the PC and the *desktop* revolution, and the 1990s is generally heralded as the *networking* decade. This is probably so at a superficial inspection of developments. Software and the ingenuity of human intellectual capacity now set the limits of computing and define the range of applications available. But the evolution of the computer as a *network* or decentralized computing has hit the clippings of the Chronicle only very recently. Networked computing is the extremely complex organizational technology of computing, data communication, switching and telecommunications combined that all players, including IBM and AT&T have understood that they have to master, but that so far no one has developed or acquired. Some of the technologies related to high capacity digital transmission of voice, data and video combined are only recently beginning to become operational.

Deregulation Saved the U.S. IT Industry

Distributed processing (as distinct from unintelligent terminals) paved the way in the 1970s for an explosion in the 1980s in networking and communications, which was the first step towards gradually merging telecommunications with computing. The intersection between computing and telecommunications, as mentioned, appears to have been extremely fertile land for innovations, witness the explosion of innovative activity that occurred after lifting (in 1982) in the U.S. the enforced (through antitrust regulation) separation of the two fields. After having been limited for antitrust reasons to a particular technology and defined markets, AT&T was now allowed to enter computing and IBM to enter tele-communications. It is tempting to draw rather strong conclusions about misdirected policies. This innovative merge might have come about gradually long before, if there had been no restrictions. I would argue that the removal of the legally enforced market segmentation of computing and telecommunications saved the U.S. computer industry from destructive Japanese competition by releasing extremely active innovative behavior. This innovative behavior occurred, however, in new firms that based their ventures on research and development done, not in university laboratories, but in the large established firms like AT&T, HP, TI and *Xerox*. It is also, still, an open question in what shape the earlier giants will survive the enormous innovative technology shift they have been instrumental in creating.

The new systems architectures developing in the intersection between computing and communications technology are based on decentralized computing, presentation and database technology and applications portability, integrated data access and manipulation, and electronic data interchange (EDI). Graphical presentation and instrumentation are playing an increasingly important rôle, as multimedia technology is making the graphics format possible. The key concepts are *connectivity* and *organizational computing*.

The Core Technologies upon which Most UBIS's Attempts Have Been Based

While the overambitious search for an analytically based, universal information system went on in about 40 large firms through most of the 1980s (see Supplement 1 and Chronicle under 10b), a virtual explosion in special applications occurred, many of them based on the combined networking and computing capability that had been developed. These attempts -- as the Chronicle tells -- were organized around certain in-house technologies of the firms, notably (1) *computing*, (2) PBXes and/or *local networking* (LAN) technologies, (3) *electronic mail* systems, (4) *wordprocessing* or (5) *copying or document management*. The key words were "office automation", "office information systems", "the office of the future" or the "business information system". All these approaches attempted by some 40 firms just before and just after 1980 had a strong rationalization orientation. The early attempts to organize the business information system around computer-based copying and document technology (notably by *Xerox*) failed, but may be returning, as computing, networking and database technology are gradually merging into a separate, digitally based document management technology. Considering the nature of internal business information requirements and recent technology developments one may envision a sixth (6) clustering of attempts to develop a broad-based business information system around a *multimedia format* where graphics plays an important rôle. Multimedia in fact merges all the above technologies on a digital mode (computing, networking, storage), but adds a personal communications, graphics presentations and interactive format (video, voice, data). The rapid advance of a digitally based graphics technology has been instrumental in this development.

Firms having failed to develop a full-scale (universal) information product have gradually settled down for specialties. The total cost of failed attempts is large but probably reasonable if viewed as a cost for technological advance of an entire industry.

Enormous Technological Variety ....

The listing of categories (below) gives an inkling only, of the enormous differentiation of the whole information technology area, and the impossible task of developing inhouse (IBM has *not* succeeded) all the specialist technologies needed for a full-scale information product, whether (mistakenly) analytically oriented, or more useful and user oriented, as it is currently taking shape. What is now emerging as a comprehensive information systems product was totally impossible to predict or design ahead of time. The technologies integrated were too differentiated, complex or unknown and the use to which such a product might be put was misunderstood. The Chronicle tells a story about how some of the big, intellectually minded firms like IBM understood in principle and quite early where both technologies and markets were heading, but that they were unable to foresee some particular hurdles and, above all, to execute the necessary change of staff and reorientation of their organization necessary to exploit this understanding industrially. Instead new start-up firms or small firms may be doing it.

.... Turns Conventional Truths Upside Down

There is a tricky catch 22 situation. On the one hand, no firm may be capable of doing it all alone in the business information systems market. Enormous resources may be needed but the established, giant firms with large resources have their minds hung up on an old technology. On the other hand, solutions gradually appearing are based on the standardization and "commodization" of major parts of hardware and software, lowering the entry barrier and allowing small innovators with fresh minds to enter to design a UBIS product based on standardized subsystems designed and produced by other firms, an end product that requires the right idea, but not necessarily enormous resources to develop. This product, as it can be seen now was not feasible to develop until innovations had appeared that were "released" by the deregulation of the U.S. telecommunications market.

Figure VII.1   Early entrants into the business and office information markets

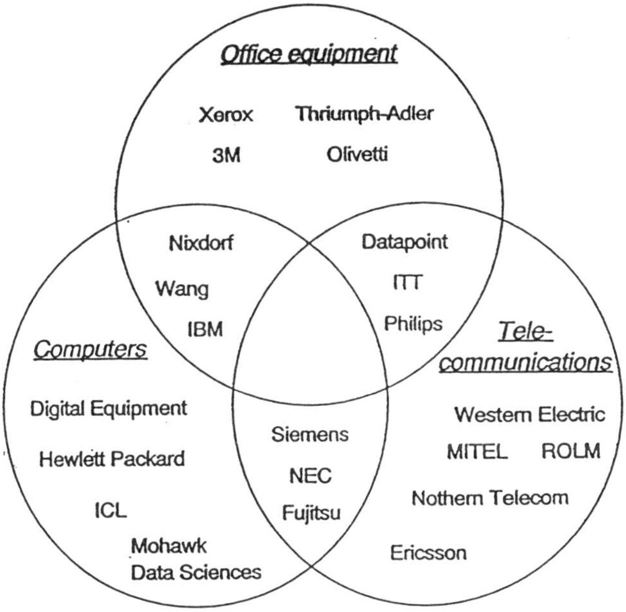

Note: Cf, Figure VI.1.

Technology Wars

A special, and very dramatic story is evolving within the hardware, processing field B (see classification in Table VII.1). Earlier, rather clear borderlines between different computer categories have been blurred. A big "war" has occurred in the area between mainframes and PCs. Mini and micro computer manufacturers that did not understand were washed out in the late 1980s (like *Wang, Nixdorf, Norsk Data, Prime,* etc.) and disappeared or specialized on more narrow products, like Prime on CAD technology and Wang on graphics. *Digital,* once the second largest computer maker in the world, has gone through several dramatic restructurings, and has shrunk enormously. It is still in a distressed situation (in 1995). The PC has been upgraded through the workstation (*Sun Micro Systems, Apollo,* HP and IBM). Many workstations, based on new microprocessors (*Risk* technology that is good at handling lots of information from several sources) and the *Unix* operating system have surpassed minicomputers in performance. The Unix operating system, furthermore, is designed for networking applications, but as the

Chronicle shows, strong windows applications are now hitting back. Workstation networks are currently threatening the mainframe business. HP has succeeded in changing from a minicomputer to a workstation maker. IBM has moved up into supercomputing and down into workstations, networking and Unix-based open systems. One of its ambitions has been to use its mainframe technology to drive the entire communications system. With mainframe capacity being moved via minis, workstations and PCs to your portable lap top the new obvious development will occur in networking and integrated computing, a software-based technology where the old hardware-based producers may find themselves at a disadvantage.

Standardization and "Commodization"

Standardization of the hardware field began already in the mid-1970s with the appearance of the microprocessor and fourth generation computers. By the mid-1980s "the computer was becoming a commodity". The earlier trend towards customized chips was halted and turned towards standardized off-the-shelf components. Advanced computer systems could be put together from standardized components (see *BW*, Dec. 1, 1986, pp. 72-78, *BW*, March 6, 1989, pp. 45-49).

Standardization of internal software (operating systems, networking protocols) from proprietary to open systems is currently changing the direction of development. The "Unix war" that was a gigantic, experimentally based development of a "language standard" for "open computing" illustrates this. It is also instructive to observe here that the case for one version of the open standard against another version is so complex that cooperation among firms doesn't seem to work. The solution is being slugged out in the market. The rift in the IBM/Microsoft relation over a new operating system design for PCs is another illustration. Microsoft went out alone with its very successful Windows (a version of "old" Apple technology), leaving IBM behind and delayed with its OS/2 system, originally to have been developed together with Microsoft. Microsoft was apparently attempting to integrate the entire software agenda of operating systems and applications packages (Database, Networks etc.; see Chronicle). But as its ambitions grew so did also the problems it had to take on. Many believe (when this manuscript is being finalized in June 1995) that the delay of Microsoft's new "Apple killer", the new version of Windows, Windows 95, also called "Chicago" will have given an opportunity for IBM's OS/2.

Technological Locking-In

Technological lock-in effects appear to be typical of development. Entire firms get their minds locked into a particular technology that it cannot get out of when a new and better technology is developed. Entire markets get stuck in particular technologies, established standards being the best example. Users learn particular technologies associated with particular firms, and have difficulties upgrading to improved systems offered by other vendors. As already observed these intellectual constraints on individuals, firms and markets make for fast business failure in innovative markets, and explain why new technology tends to be introduced through new business establishment, and phased out through exit, rather than being learned and adopted systematically by the existing large firms.

The Three Dominant Structural Changes

a) Integrating computing and communications
Three systematic structural changes can be observed. *First*, while large computer makers (like IBM) have been unable to acquire and successfully integrate telecommunications technology with computing, telecommunications vendors (like AT&T) have, in turn, not been successful in acquiring computer technology. The tendency towards *organizational computing* means *integrating* the two technologies. (The network is the computer), and a host of small, new and old competitors are appearing in the market. NCR has to some extent succeeded here, based on a strategy conceived already in 1983. Apparently NCR has learned what both IBM and AT&T have been striving to learn, to the extent that AT&T acquired NCR through a semi-hostile takeover in 1991. My interviews, however, indicate that fully integrated computing is still far off, since there is a lack of critical technologies, notably on the computing side, needed to coordinate computing on the network. Even though IBM has recently unloaded its costly mistaken experiment with *Rolm*, IBM still considers itself viable in the integrated computing and telecommunications market.

b) Standardization
Second, there is a large temporary rent to be captured from "imposing a *standard*" on the market. Earlier IBM was the only firm large enough to do this, but others, like *Microsoft*, now appear to be capable. IBM established a standard in the PC market, and has been trying to do it again in the networking field, while a group of companies, consisting of DEC, AT&T, NCR etc., beginning in the early 1980s, tried to beat IBM through joining forces in developing a new open standard, based on Unix, the Common Applications Environment (see *Datamation*, June 1, 1988, p. 60. Also see Chronicle).

c) Downstream user interface technology

A *third* interesting "evolution" -- or rather understanding -- is currently occurring in the *user interface area* (D in Table VII.1). There are two sides to it. First, a plethora of specialist applications are being steadily introduced. Second, with IBM moving the field, the large information companies are realizing that if you want to stay in the market as a big competitor, you have to refocus on the *deficient receiver competence* of large-scale information systems among users and the kind of business problems all these systems are to be used for. While hardware producers are in for a (continuing) slump, the *computer services* market has been booming, with EDS, competing with IBM, DEC and Anderson Consulting, being the dominant players. Two consequences can be observed already. Computer manufacturers tend to move through the technology of information processing *into information service business, consulting and the design, introduction and setting up of tailor made systems*. IBM has been trying to rapidly reorient itself in this direction since the late 1980s, but it meant a radical change in "its mind" of a magnitude that the (at the time) almost 400 thousand employee organization was incapable of. This, furthermore, meant building a bridge across the entire "analytical system" (Sections B and C in Table VII.1) to connect the "objects of manipulation" (the firm and its process representation, i.e. A) with the user (in D), essentially understanding what kind of user the system should be designed for. A first realization of this has been observed since the early 1980s, witnessing an explosion in database technology. However, the more general problem of how to *represent business problems* in the information system (A) is still more or less lacking in the product development survey of the Chronicle, excepting well structured applications within manufacturing process automation and computer aided design.

The Access Feature

I do see, however, where the evolution will head. This prediction is based on the first theoretical chapters of this book and interviews with users. The early analytical process control approach to information systems design for entire firms is useful only in special, well structured contexts but of little use in higher level decision making, where decision situations are extremely shifty and the analytical side is dominated by the *monitoring* (control) problem. These two, fundamentally different sides of the information problem, relating to organizational innovation and short-term ("static") coordination have not been kept apart in the development of business information technologies. This, to sidetrack slightly from my main theme, illustrates the imposing force of conventional thinking about matters economic and standard economic theory, which maintains the idea that everything can eventually be learned, and that such learning of the one truth can be enhanced by information technology.

My argument -- outlined in the early part of the text -- is that high-level decisions are characterized by the constant changing of the (or the choice of) decision model, but that the bulk of raw information (transactions) processing in firms ultimately serves such top level decisions. This means that there is no Universal Business Information Systems product (UBIS). For one thing transactions processing related to ("static") operations coordination will follow one analytical ("automation") track, and the selection, organization choice decision will be dealt with in an entirely different manner. The latter information product will support human (team) decision making and will be designed to (1) optimize *access to information on the format needed* and to (2) *organize access to people.*

Part I arrived at that conclusion on theoretical grounds. Part II demonstrated how business information systems in practice had been gradually reorganized during the 1970s and 1980s, away from analytical devices towards access systems. Part III and the Chronicle of events to follow on the diskette shows how this awareness has dawned on the IT industry through sequences of business mistakes intersected by successful business and technological experiments that have eventually taken the enormous IT and communications industries to where they currently are. The Chronicle has been structured on the further break down of Table VI.6 (in Chapter VI) in Table VII.1 allowing also the enormous technology demands of the new Universal Business Information Systems product to be clearly exhibited.

Lessons for Policy Makers

The main lesson for the government policy maker to learn from this discussion and the Chronicle is the pronounced experimental nature of innovative activity and economic development. The set of opportunities facing the business decision maker is immense, and particularly so in an innovative new technology with generic potential. The probability of coming out on top on the basis of systematic analysis of previous experience is not great. One business success in the market requires creative imagination, bold initiatives, many attempts (business experiments) and a large number of business mistakes. Policy attempting to minimize the mistakes[1] or to control (regulate) the largely unpredictable consequences of the experimental innovative process, either stops the innovative process or cuts out the good solutions, while generating bad solutions with a high probability.

Even though the large, existing firms are close to the market and should be better equipped to make headway in this innovative process, they face the same principal problems as government. Large bureaucracies are not good environments for innovative activity and large resources only help for a while. A large business organization with large resources, that has understood the business potential of an innovation, on the other hand can move much faster than the small, independent entrepreneur, to industrial scale production. Thus, the conclusions from the Chronicle can be restated in a policy context.

First, new technology predominantly appears to be realized successfully in the form of business ventures in newly started firms that are independent of existing producers. To "mature into" industrial scale production, ambitions to build large commercial enterprises or very perceptive large business firms have to be present. The IT market has demonstrated an enormous potential for new firms to become industrial giants in a very short time, challenging the very existence of giant established players like IBM.

It is, however, very clear from the Chronicle that, excepting perhaps a few basic technological break throughs, new technology products introduced through new firms have their origin in the research laboratories of already existing firms, or a group of people that has left such a laboratory to start a new firm. The reason probably is the very large economic or commercial, as distinct from technological content in IT products. Innovative product development has to be guided by information on, or intuition for what the market wants, and such knowhow can only be developed in the market, through direct confrontations between the very best competitors (Eliasson 1994d). Most of the new start-ups, however, appear to fail even though the Chronicle is very incomplete on the failure side.

This means that *the large established, high-technology firms serve as infrastructure providers* of the rest of the market through research results they have not been able to exploit themselves, and through the training of people, who then leave. The Chronicle, on the other hand, supplies little evidence of public or university laboratories serving the same function in the IT market. Among several possible reasons distance from the market is probably most important, and a deficient sense for what customers want, rather than what scientific standards prescribe for the researcher. Closeness to commercially advanced and resourceful customers, users, appears to be the explanatory feature that university laboratories lack. Applications-oriented minds develop in industry laboratories not in university laboratories. Another factor is the absence of competition that relieves researchers of the pressure of urgency.

Second, regulation slows down or strangles commercial innovative activity. When the regulatory constraint on telecommunications and computing industries was removed in the U.S. in the early 1980s the enormous technological potential of merging the two technologies revealed itself in the form of extremely rapid innovative initiatives. This deregulation, opening the gates for a new communications technology probably and unexpectedly saved the U.S. IT industry from the Japanese onslaught. At the time European technology was very much government dominated and locked into mainframe and hardware thinking, and it still is. With the telecommunications market of major countries like France and Germany still wired by regulations, there is no wonder that European IT industry has a problem, perhaps leading to its extinction, as U.S. industry is rapidly shifting, through the creation of new firms, into distributed PC- and workstation-based networked computing.

Third, while government policy makers and academic laboratories have been aloof from the trends of new technology the big firms in the market, like IBM, appear to have been aware in principle of where the technology and commercial potential were leading, but they have been unable to transform this principal awareness into operational reality in 100 thousand plus employee organizations, shaped in a different mode of thinking. There are many entries in the Chronicle reflecting attempts by IBM, Digital, Xerox and other firms to reorient themselves in directions that later set the tune of the market. In addition, unforeseen consequences of seemingly sound decisions that changed the nature of the market, proved disastrous in the long run for the big firms that initiated the change. IBM prepared for its own "destruction" by introducing open, non-proprietary computing on the PC on the basis of MS-DOS. By delegating control of "its" extremely successful operating system to Microsoft it lost control of the market. Without capacity to take initiatives based on its own operating system it was left behind in the technology race, despite its enormous resources. The Chronicle tells about IBM's attempts to correct the situation and the enormous complexity of technology and markets, where a few new players, among hundreds of competitors, began to gain dominance. In this experimental setting, perhaps there was no other way for IBM. By withholding its unique proprietary operating system from outside users, *Apple* may, however, have made a similar mistake.[2] By refusing to license Macintosh ingenious operating system it left the field open for Microsoft to enter with its competing system Windows and eventually gain dominance. The long story of Xerox is similarly sad. Principal insight even if right, may not help when tried in operational practice, either because a competitor gets the fine details right earlier or because the hidebound staff of a large corporation resists the change of organizational practice that will make the new ideas operational.

On this final score *the giant, once successful corporation has the same problem as government bureaucracy. The bulk of its knowledge capital is dominated by what was good in the past. And in an innovative, rapidly changing market what was good in the past is a bad predictor of the future.* The advantage of the private business organization over government bureaucracy, or the protected or regulated firm is that bureaucracy and policy authorities by the nature of their "charters" do not readily admit and correct mistakes, while *even the big resourceful private players in the experimentally organized market economy have their resources limited by impatient owners concerned about the future value of their assets* (Eliasson 1990b). In the experimentally organized economy mistakes are part of the standard costs of economic development. Firms not only have to learn to live with them, but also to cope with them if they want to survive (see Chapter III). And only very few large firms have coped successfully with major mistakes.

NOTES

1.   or "waste", as it was called in the centralist, industrial policy debate of the 1960s.

2.   Note that *Apple* has recently changed that policy.

OFFICE AUTOMATION OR BUSINESS INFORMATION SYSTEMS MARKET -- ANNOUNCEMENT OF ENTRY

Year	through (technology)

1975
Xerox — copying
IBM — computing etc.
Burroughs — computing

1977
DEC — word processing + computing
UNIVAC — computing

1979
Olivetti — minicomputers + typewriters
3M — word processing + other office equipment
Wang — word processing + computing
CTP Corp. — word processing
NBI Inc. — word processing
Lanier Business
  systems — word processing
Systems Development
  Corp. (SDC) — electronic filing cabinets
Oyx (of Exxon) — typewriters/word processing
Datapoint Corp. — computing + filing + typing
Harris — word processing
Siemens — PBXs
Northern Telecom — PBXs

1980
AB – Dick
CGE (France) — from Facsimile machines
Electronic
  Communications
  Systems Inc. — electronic mail
Exxon Information
  Systems — word processing
Systems Forms
  Makers — makers of business forms
Olivetti — CH–Honeywell–Bull partnership (computing etc.)
Prime — minicomputers + workstations

Raytheon Data	
Systems	— computing and word processing
Sony	
Volkswagen	— VW money and Adler customer base (VW owns: Royal, Triumph-Adler, Pertic Computers etc.)

1981
HP	— integrated computing and word processing
Mitel (Canada)	— PBXs
Rolm Corp.	— PBXs
Syntrex	— word processing

1982
Ericsson	— PBXs and telecommunications
Nixdorf	— distributed processing
Sperry	— word processing and PCs

1983
AT&T	— PBXs and telecommunications
Philips	— computers and office equipment
American Bell	— PBXs

1984
Compugraphic	
Corp.	— technical publishers
McDonnel Douglas	— information systems (through Tymshare subsidiary)

1985
| Canon | — copying |
| Ricoh | — copying |

Not dated entries before end of June 1982
Data Sciences
Fujitsu
ICL
ITT
Mohawk
NEC
Western Electric

Source: The Chronicle.

Supplement 2

SPIN-OFF, START-UP AND MAJOR INNOVATIONS CHRONOLOGY

1911;	*Computing, Tabulating, Recording* (changed to IBM in 1924) is founded as a merge between *Tabulating, Machine Company, International Time Recording Company* and *Computing Scale Company.*
1939;	David Packard and William, R. Hewlett form partnership *Hewlett-Packard* (HP) in a garage in Palo Alto. Production began already 1938. First product: audio oscillator. First major customer; Walt Disney who ordered eight oscillators in 1938 for the production of "Fantasia". HP grows soon to become the largest manufacturer in the world of test and measurement instruments.
1947;	The *transistor* is invented by Bell Labs and becomes the foundation of the *second generation of computers* in the 1960s.
1951;	An Wang (Phil.dr from Harvard) founds *Wang Laboratories Inc.* First EDP products introduced in 1964.
1951;	IBM decides to produce the 701, the first electronic binary computer (*Datamation*, March 15, 1991).
1953;	First *magnetic core memory* designed by Jay Forrester, MIT, goes into MIT's *Whirlwind* computer.
1955;	Sperry-Univac was founded in 1955 (A merge between *Sperry Remington* and *Rand's Univac* division, *BW*, Sept 9, 1985, pp. 77-78).
1955;	IBM announces *magnetic disk* memory.
1955;	*Bell Labs* solves the technical diffusion problem of placing several transistor functions on a simple silicon chip (Sobel 1981, p. 211).
1955;	William Shockley (MIT Ph.Dr, and 1936 Nobel Prize winner for his work on the transistor) leaves *Bell Labs* to found *Shockley Semiconductor Laboratory* from which the "big eight" engineers (e.g. Noyce and Moore) later (1959) leave to start *Fairchild Semiconductor* (*BW*, Dec. 9, 1991, pp. 40-45 and *Datamation*, Sept. 15, 1987, p. 71).
1955;	IBM starts work on its innovative *Stretch* computer.
1956;	IBM introduces first *Fortran* version.
1956;	*General Electric* enters computer business.

1956;	IBM agrees with Justice Department's Antitrust Division to certain restrictions in its marketing practices; the so-called *Consent Decree.*
1957;	William Norris and Seymour Cray leave *Sperry Rand* to form *Control Data Corporation* (CDC), because, as he testified, Sperry Rand failed to focus its efforts on the EDP business (*Datamation*, Sept. 15, 1989, pp. 56 ff).
1957;	DEC is founded by Kenneth H. Olsen, who steps out of MIT.
1958;	*Texas Instruments* invents crude version of the *integrated circuit* (*BW*, Aug. 2, 1993, pp. 38 f) that becomes the foundation of the *third generation of computers.*
1959;	*Fairchild Semiconductor* started as a subsidiary to *Fairchild Camera.*
1959;	Robert Noyce invents the planer technique for integrated circuits at *Fairchild Semiconductor* (Sobel 1981, p. 211).
1959;	*Haloid* (1961 Xerox) introduces plain paper copier.
Late 1960s;	*Intel, Signetics, National Semiconductor* and *Advanced Semiconductors* are started by engineers from *Fairchild Camera and Instrument Cooperation* (*BW*, Dec. 6. 1982, p. 75 and Dec. 9, 1991, pp. 40-45).
1961;	IBM introduces *Selectric* "golf ball" electric typewriter.
1962;	Ross Perot leaves IBM to start EDS.
1962;	AT&T launches first communication Satellite, *Telestar.*
1964;	*General Electric* (GE) wins contract to develop "an extremely advanced *time-sharing* system" for an MIT project founded by ARPA (Fisher, Mackie and Mancke 1983, p. 160).
1964;	IBM announces its unified *System/360*-family. Builds on architectural features from *Stretch* computer.
1968;	de Castro leaves DEC to found *Data General Corporation* (*BW*, Nov. 25, 1985, pp. 82-85).
1968;	*Intel*, founded by Andy Grove, Gordon E. Moore and Robert Noyce from *Fairchild Camera and Instrument Corporation.*
1968/69;	IBM develops microprocessor for internal use. Some of the development group at the IBM San José Laboratory later left for *Intel.*
1969;	Justice Department files its suit against IBM, based on its dominance in mainframe market.
1969;	Xerox acquires *Scientific Data Corporation* (SDS) for $100 Million to merge copying and computing.
1969;	*General Electric* sells computer business to *Honeywell.*
1969;	ARPA net connects scientists at U.S. universities; beginning of *Internet.*
1969;	*Unix* invented by *Bell Labs.*

1970;	Gene M. Amdahl leaves IBM to found *Amdahl Corp.* Starts plug compatible mainframe market (*Datamation*, March 1991).
1970;	IBM releases its first "Xerox" type copier.
1970;	Xerox sets up its *Palo Alto Research Center* (PARC) (*BW*, Mar. 28, 1983, p. 47).
1970;	The IBM 370/145 system; the first computer with memories in integrated circuits (Pugh 1995, p. 306).
1971;	*Intel* invents *microprocessor*. Engineers from the IBM San José Laboratory who developed the IBM "desktop computer" 1130, announced in 1964 had joined Intel and transformed parts of the 1130 design to the Intel micro processor architecture (see Pugh 1995, op. cit.).
1971;	*Honeywell*, a controls manufacturer, enters computer business.
1971;	*Prime* started by William Poduski.
1972;	Seymor Cray leaves CDC to set up *Cray Research Inc.* to design vector processing supercomputer (*Datamation*, Sep. 15, 1987, p. 60).
1972;	EMI of Britain introduces CT scanner.
1972;	The user-friendly *Dynabook* computer (later called *Alto*) is created in the Xerox Parc Research Center.
1973;	PLM code for micro processors developed by *Intel*.
1973;	IBM introduces *floppy disk*.
1973;	IBM introduces *Winchester disk memory*, invented in 1969 by IBM (Fisher, Mackie and Mancker 1983, pp. 338 f).
1973;	*Philips, Siemens* and *CII* bond together in *Unidata Consortium*.
1973;	*Ethernet* invented at *Xerox Parc*.
1974;	*Altair* 8800, the "very first personal computer" is announced by MITS (see *MikroDatorn* No. 15, 1993, p. 46 and *Popular Electronics*, Jan. 1975).
1974;	J.G. Treybig, trained at HP starts *Tandem* (*BW*, Dec. 6, 1982, p. 75).
1974;	Intel's second generation micro processor makes the PC possible.
1975;	*Philips* leaves mainframes. *Honeywell Bull* merges with CII.
1975;	*Microsoft* founded by Bill Gates and Paul Allen.
1975;	*Wang* delivers complete word processing product.
1975;	*Zilog* started by people leaving *Intel*, and almost wins over Intel. Soon after its start it receives financing from *Exxon*.
Ca 1975;	NCR [National (electromechanical) Cash Registers], changes into full line computer maker.
1976;	*Apple* started by Stephen G. Wozniak, who left HP, and Steve Jobs.
1977;	The first PC (*BW*, May 16, 1977, p. 50 f).

1977;	*Xerox* introduces high-speed *laser printer*.
1977;	*Computer Associates* (CA) founded by Charles Wang.
Late 1970s;	First LAN, *Ethernet* developed by *Xerox* (*BW*, Oct. 28, 1985, p. 68).
1979;	*Fairchild Camera and Instruments Corp.* is acquired by *Schlumberger*, the oil services giant.
1979;	Jim H. Clark and six students at Stanford University come up with novel ways for building a cheap graphics computer; the beginning of *Silicon Graphics*. First workstation sold.
1979;	*Software Arts Inc.* introduces *VisiCalc*, the first electronic spreadsheet for PCs (*Datamation*, Mar. 15, 1991).
1980;	Software Publishers, *Cary Research, Integrated Devices Technology* and *Ridge Computer* started by people from HP (*BW*, Dec. 6, 1982, p. 75).
1980;	*Apollo*, started in a basement by William Poduski. Creates workstation market (*BW*, July 30, 1989, p. 88).
1981;	*Silicon Graphics* is founded by Jim H. Clark. Goes public in 1986.
1981;	IBM enters PC market, using *Microsoft* as supplier of operating system (*BW*, Aug. 24, 1981, p. 38).
1981;	Xerox' *Parc* introduces *graphical user interface*.
1981;	*Burroughs* acquires *Memorex*.
1981;	*Pyramid Technology* is started by Robert Regen-Kelley from HP (*BW*, Dec. 6, 1982, p. 75).
1981;	*Micro Source* started by people from HP.
1982;	US telecommunications industry deregulated.
1982;	US Justice Department drops the 1969 antitrust case against IBM.
1982;	*Sydis* and *Insight Systems* started by people from HP (*BW*, Dec. 6, 1982, p. 75).
1982;	*Sun* introduces high-performance *workstation*.
1982;	*Compaq* is founded by a group of TI engineers (Canion, Harris etc.) to build portable IBM PC clones (*BW*, Nov. 2, 1992, pp. 66-71).
1982;	*Metaphor Computer Systems* founded (*BW*, Sep. 17, 1984, p. 45).
1982;	*Motorola* buys *Four-Phase Systems*.
1983;	IBM buys *Rolm Corp.* after a series of failed attempts of its own to mix voice and data (*BW*, June 15, 1983, pp. 23 ff).
1983;	Philippe Kahn, a French-born mathematician, founds *Borland*. Markets database products.
1983;	*Lotus* introduces *spread sheet software* (*BW*, Aug. 12, 1991, pp. 44-50).
1983;	*Thinking Machines Corporation* founded by Daniel Hillis and others from the MIT AI Laboratory.
1983;	17 key *Intel* employees found *Sequent Computer Systems Inc.* to

build a supercomputer, based on parallel processing (*BW*, Sept. 17, 1984, p. 46, and May 25, 1987, p. 69).

1984;   The Federal Government breaks up AT&T.

1984;   *McDonnel Douglas* acquires *Tymeshare Inc.* to obtain its larger communications services operation to make its information systems group the biggest part of the company in the late 1990s (*BW*, May 21, 1984, p. 54).

1984;   Raymond Ozzie leaves *Lotus*. Starts *Iris Associates* to develop groupware program *Notes*.

1984;   Michael S. Dell starts "PC Limited" in Austin, Texas and later changes the name to *Dell Computer Corp.*

1984;   *Encore Computer Corp.* is founded by a cadre of people from *Prime* and *Gordon Bell* to produce a supermini machine that will be able to work in parallel and process data like a mainframe (*BW*, Aug. 27, 1984, p. 51).

1984;   *VPC Research* is founded.

1985;   GM buys EDS.

1985;   *Simigraphics* is founded.

1986;   *Burroughs* (world's No. 3 computer maker) acquires *Sperry* (No. 4) and forms *Unisys Corp.* (*BW*, June, 9, 1984, p. 28).

1986;   Jobs starts *Next Inc.* to build workstations for higher education (*BW*, June 27, 1986, p. 65).

1986;   *Stella Computer Inc.* and *Dana Group* founded to develop superworkstations.

1986;   *Sperry* is buying *Burroughs* (*BW*, May 26, 1986, pp. 28-29).

1987;   *Unisys* is created out of Burroughs' acquisition of *Sperry* (*BW*, Mar. 2, 1987, p. 50).

1987;   *Bull* acquires *Honeywell's* computer business.

1987;   IBM sells copying business to *Kodak*.

1988;   *Greenleaf Medical Systems* is founded.

1988;   *EXOS* is founded.

1988;   *Cyrix Corp.* is founded by Rogers leaving *Texas Instruments* to produce new risk chip (*BW*, Sept. 19, 1994, pp. 62A-E).

1989;   HP buys *Apollo* (*BW*, April 24, 1989, p. 30).

1989;   First copy of *Notes* groupware introduced.

1989;   *Fake Space Labs* is founded.

1989;   *Bull* buys *Zenith*'s PC division.

1989;   *IBM* sells 50% of Rolm to *Siemens* (*BW*, July 10, 1989, pp. 40-45) and the rest in 1992.

1989;   Seymor Cray leaves *Cray Research Inc.*, who could not fund his ambitious parallel supercomputer based on hundreds of microprocessor chips. Starts *Cray Computer Corp.*

1989;   AT&T acquires *Pyramid Technology Corp.*
1990;   *Sense 8* is founded.
1991;   The founder of *Apollo* (and also of *Prime*; William Poduski) leaves HP (-Apollo) to start *Stellar Computer* to create a "Super workstation" (*BW*, Feb. 18, 1991, pp. 78-79). In fact 9 start ups have originated in Apollo.
1991;   *Borland* acquires ailing *Ashton-Tate Corp.* and its *dBase* database technology.
1991;   IBM turns its no longer successful typewriter division into a separate company; *Lexmar.*
1991;   IBM and *Apple* agree to work together (*BW*, Aug. 12, 1991, pp. 44-50).
1991;   *General Magic Inc.* founded by ex-Apple executives to develop handheld PC and communicating devices (*BW*, Dec. 23, 1991, p. 83).
1992;   IBM spins off IBM PC Co.
1993;   *Dell Computer Corp.* with $2 billions in sales and 4654 employees is the fourth largest PC maker in the U.S., after IBM, *Apple* and *Compaq* (*BW*, Mar. 22, 1993, pp. 48-53).
1994;   Narc Andressen and Jim Clark, earlier CEO of Silicon Graphics, found *Mosaic Communications.* The name is then changed to *Netscape Communications.*
1994;   *Lotus* acquires *Iris Associates* and *Notes.*
1995;   *Cray Computer Corporation* files for Chapter 11.
1995:   IBM acquires *Lotus.*
1995;   On January 17 a Federal appeals court orders district judge Edelstein, who has overseen the Justice Department antitrust settlement with IBM for almost 40 years, to remove himself from the case, saying he does not appear impartial. IBM has repeatedly asked the judge, without success, to lift the 1956 *Consent Decree* that restricts company operations, notably in computer services business, saying the settlement was obsolete (IEEE *Spectrum*, Mar. 1995, *Newslog*, p. 1).

Supplement 3

INTERVIEWED FIRMS

Producers of information systems

Altogether 68 interviews of 51 companies

Apple Computer Inc., Cupertino, CA, 1989
AT&T, Berkeley Heights, NJ, 1987
Celsius, Järfälla, 1995
Datema, Stockholm, 1982
Digital Equipment Corporation, Maynard, MA, 1982
Ericsson, Stockholm, 1982, 1986, 1995
Esselte, Stockholm, 1982, (1995)
Exxon, New York, 1985
Factorial Systems, 1986
Fuji Xerox, Tokyo, 1992
Hewlett Packard, CA, 1994
IBM, Sweden, 1982, 1989, 1990, 1992, (1995)
IBM, Paris, World Trade HQ, 1986
IBM, La Hulpe, Belgien, 1986
IBM, Program Development Laboratory; San José, 1987
IBM, Thomas J. Watson, Research Center, New York, 1994
IBM, Tokyo, Japan, 1992
Industrimatematik AB, Stockholm, 1988, 1995
Microsoft, Washington, 1995
Millicom, Greenwich, Conn., 1989
Nokia, Espod, Finland, 1994
Nolan & Northon, Lexington, MA, 1987
Northern Telecom, Toronto, Canada, 1985
Nynex, White Plains, NY, 1987
Olivetti, Ivrea, Italien, 1989
Oracle, CA, 1994
Philips, Apeldorn and Eindhoven, Holland, 1988
Programator, Stockholm, 1982
Xerox, Palo Alto Research Center, CA, 1986
The Rand Corporation, Santa Monica, CA, 1985
Seiko Instruments, Tokyo, 1992
Sun Micro Systems, Mountain View, CA, 1985

Systems Solutions Technologies Inc., 1986
Tandem, Cupertino, CA, 1983
Thinking Machines Corporation, Boston, 1994

Users

ABB, Västerås, 1991, 1995
ABB, Mexico City, 1990
Electrolux, Stockholm, 1982
Ericsson, Stockholm, 1988
Ericsson, Mexico City, 1990
Korsnäs, 1991
Nissan, Tokyo, 1992
Pharmacia Biotechnology AB, Uppsala, 1988
The Rand Corporation, 1985
Robo AB, Linköping, 1990, 1991
Saab-Scania, 1991, 1994, 1995
Sandvik, 1982, 1987
SKF, Göteborg, 1988
White Consolidated Inc. (Electrolux Subsidiary), Columbia, Ohio, 1987
Volvo, Göteborg, 1987
Volvo, Uddevallaverken, 1989

SUBJECT INDEX

Some terms used in the text and in the *Chronicle* are explained. Whenever there is an exhaustive discussion in the text a page or section reference is given.

PCM;   Plug Compatible Market
PDA;   Personal Digital Assistant
PDF;   Portable Document Format
Public ownership (of industry); Section III.1
QBIC;   Query By Image Content
RAID;   Redundant Arrays of Inexpensive Disks
Rate of return; Section III.11
Receiver competence; Section VI.7, pp. 8, 14 ff, 18 f, 212 ff, 216, 229, 238
Risk technology; p. 235
SAA;   Systems Applications Architecture (IBM) lets the same software
          package run or all IBM machines
Separable additive (profit) *targeting*; Section III.11, pp. 81 f, 99, 138

SNA;   Systems Network Architecture, IBM's standard that "competes"
          with OSI
Sonet;   Synchronous Optical Network Technology, high-speed transmission
          architecture to exploit huge bandwidth in fibre-optic networks
SQL;   Structured Query Language (IBM)
Standardization; Chapter VII, p. 236 f and *Chronicle*, Sections 4d, 6b and 9k,
          pp. 110, 164, 174, 181, 201, 212 ff, 236
State space; pp. 3 ff, 8,, 14 ff, 24 ff, 42, 52, 60, Section V.3
Särimner effect; p. 27 f
Tacit knowledge; Sections I.8, II.3, II.6
TDMA;   *Time Division Multiple Access* (digital standard in cellular
          telecom)
Technology wars; p. 235
Time sharing; pp. 180 f
(Top) competent team; pp. 54, 68, 71, 99, 108 ff, 122 f, 150
Top view; IBM non-graphical easy-to-use software environment
          for PC
Total factor productivity; Section III.15 and Appendix to Chapter III
UBIS;   Universal Business Information System; Chapter V and Section VI.7
Universal (business) *information system*; Chapter V and Section VI.7
Unix;   Operating system developed at Bell Labs
VAN;   Value Added Network services
vBNS;   very high speed Backbone Network Service
VIS;   Visual Information Systems
VLSI;   Very Large Scale Integrated circuits
VR;   Virtual Reality; Section 9c in *Chronicle*
WAN;   Wide Area Network. Enterprise-wide communication between LANs
          over public or private lines
Windows; Graphics-based easy-to-use software environment developed
          by *Microsoft*

BIBLIOGRAPHY

Akerlof, G.A., 1970. The Market for 'Lemons': Qualitative Uncertainty and the Market Mechanism. *Quarterly Journal of Economics*, 84 (3), 488-500.

Albrecht, J., 1978. Expectations, Cyclical Fluctuations and Growth -- Experiments on the Swedish Model; in G. Eliasson (ed.), 1978, *A Micro-to-Macro Model of the Swedish Economy*, Conference Reports, 1978:1. Stockholm: IUI.

Albrecht, J. and Lindberg, T. 1989. The Micro Initialization of MOSES; in J. Albrecht et al., 1989, *MOSES Code*. Research Report No. 36. Stockholm: IUI.

Alchian, A.A., 1950. Uncertainty, Evolution and Economic Theory. *Journal of Political Economy*, 58, 211-221.

Alchian, A.A. and Demsetz, H., 1972. Production, Information Costs and Economic Organization. *American Economic Review*, 62 (5), 777-795.

Allais, M., 1962. The Influence of the Capital-Output Ratio on Real National Income. *Econometrica*, 30, (4), 700-728.

Andersson, T., Braunerhjelm, P., Carlsson, B., Eliasson, G., Fölster, S. and Kazamaki Ottersten, E., 1993, *Den långa vägen – om den ekonomiska politikens begränsningar och möjligheter att föra Sverige ur 1990-talets kris* (The Long Road – about the limitations and possibilities for policy makers to take the Swedish economy out of the crisis of the 90s). Stockholm: Industriens Utredningsinstitut (IUI).

Antonelli, C., 1995. *The Economics of Localized Technological Change and Industrial Dynamics*. Boston: Kluwer Academic Publishers.

Antonov, M. and Trofimov, G., 1993. Learning through Short-Run Macroeconomic Forecasts in a Micro-to-Macro Model, *Journal of Economic Behavior and Organization*, 21 (2), June.

Aoki, M., 1986. Horizontal vs. Vertical Information Structure of the Firm, *American Economic Review*, 76 (5), 971-983.

Aoki, M., 1988, *Information, Incentives, and Bargaining in the Japanese Economy*. Cambridge: Cambridge University Press.

Arrow, K.J., 1959. Toward a Theory of Price Adjustment; in M. Abramovitz et al., *The Allocation of Economic Resources*, Stanford, CA.

--------, 1962a. The Economic Implications of Learning by Doing. *Review of Economic Studies*, 29, (3), 155-173.

--------, 1962b. Economic Welfare and the Allocation of Resources for Invention; in R. Nelson (ed.), 1962, *The Rate and Direction of Inventive Activity: Economic and Social Factors*. Princeton: NBER, Princeton University Press, 609-626.

--------, 1971. The Firm in General Equilibrium Theory; in R. Marris and A. Wood, eds., *The Corporate Economy: Growth, Competition and Innovative Potential*. Edinburgh.

--------, 1974. *The Limits of Organization*. New York.

--------, 1975. Vertical Integration and Communication. *Bell Journal of Economics*, 6 (19), 173-183.

--------, 1986. Rationality of Self and Others in an Economic System. *Journal of Business*, 59 (4), Part 2 (Oct.), S385-S398.

Arrow, K.J. and Hurwicz, L.. 1958. On the Stability of the Competitive Equilibrium, Part I. *Econometrica*, 26 (4), 522-552.

Bairstow, J., 1987. Personal Workstations Redefine Desktop Computing. *High Technology* (March)

Barnard, C.I., 1938. *The Functions of the Executive*. Cambridge, MA: Harvard University Press.

Bauer, R.J., Jr. and Griffiths, M.D. 1988, Evaluating Expert System Investment: An Introduction to the Economics of Knowledge. *Journal of Business Research*, 17 (2), 223-233.

Bergholm, F., 1989. *MOSES Handbook*, Research Report No. 35. Stockholm: Industriens Utredningsinstitut (IUI).

Berndt, E.R., Morrison, C.J. and Rosenblum, L.S., 1992. *High-Tech Capital Formation and Labor Composition in U.S. Manufacturing Industries: An exploratory analysis*, NBER Working Paper No. 4010, Cambridge, MA.

Bishop, J., 1988. *The Productivity Consequences of What is Learned at High School*. Working Paper No. 88-18, Cornell University, Ithaca, N.Y.

--------, 1989, Is the Test Score Decline Responsible for the Productivity Growth Decline?, *American Economic Review*, (March).

Boulding, K.E., 1950. *A Reconstruction of Economics*. New York: Wiley & Sons.

Boult, R., 1989. France's ISDN Hors d'Oeuvre. *Datamation*, April 1, pp. 88 ff.

Braunerhjelm, P., 1993a. Nyetablering och småföretag i svensk tillverknings-industri; in *Marknadsekonomins gränsvillkor, årsbok och verksamhetsberättelse 1992-1993*. Stockholm: Industriens Utredningsinstitut (IUI).

Braunerhjelm, P., 1993b. Nyetablering och småföretagande i svensk industri (New Establishment and Small firms in Swedish Industry); Chapter 4 in T. Andersson et al. (1993).

Brody, H., 1987. CAD meets CAM. *High Technology* (May).

Brousell, D.R., 1988. The New Era of DBMs Integration. *Datamation*, Aug. 15.

Bryan, M., 1989. Shopping for PC DBMs. *Datamation*, March 15.

BW; *Business Week*. All references to Business Week in the text and in the Chronicle are given as *BW*.

Bunker, T., 1991. DEC's Ambitious Software Strategy, *Datamation*, Mar. 15, 1991, pp. 66-72.

Campbell, J., 1982. *Grammatical Man*. New York.

Camacho, A., 1988. *A Partial Theory of the Optimal Size of Teams*; mimeo, Feb.), Dep. of Economics, University of Illinois, Chicago.

Camacho, A., 1991. Adaptation Costs, Coordination Costs and Optimal Firm Size. *Journal of Economic Behavior and Organization*, 15 (1), 137-149.

Camacho, A. and Persky, J.J., 1988. The Internal Organization of Complex Teams: Bounded Rationality and the Logic of Hierarchies. *Journal of*

Economic Behavior and Organization, 9 (4), 367-380.

Camacho, A. and White, D.W. 1981. A Note on Loss of Control and the Optimum Size of the Firm. *Journal of Political Economy*, 89 (2), 407-410.

Carleson, L., 1991. Stochastic Behavior of Deterministic Systems. *Journal of Economic Behavior and Organization*, 16, (1-2), 85-92.

Carlsson, B., 1981. The Content of Productivity Growth in Swedish Manufacturing; in *The Firms in the Market Economy, IUI 40 years 1939-1979*. Stockholm:Industriens Utredningsinstitut (IUI).

--------, 1983a. Industrial Subsidies in Sweden: Macro-Economic Effects and an International Comparison. *Journal of Industrial Economics*, XXXII (1), Sept.

--------, 1983b. Industrial Subsidies in Sweden: Simulations on a Micro-to-Macro Model; in *Microeconometrics, IUI Yearbook 1982-1983*. Stockholm: Industriens Utredningsinstitut (IUI).

--------(ed.), 1989a. *Industrial Dynamics. Technological, Organizational, and Structural Changes in Industries and Firms*. Boston/Dordrecht/London: Kluwer Academic Publishers.

--------, 1989b. The Evolution of Manufacturing Technology and Its Impact on Industrial Structure: An International Study. *Small Business Economics*, 1, (1), 21-37.

--------, 1991. Productivity Analysis: A Micro-to-Macro Perspective; in E. Deiaco, E. Hörnell and G. Vickery (eds.), *Technology and Investment. Crucial Issues for the 1990s*. London:Pinter Publishers.

--------, 1992a. *Industrial Dynamics and the Role of Small Plants in Swedish Manufacturing Industry*, 1968-1988, Working Paper No. 348. Industriens Utredningsinstitut (IUI), Stockholm.

--------, 1992b. The Rise of Small Business: Causes and Consequences; in W.J. Adams (ed.), *Singular Europe: Economy and Polity of the European Community after 1992*. Ann Arbor:University of Michigan Press.

Carlyle, R.E., 1987. Midrange Shoot-out: Mini/Micro Survey. *Datamation*, Nov. 15, pp. 61 ff.

--------, 1988a. Sins of Omission. *Datamation*, Jan. 1.

--------, 1988b. Open Systems: What Price Freedom. *Datamation*, June 1.

--------, 1988c. RISC and UNIX: The Signs of Transitional Times. *Datamation*, Sept. 1.

--------, 1988d. CIO: Misfit or Misnomer. *Datamation*, Aug. 1.

--------, 1988e. Advanced Technology Groups. *Datamation*, Nov. 1.

--------, 1988f. Where Methodology Falls Short. *Datamation*, 34, (24), pp. 43-48.

--------, 1989. Careers in Crisis, *Datamation*, Aug. 15.

--------, 1990. The Out of Touch CIO, *Datamation*, Aug. 15, pp, 31-34.

Carlyle, R.E. and Moad, J., 1988. IBM and the Control of Information, *Datamation*, June 1.

--------, 1989. The Rise of an Information Utility, *Datamation*, Jan. 1.

Cattela, R.C.S., 1981. Accounting and Information from the Viewpoint of the Concern. *Philips Administrative Review* (Theme-Number: Accounts and Information), 35 (1/2), 1981.

Cerf, V.G., 1991, Networking, *Scientific American* (Sept.).

Chamberlin, E.H., 1933. *The Theory of Monopolistic Competition. A Re-orientation of the Theory of Value*. Cambridge, MA: Harvard University Press.

Chandler, A.D., 1962. Strategy and Structure; *Chapters in the History of the American Industrial Enterprise*. Cambridge, MA: MIT Press.

Chandler, A.D., 1977. *The Visible Hand: The Managerial Revolution in American Business*. Cambridge, MA: Harvard University Press.

Chandler, A.D., 1990. *Scale and Scope: The Dynamics of Industrial Capitalism*. Cambridge, MA and London, England: The Belknap Press of Harvard University press.

Chomsky, N., 1965. *Aspects of the Theory of Syntax*. Cambridge, MA: MIT Press.

Clark, J.B., 1887. The Limits of Competition. *Political Science Quarterly*, II, (1), 45-61.

Clark, J.M., 1961. *Competition as a Dynamic Force*. Washington, D.C.: The Brookings Institution.

Coase, R.H., 1937. The Nature of the Firm. *Economica*, New Series, IV, (13-16), 386-405.

Codd, E.F., 1988. Total Flaws in SQL. *Datamation*, Sept. 1.

Cohen, W.M. and Levinthal, D.A., 1989. Innovation and Learning: The Two Faces of R&D. *Economic Journal*, 99, 569-596.

Cohen, W.M. and Levinthal, D.A., 1990. Absorptive Capacity: A New Perspective on Learning and Innovation. *Administrative Science Quarterly*, 35, 128-152.

Cole, R., 1981. *Computer Communications. London*/Macmillan.

Cornet, B., 1988. General Equilibrium Theory and Increasing Returns: Presentation. *Journal of Mathematical Economics*, 17, (2/3), 103-118.

Dahlin, K., 1995, Diffusion and Industrial Dynamics in the Robot Industry; in Carlsson, B. (ed.), *Technological Systems and Economic Performance: The Case of Factory Automation*, Boston/Dordrecht/London: Kluwer Academic Publishers.

Datta, S.K. and Nugent, J.B., 1986. Adversary Activities and per Capita Income Growth. *World Development*, 14 (12), 1457-1461.

Davis, L., 1989. Can Education Meet IS Career Demands?. *Datamation*, March 15.

Davis, L., 1989b. Point of Access, *Datamation*, July 15.

Davis, L., 1990. Which Network Operations Systems Is Right for You?. *Datamation*, July 1, p. 34.

Davis, P.B., 1987. Managing Computer Communications. *High Technology*, March.

Davis, S.G., 1989. Can Stand-Alone EISs Stand Up?. *Datamation*, July 1.

Day, R.H., 1967. Profits, Learning and the Convergence of Satisficing to Marginalism. *Quarterly Journal of Economics*, LXXXI, (2), 302-311.

--------, 1971. Rational Choice and Economic Behavior. *Theory and Decision*, 1, 229-251.

--------, 1975a. Adaptive Processes and Economic Theory; in R.H. Day and T. Groves, eds. (1975).

--------, 1975b. Orthodox Economists and Existential Economics. *Journal of Economic Issues*, IX (June).

--------, 1982a. Irregular Growth Cycles. *American Economic Review*, 72, 406-414.

--------, 1982b. *Dynamical Systems Theory and Complicated Economic Behavior.*, Working Paper 8215, Dep. of Economics. Los Angeles, CA.: University of Southern California.

--------, 1983. The Emergence of Chaos from Classical Economic Growth. *Quarterly Journal of Economics*, 98 (May), 201-213.

--------, 1986a. Disequilibrium Economic Dynamics: A Post-Schumpeterian Contribution; in R.H. Day and G. Eliasson, eds. (1986).

--------, 1986b. On Endogenous Preferences and Adaptive Economizing; in R.H. Day and G. Eliasson, eds. (1986).

--------, 1993. Bounded Rationality and the Coevolution of Market and State; Chapter 4 in R.H. Day, G.E. Eliasson and C. Wihlborg, eds. (1993).

Day, R.H. and Eliasson, G. (eds.), 1986. *The Dynamics of Market Economies*, Stockholm: IUI and Amsterdam: North-Holland.

Day, R.H., Eliasson, G. and Wihlborg, C. (eds.), 1993. *The Markets for Innovation, Ownership and Control.* Stockholm: Stockholm: Industriens Utredningsinstitut (IUI) and Amsterdam: Elsevier Science Publishers B.V.

Day, R.H. and Groves, Th. (eds.), 1975. *Adaptive Economic Models*, New York: Academic Press Inc.

Day, R.H., Morley, S. and Smith, K.R., 1974. Myopic Optimizing and Rules of Thumb in a Micro-Model of Industrial Growth. *American Economic Review*, LXIV (1), 11-23.

Day, R.H. and Tinney, E.H., 1968. How to Cooperate in Business without Really Trying: A learning model of decentralized decision making. *Journal of Political Economy*, (76), 583-600.

Debreu. G. 1959. *The Theory of Value*. New Haven: Yale University Press.

Denison, E.F., 1967. *Why Growth Rates Differ*. Washington, D.C.: The Brookings Institution.

Dunn, A., 1988. IBM and Telecom: Glimmer of a Grand Design, *Datamation*, Feb. 1, pp. 77-81.

Eliasson, G., 1967. *Kreditmarknaden och industrins investeringar*. Uppsala: Industriens Utredningsinstitut (IUI).

--------, 1969, *The Credit Market, Investment, Planning and Monetary Policy -- an Econometric Study of Manufacturing Industries*. Stockholm: Industriens

Utredningsinstitut (IUI).
--------, 1976a. *Business Economic Planning -- Theory, Practice and Comparison.*
London etc.: John Wiley & Sons.
--------, 1976b. *A Micro-Macro Interactive Simulation Model of the Swedish
Economy -- Preliminary Documentation.* Economic Research Report B15,
Stockholm: Federation of Swedish Industries (with the assistance of Gösta
Olavi and Mats Heiman).
--------, 1977. Competition and Market Processes in a Simulation Model of the
Swedish Economy. *American Economic Review*, 67 (1), 277-281.
--------, 1978. *A Micro-to-Macro Model of the Swedish Economy.* Conference
Reports 1978:1. Stockholm: Industriens Utredningsinstitut (IUI).
--------, 1979. *Technical Change, Employment and Growth. Experiments on a Micro-
to-Macro Model.* Research Report No. 7. Stockholm: Industriens
Utredningsinstitut (IUI).
--------, 1980. Elektronik, teknisk förändring och ekonomisk utveckling; in
Datateknik, ekonomisk tillväxt och sysselsättning (Electronics, technical
change and employment). Stockholm: Data- och Elektronikkommittén
(DEK).
--------, 1982. Electronics, Economic Growth and Employment -- Revolution or
Evolution; in H. Giersch (ed.), *Emerging Technologies: Consequences for
economic growth, structrual change and employment*, Kiel.
--------, 1983. On the Optimal Rate of Structural Adjustment; in G. Eliasson, M.
Sharefkin and B.-C. Ysander (eds.), 1983. *Policy Making in a Disorderly
World Economy,*Conference Reports 1983:1. Stockholm: Industriens
Utredningsinstitut (IUI).
--------, 1984a. The Micro-Foundations of Industrial Policies; in J. Jacquemin (ed.),
European Industry, Public Policy and Corporate Strategy, Oxford University
Press.
--------, 1984b. Micro Heterogeneity of Firms and the Stability of Industrial
Growth. *Journal of Economic Behavior and Organization*, 5, (3-4).
--------, 1984c. Informations- och styrsystem i stora företag (Information and
control systems in large firms); in *Hur styrs storföretag?* (How are large firms
run?), Stockholm: Industriens Utredningsinstitut (IUI).
--------, 1985a. *The Firm and Financial Markets in the Swedish Micro-to-Macro
Model -- Theory, Model and Verification.* Stockholm: Industriens
Utredningsinstitut (IUI).
--------, 1985b. The Swedish Micro-to-Macro Model: Idea, Design and Application;
in G. Orcutt, J. Merz & H. Quinke (eds.), 1986. *Microanalytic Simulation
Models to Support Social and Financial Policy.* Amsterdam: North-Holland.
--------, 1986a. A Note on the Stability of Economic Organizational Forms and the
Importance of Human Capital; in R.H. Day and G. Eliasson, eds. (1986).
--------, 1986b. Kompetens, kommunikation och kunskapsuppbyggnad --

sammanfattning och arbetshypotes för industripolitiken; in G. Eliasson, B. Carlsson et al. (1986).

--------, 1986c. Innovative Change, Dynamic Market Allocation and Long-Term Stability of Economic Growth. Working Paper No. 156, Stockholm: Industriens Utredningsinstitut (IUI); to be published in David–Dosi (eds.), *Innovation and the Diffusion of Technology*. Oxford: Oxford University Press.

--------, 1987. *Technological Competition and Trade in the Experimentally Organized Economy*, Research Report No. 32. Stockholm: Industriens Utrednings-institut (IUI).

--------, 1988a. Ägare, entreprenörer och kapitalmarknadens organisation -- en teoretisk presentation och översikt; in J. Örtengren et al. (1988).

--------, 1988b. *The Knowledge Base of an Industrial Economy*, Research Report No. 33, Stockholm: Industriens Utredningsinstitut (IUI). Also published in 1987 as Part I, (Chapters I through IV in "The Human Factor in Economic and Technological Change" in OECD Educational Monograph Series No. 3, Paris, 1987.

--------, 1988c. Schumpeterian Innovation, Market Structure and the Stability of Industrial Development; in H. Hanush (ed.), *Evolutionary Economics, Applications of Schumpter's Ideas*. Cambridge: Cambridge University Press.

--------, 1989a. Modeling the Experimentally Organized Economy; in J. Albrecht et al., *MOSES Code*. Stockholm: Industriens Utredningsinstitut (IUI).

--------, 1989b. The Dynamics of Supply and Economic Growth -- how industrial knowledge accumulation drives a path-dependent economic process; in B. Carlsson (ed.), *Industrial Dynamics -- Technological, Organizational, and Structural Changes in Industries and Firms*. Boston/Dordrecht/London: Kluwer Academic Publishers.

--------, 1989c. *The Economics of Coordination, Innovation, Selection and Learning -- a theoretical framework for research in industrial economics*. Working Paper No. 235, Stockholm: Industriens Utredningsinstitut (IUI).

--------, 1990a. The Knowledge-Based Information Economy; in G. Eliasson (1990).

--------, 1990b. The Firm as a Competent Team. *Journal of Economic Behavior and Organization*, 13 (3), 275-298.

--------, 1991a. Modeling the Experimentally Organized Economy. *Journal of Economic Behavior and Organization*, 16 (1-2), 153-182.

--------, 1991b. Deregulation, Innovative Entry and Structural Diversity as a Source of Stable and Rapid Economic Growth. *Journal of Evolutionary Economics*, (1), 49-63.

--------, 1991c. Modeling Economic Change and Restructuring. The Micro Foundations of Economic Expansion; in P. de Wolf (ed.), *Competition in Europe. Essays in Honour of Henk de Jong*. Dordrecht/Boston/London: Kluwer Academic Publishers.

--------, 1991d. The International Firm: A Vehicle for Overcoming Barriers to Trade and a Global Intelligence Organization Diffusing the Notion of a Nation; in L.-G. Mattson and B. Stymne (eds.), 1991. *Corporate and Industry Strategies for Europe*. Amsterdam: Elsevier Science Publishers B.V.

--------, 1991e. Financial Institutions in a European Market for Executive Competence; in C. Wihlborg, M. Fratianni and T.D. Willett (eds.), 1992, *Financial Regulation and Monetary Arrangements after 1992*. Amsterdam: Elsevier Science Publishers B.V.

--------, 1991f. Produktivitet och vinster som prestandamätare för företaget och den nationella ekonomin; in G. Eliasson and L. Samuelson (eds.), 1992, *Produktivitet och lönsamhet*. Lund: Studentlitteratur.

--------, 1992a, The MOSES Model -- Database and Applications, Chapter 1 in J. Albrecht et al., *Moses Database*. Research Report No. 40, Industriens Utredningsinstitut (IUI), Stockholm.

--------, 1992b. Business Competence, Organizational Learning and Economic Growth: Establishing the Smith-Schumpeter-Wicksell Connection; in F.M. Scherer and M. Perlman (eds.), *Entrepreneurship, Technological Innovation, and Economic Growth. Studies in the Schumpeterian Tradition*. Ann Arbor: The University of Michigan Press.

--------, 1992c. *Arbetet -- dess betydelse, dess innehåll, dess kvalitet och dess ersättning* (Work). Stockholm: Industriens Utredningsinstitut (IUI).

--------, 1992d. Affärsmisstag och konkurser. *Ekonomiska Samfundets Tidskrift*, (4), 201-216.

--------, 1993a. A Note: On Privatization, Contract Technology and Economic Growth; in R.H. Day, G. Eliasson and C. Wihlborg, eds. (1993).

--------, 1993b. Företagens, institutionernas och marknadernas roll i Sveriges ekonomiska kris (The rôle of the firm, institutions and markets in the Swedish economic crisis); Bilaga 6 in *Nya villkor för ekonomi och politik*. Ekonomikommissionens förslag, SOU 1993:16, 195-233.

--------, 1993c. *Endogenous Economic Growth through Selection*. Working Paper No. 397, Industriens Utredningsinstitut (IUI), Stockholm.

--------, 1994a. Technology, Economic Competence and the Theory of the Firm -- discussing the economic forces behinc long-term economic growth; in O. Granstrand (ed.), *Economics of Technology*. Amsterdam: Elsevier Science Publishers B.V.

--------, 1994b. The Theory of the Firm and the Theory of Economic Growth -- an essay on the economics of institutions, competition and the capacity of the political system to cope with unexpected change; in L. Magnusson, ed. (1994).

--------, 1994c, *The Macroeconomic Effects of New Information Technology, with Special Emphasis on Telecommunications*. Paper presented to the "Tenth International Conference of the International Telecommunications Society (ITS)", Sydney, Australia, July 3-6 1994. To be published in D. Lamberton (ed.), 1995, *Beyond Competition*, Amsterdam: Elsevier Science Publishers B.V.

--------, 1994d. General Purpose Technologies, Industrial Competence and Economic Growth. TRITA-JEO R1994:2. Stockholm: Kungl. Tekniska Högskolan, Industriell ekonomi och organisation; to be published in B. Carlsson (ed.), *Technological Systems and Economic Development Potential*. Boston/Dordrecht/London: Kluwer Academic Publishers.

--------, 1994e. *Högre utbildning i företag* (The Employment of highly educated people in firms). Report No. 14, Agenda 2000. Stockholm: Swedish Ministry of Education.

--------, 1994f, *Markets for Learning and Educational Services – a micro explanation of the rôle of education and development of competence*. Paris: OECD, DEELSA/ED/CERI/CD, (94) 9 (04-Nov.).

--------, 1995a, The Economics of Technical Change -- The macroeconomic consequences of business competence in an experimentally organized economy, *Revue d'Économie Industrielle, Numero Exceptionnel*.

--------, 1995b. *Communication, Information Technology and the Firm*. Paper presented to the Conference "Telecommunications, Infrastructure and the Information Economy: Interactions between public policy and corporate structure" in Ann Arbor, Michigan, March 10-11, 1995.

Eliasson, G., Bergholm, F., Horwitz, E.C. and Jagrén, L., 1985. *De svenska storföretagen – en studie av internationaliseringens konsekvenser för den svenska ekonomin* (The Giant Swedish Groups – a study of the consequences of internationalization for the Swedish economy). Stockholm: Industriens Utredningsinstitut (IUI).

Eliasson, G., Carlsson, B., Deiaco, E., Lindberg, T. and Pousette, T., 1986. *Kunskap, information och tjänster* (Knowledge, Information and services). Stockholm: Industriens Utredningsinstitut (IUI).

Eliasson, G., Fries, H., Jagrén, L. and Oxelheim, L., 1984. *Hur styrs storföretag? - - en studie av informationshantering och organisation* (How are large business groups managed? -- A study of information handling and organization). Stockholm: Industriens Utredningsinstitut (IUI) and Kristianstad: Liber.

Eliasson, G., Fölster, S., Lindberg, T. and Pousette, T., 1989. *The Knowledge Based Information Economy*. Stockholm: Industriens Utredningsinstitut (IUI).

Eliasson, G. and Granstrand, O., 1983. *Venture Capital and Management -- A study of venture development units in four Swedish firms* (mimeo, Jan.). Industriens Utredningsinstitut (IUI), Stockholm.

Eliasson, G. and Lindberg, T., 1981. Allocation and Growth Effects of Corporate Income Taxes; in G. Eliasson and J. Södersten (eds.), 1981, *Business Taxation, Finance and Firm Behavior*, Conference Reports 1981:1. Stockholm: Industriens Utredningsinstitut (IUI).

Eliasson, G. and Lindberg, T., 1986. *Economic Growth and the Dynamics of Wage Determination -- A micro simulation study of the stability consequences of deficient variation in factor prices and micro structures*, Working Paper No. 170. Stockholm: Industriens Utredningsinstitut (IUI).

Eliasson, G. and Taymaz, E., 1992. *The Limits of Policy Making: An analysis of the consequences of boundedly rational Government using the Swedish micro-to-macro model (MOSES)*. Working Paper No. 333. Industriens Utredningsinstitut, Stockholm.

Eliasson, U., 1981. *Understanding of Annual Reports*, Department of Nordic Languages. (Report No. 2 to the project "Understanding of Annual Reports"). Stockholm: Stockholm University.

Ewald, L. and Westman, S., 1983.*Datakommunikation. Datanät, protokoll och design*. Lund: Studentlitteratur.

Fama, E.F., 1980. Agency Problems and the Theory of the Firm, *Journal of Political Economy*, 88 (2), 288-307.

Feigenbaum, E.A. and Feldman J. (eds.), 1963. *Computers and Thought*. New York etc.: McGraw-Hill Book Company.

Fisher, F.M., McKie, J.W. and Mancke. R.B., 1983. *IBM and US Data Processing Industry -- An Economic History*. New York: Praeger.

Foster, R.N., 1986. *Innovation: The Attacker's Advantage*. New York: Summit Books, p. 133.

Fosdick, H. and Garcia-Rose, L., 1988. DB2 Users Stand Up to be Counted. *Datamation*, Oct. 15, pp. 45-58.

Francis, B., 1989a. Desktop Tugs of War, OS/2 vs. Unix. *Datamation*, Feb. 15.

--------, 1989b. Climbing the PC Ladder. *Datamation*, May 1.

--------, 1989c. Competitiveness: A New Standard. *Datamation*, July 15.

Francis, B. and McMuller, J., 1990. Apple Breaks Through. *Datamation*, July 1, pp. 24ff.

Friedman, M., 1953. *Essays in Positive Economics*. Chicago: The University of Chicago Press.

Gershefski, G.W., 1968. *The Development and Application of a Corporate Financial Model*. Oxford, Ohio: Planning Executives Institute Research series.

Gibrat, R., 1930. Une loi des répartitions économiques: L'éffet proportionnel, *Bulletin de la Statistique Général de la France*, 19, 469 ff.

Gibrat, R., 1931. *Les inégalités économiques*. Paris: Recueil Sirey.

Granstrand, O., 1986. A Note: On Measuring and Modelling Innovative New Entry in Swedish Industry; in R.H. Day and G. Eliasson, eds. (1986).

Granstrand, O. and Sjölander, S., 1987. *Managing Innovation in Multi-Technology Corporations*, mimeo, Aug., Dept. of Industrial Organization, Götcborg: Chalmers University of Technology.

Granstrand, O. and Sjölander, S., 1993. The Acquisition of Technology and Small

Firms by Large Firms; in R.H. Day, G. Eliasson and C.G. Wihlborg, eds. (1993).

Greenstein, S.M., 1994. *Did Computer Technology Diffuse Quickly?: Best and Average Practice in Mainframe Computers 1968-1983.* NBER Working Paper No. 4647, Cambridge, MA.

Göranzon, B., 1993. *The Practical Intellect: Computers and Skills,* UNESCO. London, Berlin etc.: Springer-Verlag.

Halper, M., 1988. Portable Gets Raves on the Road. *Datamation,* Nov. 15.

Hanson, K.A., 1986. On New Firm Entry and Macro Stability; in *The Economics of Institutions and Markets, IUI Yearbook 1986-1987.* Stockholm: Industriens Utredningsinstitut (IUI).

Harris, M. and Raviv, A., 1990. Capital Structure and the Informational Role of Debt. *Journal of Finance,* 45 (2), 321-349.

Harris, M. and Raviv, A., 1991. *Financial Contracting Theory.* Paper prepared for the 6th World Congress of the Econometric Society, Barcelona, Spain, Aug. 22-28, 1990.

Hart, O. and Moore, J., 1990. Property Rights and the Nature of the Firm. *Journal of Political Economy,* 98 (6), 1119-1158.

Hartog, C. and Rouse, R.A., 1987. A Blue Print to the New ID Professional. *Datamation,* Oct. 15, pp. 64ff.

Haugeland, J., 1985. *Artificial Intelligence: The Very Idea,* A Bradford Book. Cambridge, MA: The MIT Press.

von Hayek, F.A. (ed.), 1935-36. *Collectivist Economic Planning.* London: George Routledge & Kegan Paul.

--------, 1940. Socialist Calculation, *Economica,* VII (26).

--------, 1945. The Use of Knowledge in Society, *American Economic Review,* XXXV (4), 519-530.

Hedenklint, J., 1991. *Att fatta beslut om IT - investeringar i industriföretag,* Booklet from 1991.

Henderson, D.A. Jr., 1986. *The Trillion User Interface Design Environment.* Paper presented at CHI, 86 Conference on Human Factors in Computing Systems, April 13-17, 1986, Boston, MA.

Hicks, J., 1932. *Theory of Wages.* London: Macmillan.

--------, 1979. *Causality in Economics.* New York: Basil.

Hirschleifer, J., 1966. Investment Decison under Uncertainty: Applications of the State-Preference Approach. *Quarterly Journal of Economics,* May, pp. 252-277.

--------, 1981. The Decline in Aggregate Share Values: Taxation, Valuation Errors, Risk and Profitability, *American Economic Review,* 71 (5).

Holmström, B., 1993. The Agency Cost and Innovation; in R.H. Day, G. Eliasson and C.G. Wihlborg, eds. (1993)

Holmström, B. and Tirole, J., 1989, The Theory of the Firm; in Schmalensee and

Willig (eds.), 1989, *Handbook of Industrial Organization*, Amsterdam: North-Holland.

Hotelling, H., 1929. Stability in Competition. *Economic Journal*, 39, 41-57.

Hägglund, S., 1986. *Datorstödda kunskapssystem i framtidens kontor*. Teldok Rapport 26, Stockholm (Dec.).

Jagrén, L., 1986. Concentration, Exit, Entry and Reconstruction of Swedish Manufacturing; in *The Economics of Institutions and Markets, IUI Yearbook 1986-1987*. Stockholm: Industriens Utredningsinstitut (IUI).

--------, 1988. Företagens tillväxt i ett historiskt perspektiv; in J. Örtengren et al. (1988).

--------, 1993. De dominerande storföretagen (The Dominant Large Firms); Chapter 3 in T. Andersson et al. (1993).

Jenkins, A., 1989. The Longer Reach of Apple Talk. *Datamation*, Aug. 1, pp. 50-60.

Jensen, M.C. and Meckling, W.H., 1976. Theory of the Firm: Managerial Behavior, Agency Costs, and Ownership Structure. *Journal of Financial Economics*, 3 (4), 305-360.

Jensen, M.C. and Meckling, W.H., 1979. Property Rights and Production Functions: An Application to Labor-Managed Firms and Codetermination, *Journal of Business*, 52, 469-506.

Johanneson, O., 1968. *The Great Computer -- A vision*. London.

Johnson, R.C., 1989. That Fuzzy Feeling. *Datamation*, July 1.

Jorgenson, D.W. and Griliches, Z., 1967. The Explanation of Productivity Change, *Review of Economic Studies*, XXXIV (3), 249-282.

Jorgenson, D.W. and Stiroh, K., 1994, *Computers and Growth*, Hier Discussion Paper No. 1707 (Dec.), Cambridge, MA: Harvard University.

Keynes, J.M., 1921. *A Treatise on Probability*. London: McMillan.

--------, 1936. *The General Theory of Employment, Interest and Money*. London: Macmillan.

Kerr, S., 1988. The Politics of Network Management. *Datamation*, Sept. 15.

Kim, J.I. and Lau, L.J., 1993. *The Role of Human Capital in the Economic Growth of the East Asian Newly Industrialized Countries*. Mimeo, Department of Economics. Stanford CA: Stanford University, (Dec.).

Klevmarken, A., 1989. *Supercomputing and Econometrics*. Paper presented at the IBM-conference on super computing at Cirkus, Stockholm 1989-09-18 (Mimeo, Dep. of Economics, University of Gothenburg, Göteborg.

Knight, F., 1921. Risk, *Uncertainty and Profit*. Boston: Houghton-Mifflin.

--------, 1944. Diminishing Returns from Investment. *Journal of Political Economy*, LII (Match), 26-47.

Lamb, J., 1988. IBM Eyes EDI in Europe. *Datamation*, July 1.

Latamore, G.B., 1988. CAD/CAM's 800 Million Winners, *High Technology*, (Jan.)

Lazear, E.P., 1981. Agency, Earnings Profiles, Productivity, and Hours

Restrictions. *American Economic Review*, 71 (4), 606-620.

Lazear, E.P. and Rosen, S., 1981. Rank Order Tournaments as Optimal Labor Contracts. *Journal of Political Economy*, pp. 841-864.

Ledin, H., 1988. Building a Dynamic Intelligent Network, Lessons from the Telecommunications Revolution for the MNC Organization of the Future, mimeo, Sept. 1988, Stockholm.

Leibowitz, M.R., 1990. Unix Workstations Arrive. *Datamation*, June 1, pp. 24-30.

LeRoy, S.F. and Singell, L.D., Jr, 1987. Knight on Risk and Uncertainty. *Journal of Political Economy*, 95 (2), 394-406.

Lewis, T.R. and Sappington, D.E.M., 1991. Technological Change and the Boundaries of the Firm. *American Economic Review*, 81, (4), 887-900.

Lindh, T., 1993. Lessons from Learning to have Rational Expectations; Chapter 5 in R.H. Day, G. Eliasson and C.G. Wihlborg (1993).

Lichtenberg, F.R., 1993. *The Output Contributions of Computer Equipment and Personnel; A Firm-Level Analysis*. NBER Working Paper No. 5440, Cambridge, MA.

Lucas, R.E., Jr., 1988. On the Mechanics of Economic Development. *Journal of Monetary Economics*, Vol. 22, No. 1, pp. 3-41.

Lundberg, E., 1961. *Produktivitet och räntabilitet*. Stockholm: Studieförbundet Näringsliv och Samhälle (SNS).

Machlup, F., 1967. Theories of the Firm: Marginalist, Behavioral, Managerial. *American Economic Review*, LVII (1), 1-33.

Magnusson, L. (ed.), 1994. *Evolutionary and Neo-Schumpeterian Approaches to Economics*, Boston/ Dordrecht/London: Kluwer Academic Publishers.

Manne, H.G., 1965. Mergers and the Market for Corporate Control. *Journal of Political Economy*, LXXIII (2), 110-120.

--------, 1966. *Insider Trading and the Stock Market*. New York: Free Press.

March, J.G. and Simon, H.A., 1958. *Organizations*. New York: Wiley & Sons.

Markowitz, H.M., 1952. Portfolio Selection. *Journal of Finance*, 7, 77-91.

Marris, R., 1963. A Model of the 'Managerial' Enterprise. *Quarterly Journal of Economics*, 77 (May), 185-209.

--------, 1964. *The Economic Theory of 'Managerial' Capitalism*. Glencoe, N.Y.: Free Press.

--------, 1971a. An Introduction to Theories of Corporate Growth, Chapter 1 in R. Marris and A. Wood, eds. (1971), pp. 1-37.

--------, 1971b. The Modern Corporation and Economic Theory, Chapter 9 in R. Marris and A. Wood, eds. (1971).

--------, 1972. Why Economics Needs a Theory of the Firm. *Economic Journal*, 82, (March), 321-352.

Marris, R. and Mueller, D.C., 1980. The Corporation, Competition, and the Invisible Hand. *Journal of Economic Literature*, XVIII (March), 32-63.

Marris, R. and Wood, A. (eds.), 1971. *The Corporate Economy: Growth,*

Competition and Innovative Potential, Edinburgh.

Marschak, J. and Radner, R., 1972. *The Economic Theory of Teams*. Yale: Cowles Foundation Monograph.

Marshall, A., 1919. *Industry and Trade*. London.

Marx, K., 1867. *Das Kapital; Kritik der politischen Oekonomie*, Vol. I. Der Produktionsprocess des Kapitals, Hamburg.

Mason, R.O., 1969. A Dialectical Approach to Strategic Planning. *Management Science*, 15 (8) (April).

McCusker, T., 1989. Tracking the Wild Data Base. *Datamation*, July 1.

McKenzie, L.W., 1959, On the Existence of General Equilibrium for a Competitive Market. *Econometrica*, 27 (1), 30-53.

McMullen, J., 1991. OS/2's Second Coming. *Datamation*, April 15, pp. 49 ff.

McWilliams, G., 1987. The Mini at Middle Age: Just a Future Niche Role?. *Datamation*, Aug. 1.

--------, 1988a. Selling IBM or Solution Selling?, *Datamation*, Jan. 1.

--------, 1988b. Can Digital Stay on Track?, *Datamation*, Feb. 1.

--------, 1988c. Oracle's Olympic Challenge, *Datamation*, Nov. 15.

--------, 1988d. Banks, Network Provider, Eye EDI, *Datamation*, Nov. 15.

--------, 1988e. Integrated Computing Environments, *Datamation*, May 1.

McWilliams, G. and Kerr, S., 1989. IBM Redefines the Competition. *Datamation*, Jan. 1.

Mellander, E., 1993, *Measuring Productivity and Inefficiency without Quantitative Output Data*. Doctoral Dissertation. Stockholm: Industriens Utrednings-institut (IUI)

Meltzer, B. and Michie, P. (eds.), 1969. *Machine Intelligence 5*. Edinburgh: University Press.

Meurling, J. and Jeans, R., 1994. *The Mobile Phone Book. The invention of the mobile telephone industry*. Communications Week International, 1994.

Mill, J.S., 1848. *Principles of Political Economy with Some of Their Applications to Social Philosophy*, London.

Miller, M.H. and Modigliani, F., 1961. Dividend Policy, Growth, and the Valuation of Shares. *Journal of Business*, 34 (Oct.), 411-433.

Miller, M.H. and Rock, K., 1985. Dividend Policy under Asymmetric Information. *Journal of Finance*, XL (4), 1031-1051.

Mitroff, J.J., 1971. A Communication Model of Dialectical Inquiring Systems – a strategy for strategic planning. *Management Science*, 17 (11) (July).

Moad, J., 1988a. Promise and Promises. *Datamation*, Jan 1.

--------, 1988b. Can UNISYS Juggle Open Systems too?. *Datamation*, Sept. 1.

--------, 1989a. The Database Dimension, *Datamation*. May 15, 1989.

--------, 1989b. Workstations Win a Big Blue Case. *Datamation*, Oct. 9, pp. 37 ff.

--------, 1991, Can IBM Recast its AS/400?. *Datamation*, July 15, 1991, pp. 28 ff.

Moad, J. and McWilliams, G., 1988. SAA: The Yellow Brick Road to Cooperative

Processing. *Datamation*, July 1.

Modigliani, F. and Cohen, K., 1958. The Significance and Uses of Ex Ante Data; in M.J. Bowman (ed.), 1958, *Expectations, Uncertainty and Business Behavior*. A Conference held at Carnegie Institute of Technology, 1955, New York.

--------, 1961. *The Role of Anticipations and Plans in Economic Behavior and Their Use in Economic Analysis and Forecasting* (Studies in Business Expectations and Planning, 4), Urbana III

Modigliani, F. and Miller, M.H., 1958, The Cost of Capital, Corporation Finance and the Theory of Investment. *American Economic Review*, 48 (3), 261-297.

Monsen, R.J. Jr. and Downs, A., 1965. A Theory of Large Managerial Firms. *Journal of Political Economy*, 73 (June), 221-236.

Morgan, G., 1986. *Images of Organization*. Beverly Hills, London etc.: SAGE Publications,

Mueller, D.C., 1977. The Persistence of Profits abve the Norm. *Economica*, 44 (176), 369-380.

--------, 1986a. *Profits in the Long Run*. Cambridge: Cambridge University Press.

--------, 1986b. *The Modern Corporation*, Cambridge.

--------, (ed.), 1990. The Dynamics of Company Profits -- an international comparison. WZB-Publications & Cambridge University Press, New York, Port Chester, Melbourne, Sydney.

Muggleton , S., 1988. Encoding the Universe. *Nature*, 335 (13), 597.

Musgrave, B., 1987. Integrating the PBX into ISDN. *Datamation*, Dec. 1, pp. 59ff.

--------, 1988. Stacking up LANs. *Datamation*, Feb. 15.

Myrdal, G., 1927. *Prisbildningsproblemet och föränderligheten*, Uppsala and Stockholm.

Myrdal, G., 1939. *Monetary Equilibrium*, London.

Nadiri, I., 1978. A Dynamic Model of Research and Development Expenditure; in B. Carlsson, G. Eliasson and I. Nadiri (eds.), *The Importance of Technology and the Permanence of Structure in Industrial Growth*, Conference Reports, 1978:2. Stockholm: Industriens Utredningsinstitut (IUI).

Nelson, R.R. and Winter, S.G., 1982. *An Evolutionary Theory of Economic Change*. Cambridge, MA.: Harvard University Press.

North, D.C., 1990, *Institutional Change and Economic Performance*. Cambridge, New York, Port Chester, Melbourne, Sidney: Cambridge University Press

North, D.C. and Thomas, R., 1973, *The Rise of the Western World, A New Economic History*. Cambridge: Cambridge University Press.

O'Connell, D.R., 1988. A Matter of Semantics. *Datamation*, 34 (25), pp. 51-54.

Olley, G.S., and Ariel Pakes, 1992. *The Dynamics of Productivity in the Telecommunications Equipment Industry*. NBER Working Paper No. 3977, Cambridge, MA.

Oxelheim, L., 1988. *Finansiell ingegration – en studie av svenska marknaders internationella beroende*. Stockholm: Industriens Utredningsinstitut (IUI).

Palander, T., 1941. Om "Stockholmsskolans" begrepp och metoder, *Ekonomisk Tidskrift*, Årg. 43, 1941:1, pp. 88-143.

Pelikan, P., 1969. Language as a Limiting Factor for Centralization. *American Economic Review*, LIX (4) (Sept.).

--------, 1986a. *The Formation of Incentive Mechanisms in Different Economic Systems*. Working Paper No. 155, Industriens Utredningsinstitut (IUI), Stockholm.

--------, 1986b. Why Private Enterprise? Towards a Dynamic Analysis of Economic Institutions and Policies; in *The Economics of Institutions and Markets, IUI Yearbook 1986-1987*, Stockholm: Industriens Utredningsinstitut (IUI).

--------, 1988a. Can the Imperfect Innovation Systems of Capitalism Be Outperformed?; in G. Dosi et al., 1988, *Technical Change and Economic Theory*. London: Pinter Publishers Ltd.

--------, 1988b. *Schumpeterian Efficiency of Different Economic Systems*, Working Paper No. 194. Industriens Utredningsinstitut (IUI), Stockholm.

--------, 1989, Evolution, Economic Competence, and the Market for Corporate Control, *Journal of Economic Behavior and Organization*, 12 (3), (Dec.).

--------, 1992. The Dynamics of Economic Systems, or How to Transform a Failed Socialist Economy. *Journal of Evolutionary Economics*, 2 (1), 39-63.

Penrose, E.T., 1952. Biological Analogies in the Theory of the Firm. *American Economic Review*, XLII (5), 804-819.

--------, 1959. *The Theory of the Growth of the Firm*. Oxford: Basil Blackwell.

Pinella, P., 1991. An EIS for the Desktop. *Datamation*, May 1, 1991, pp. 26 ff.

Polanyi, M., 1967. *The Tacit Dimension*. Garden City, N.Y.: Doubleday Anchor.

Pugh, E.W., 1995, *Building IBM – Shaping an Industry and Its Technology*, Cambridge, MA: MIT Press.

Radner, R., 1986a. Can Bounded Rationality Resolve the Prisoner's Dilemma?; Ch. 20 in A. Mas-Colell and W. Hildenbrand (eds.), *Contributions to Mathematical Economics. Essays in Honor of Gerard Debreu*. Amsterdam: North-Holland.

--------, 1986b. The Internal Economy of Large Firms. *Economic Journal*, Supplement (Jan.), pp. 1-21.

Rankine, S. and Sacks, D., 1987. Electric Visions of Computer Data. *Datamation*, Dec. 1, pp. 56ff.

Rashid, R., 1989. A Catalyst for Open Systems. *Datamation*, May 15.

Ricardo, D., 1817. *On the Principles of Political Economy and Taxation*; reprinted in P. Sraffa (ed.), 1954, *The Works and Correspondence of David Ricardo*. Cambridge, MA: Cambridge University Press.

--------, 1821. *The Principles of Political Economy and Taxation* (third ed.). London.

Ricart i Costa, J.E., 1988. Managerial Task Assignment and Promotions. *Econometrica*, 56 (2), 449-466.

Ridgeway, M., 1988. Curriculum Shortfall. *Datamation*, 34 (25), Dec. 15.

Riley, J.G., 1976. Information, Screening and Human Capital. *American Economic Review*, 66 (2), 254-260.

Robinson, J., 1933. *The Economics of Imperfect Competition*. London: Macmillan.

Romer, P.M., 1986. Increasing Returns and Long-Run Growth. *Journal of Political Economy*, 94 (5), 1002-1037.

Rosen, S., 1972. Learning by Experience as Joint Production. *Quarterly Journal of Economics*, LXXXVI (3), 366-382.

Rosenberg, N., 1982. Learning by Using; in N. Rosenberg (ed.), *Inside the Black Box: Technology and Economics*. Cambridge: Cambridge University Press, pp. 120-140.

Ross, S.A., 1973. The Economic Theory of Agency; The Principal's Problem, *American Economic Review*, LXIII (2), 134-139.

Rotschild, M., 1979. Social Effects of Ability Testing; unpublished paper.

Rothschild, K., 1988. The Age of Influence. *Datamation*, 34 (25), Dec 15.

Sah, R.K. and Stiglitz, J.E., 1985. Human Fallibility and Economic Organization,, *American Economic Review, Paper and Proceedings*, 75 (2), 292-297.

Salter, W.E.G., 1960. *Productivity and Technical Change*. Cambridge: Cambridge University Press, pp. 43-44.

Schaffer, G.H., 1981. *American Machinist*, Aug. (special report), pp. 152-174.

Schatz, W., 1988. Making CIM Work. *Datamation*, 34 (24), 18-23, Dec. 1.

--------, 1989. Who's Winning the Supercomputer Race?. *Datamation*, July 15.

Schultz, B., 1988a. Workstation Graphics – Blossoming from Business. *Datamation*, March 1.

--------, 1988b. VM: The Crossroads of Operating Systems. *Datamation*, July 15.

Schumpeter, J., 1911. (English edition 1934), The Theory of Economic Development, *Harvard Economic Studies*, Vol. XLVI, Cambridge, MA: Harvard University Press (originally published in German).

--------, 1942. *Capitalism, Socialism and Democracy*. New York: Harper & Row.

--------, 1954. *History of Economic Analysis* (ed. 1986 by Allen & Unwin, London).

Sculley, I. (with Byrne, J.A.), 1987. Odyssey; *Pepsi to Apple, A Journey of Adventure, Ideas and the Future*. New York: Harper & Row.

Seaman, J. (ed.), 1985. *Data Communications: A Manager's View*. New Jersey/ Berkeley, CA: Hayden Book Company.

Sewell, A., 1987. Departmental Computing: Distributing the Power. *Datamation*, Oct. 15, pp. 82 ff.

Sharpe, W.F., 1964. Capital Asset Prices: A Theory of Market Equilibrium under Conditions of Risk. *Journal of Finance*, XIX (3), 425-442.

Shannon, C.E. and Weaver, W., 1949. *The Mathematical Theory of Communication*. Urbana: The University of Illinois Press.

Shubik, M., 1959. Edgeworth Market Games; in A.W. Tucker and R.D. Luce (eds.), 1959, *Contributions to the Theory of Games*, Vol. IV. Princeton, NY: Princeton University Press, pp. 267-278.

--------, 1960. Simulation of the Industry and the Firm. *American Economic Review*, L (5), 908-919.

--------, 1975. The General Equilibrium Model is Incomplete and Not Adequate for the Reconciliation of Micro and Macroeconomic Theory. *Kyklos*, 28 (Fasc. 3), 545-573.

Simon, H.A., 1955. A Behavioral Model of Rational Choice. *Quarterly Journal of Economics*, 69, 99-118.

Simon, 1957a. *Models of Man*. New York: John Wiley & Sons.

--------, 1957b. The Compensation of Executives. *Sociometry*, 20 (March), 32-35.

--------, 1959. Theories of Decision-Making in Economics and Behavioral Science. *American Economic Review*, 49 (3), 253-283.

--------, 1965. *The Shape of Automation for People and Management*.

--------, 1979. Rational Decision-Making in Business Organizations. *American Economic Review*, 69 (4), 493-513.

Smith, A., 1776. *An Inquiry into the Nature and Causes of the Wealth of Nations*. New York: Modern Library, 1937.

Smith, V.L., 1966. *Investment and Production -- a study in the theory of the capital-using enterprise*. Cambridge, MA: Harvard University Press.

Smith, D.K. and Alexander, R.C., 1988. *Fumbling the Future – How Xerox invented, then ignored, the first personal computer*. New York: William Morrow and Company Inc., New York.

Sobel, R., 1981. *Colossus in Transition*. London: Sidgwick & Jackson.

Solow, R.M. 1957. Technical Change and the Aggregate Production Function. *Review of Economics and Statistics*, 39 (3), 312-320.

--------, 1962. Technical Progress, Capital Formation, and Economic Growth. *American Economic Review, Papers and Proceedings*, 52 (2), 76-86.

--------, 1990. *The Labor Market as a Social Institution*. Cambridge, MA: Basil Blackwell.

Spence, A.M., 1973. Job Market Signalling. *Quarterly Journal of Economics*, 87 (3), 355-379.

Stamps, P., 1987a. Modelling with Micros. *Datamation*, April 1, pp. 85 ff.

Stamps, P., 1987b. Case: Cranking out Productivity. *Datamation*, July 1, 1987, pp. 55 ff.

Stamps, P., 1990. Mapping OSI Migration Moves. *Datamation*, July 1, 1990, pp. 79 ff.

Statskontoret, *Standardiseringsinformation* nr 7:1, 1985: Lokala nät - standarder, rekommendationer och råd, Stockholm.

Stigler, G.J., 1951. The Division of Labor is Limited by the Extent of the Market. *Journal of Political Economy*, LIX (3), pp. 185-193.

Stiglitz, J.E., 1987a. Competition and the Number of Firms in a Market: Are

Duopolies More Competitive than Atomistic Markets. *Journal of Political Economy*, 95 (5), 1041-1061.

--------, 1987b. Learning to Learn, Localized Learning and Technological Progress; in P. Dasgupta and P. Stoneman (eds.), *Economic Policy and Technological Performance*. Cambridge: Cambridge University Press, pp. 125-154.

Södersten, J., 1985. Industrins vinster, finansiering och tillgångsstruktur 1965-83; Specialstudie Nr V; in *Att rätt värdera 90-talet*. Stockholm: Industriens Utredningsinstitut (IUI).

Teece, D.J., 1980. Economies of Scope and the Scope of the Enterprise. *Journal of Economic Behavior and Organization*, 1 (3), 223-247.

Tesler, G.L., 1991. Networked Computing. *Scientific American*, Sept., pp. 54 ff.

Thorngren, B., 1970. How Do Contact Systems Affect Regional Developnent? *Environment and Planning*, 2, 409-427.

Turing, A.M., 1936. *On Computable Numbers with an Application to the Entscheidungsproblem*. Proceedings of the London Mathematical Society (Nov. 30th).

Tversky, A. and Kahneman, D., 1986. Rational Choice and the Framing of Decisions. *Journal of Business*, 59 (4), Part 2, S251-S276.

Veblen, Th., 1921. *The Engineer and the Price System*. London, 1965.

Vedin, B., 1992. *Teknisk revolt – Det svenska AXE-systemets brokiga framgångshistoria*. Stockholm:Atlantis.

Vinell, L., 1991. The Hagfors Strip Mill – the Horndal effect revisited. IUI mimeo for the Nutek project on technological systems, Stockholm.

Weezenberg, J.N., 1981. Integration of Financial and Management Information Systems from the Viewpoint of Information Supply. *Philips Administrative Review* (Theme-Number: Accounts and Information), 35 (1/2), June.

Weisman, R., 1987. Six Steps to AI-Based Functional Prototyping. *Datamation*, Aug. 9.

Wentzel, V. and Hallberg, T.J. (eds.), 1994. *Tema D21, DATASAABs Historia*. Linköping.

Westerman, J., 1768. *Om Svenska Näringarnes Undervigt emot de Utländske, förmedelst en Trögare Arbets-drift* (On the inferiority of the Swedish compared to foreign manufacturers because of a slower work organization), Stockholm.

Wicksell, K., 1898. *Geldzins und Güterpreise* (Interest and Prices), published 1965 by AMK Bookseller, New York.

Williamson, O.E., 1964. *The Economics of Discretionary Behavior: Managerial Objectives in a Theory of the Firm*. Englewood Cliffs, NJ: Prentice-Hall.

--------, 1970. *Corporate Control and Business Behavior*. Englewood Cliffs: Prentice-Hall:, N.J.

--------, 1975. *Markets and Hierarchies: Analysis and Antitrust Implications. A Study in the Economics of Internal Organization*. New York: Free Press.

--------, 1981. The Modern Corporation: Origins, Evolution, Attributes. *Journal of Economic Literature*, XIX (4), 1537-1568.

--------, 1983. Organizational Form, Residual Claimants, and Corporate Control. *Journal of Law and Economics*, (June).

--------, 1986. The Modern Corporation: Origins, Evolution, Attributes, Chapter. 8 in O.E. Williamson, 1986, *Economic Organization. Firms: Markets and Policy Control*. New York: New York University Press.

Winter, S.G., 1964. Economic "Natural Selection" and the Theory of the Firm. *Yale Economic Essays*, 4 (1), 225-272.

--------, 1986. Schumpeterian Competition in Alternative Technological Regimes, Chapter 8 in R. H. Day & G. Eliasson, eds. (1986).

Wittgenstein, L., 1922. *Traktatus Logico-Philosophicus*. London: Kegan Paul, Trench, Trubner & Co., Ltd and New York: Harcourt, Brace & Company, Inc.

Ysander, B.-C. (ed.), 1986. *Two Models of an Open Economy*. Stockholm: Industriens Utredningsinstitut (IUI).

Zygmont, J., 1987. Manufacturers Move towards Computer Integration. *High Technology* (Feb.).

Åkerman, J., 1950. Institutionalism. *Ekonomisk Tidskrift*, pp. 1-14.

Örtengren, J. et al., 1988, *Expansion, avveckling och företagsvärdering i svensk industri – en studie av ägarformens och finansmarknadernas betydelse för strukturomvandlingen*. Stockholm: Industriens Utredningsinstitut (IUI).

Economics of Science, Technology and Innovation

KLUWER ACADEMIC PUBLISHERS – DORDRECHT / BOSTON / LONDON